The Illicit Economy
in Turkey

The Illicit Economy in Turkey

How Criminals, Terrorists, and the Syrian Conflict Fuel Underground Markets

Mahmut Cengiz and Mitchel P. Roth

LEXINGTON BOOKS
Lanham • Boulder • New York • London

Published by Lexington Books
An imprint of The Rowman & Littlefield Publishing Group, Inc.
4501 Forbes Boulevard, Suite 200, Lanham, Maryland 20706
www.rowman.com

6 Tinworth Street, London SE11 5AL, United Kingdom

British Library Cataloguing in Publication Information Available

The hardback edition of this book was previously catalogued by the Library of Congress as follows:

Library of Congress Cataloging-in-Publication Data

Names: Cengiz, Mahmut, author. | Roth, Mitchel P., 1953- author.
Title: The illicit economy in Turkey : how criminals, terrorists, and the Syrian conflict fuel underground markets / Mahmut Cengiz and Mitchel P. Roth.
Description: Lanham : Lexington Books, [2019] | Includes bibliographical references and index.
Identifiers: LCCN 2019009411 | ISBN 9781498595049 (cloth : alk. paper) | ISBN 9781498595063 (pbk : alk. paper) | ISBN 9781498595056 (electronic : alk. paper)
Subjects: LCSH: Transnational crime—Turkey. | Organized crime—Turkey. | Black market—Turkey. | Corruption—Turkey.
Classification: LCC HV6252.5.T87 C458 2019 | DDC 330—dc23 LC record available at https://lccn.loc.gov/2019009411

Contents

List of Acronyms

AA	Acetic Anhydride
AKP	Adalet ve Kalkınma Partisi - Justice and Development Party
ANAP	Anavatan Partisi - Motherland Party
AQI	al Qaeda in Iraq
ASOD	Anti-Smuggling and Organized Crime Department
BKA	Bundeskriminalamt - Federal Criminal Police Office
CIS	Counterfeit Incident System
DHKP- C	Revolutionary People's Liberation Party Front
DYP	Doğru Yol Partisi - True Path Party
EPS	Erdogan's Pool System
EU	European Union
FARC	Revolutionary Armed Forces of Colombia
FATF	Financial Action Task Force
FP	Felicity Party - Saadet Partisi
FSA	Free Syrian Army
G20	Group of Twenty
GDP	Gross Domestic Product
HDP	Pro-Kurdish Peoples' Democratic Party
INCSR	International Narcotics Control Strategy Report
IRGC	Islamic Revolutionary Guards Corps
ISIS	Islamic State of Iraq and Syria
JN	Jabhat al Nusra
QF	Quds Force
MA	Methamphetamine
MASAK	Mali Suçları Araştırma Kurulu - Financial Investigation Crimes Investigation Board

MIT	Milli Istihbarat Teskilati - National Intelligence Agency of Turkey
MKP	Maoist Communist Party
MLKP	Marxist-Leninist Communist Party
PKK	Kurdistan Workers' Party
PYD	Democratic Union Party in Syria
STQF	Salam Tawhid Quds Force
TADOC	Turkish International Academy against Drugs and Organized Crime
TIKKO	Workers and Peasants Salvation Army
TNP	Turkish National Police
TOC	Transnational Organized Crime
TOGEMDER	Toplumsal Gelisim Merkezi Dernegi - Social Development Center Association
TPLP/C	Turkey People's Liberation Party Front
TURGEV	Turkiye Genclik ve Egitime Hizmet Vakfi - Turkey Youth and Education Foundation
UAE	United Arab Emirates
UK	United Kingdom
UN	United Nations
U.S.	United States
USD	United States Dollar
UYAP	Ulusal Yargi Agi Bilisim Sistemi - National Judiciary Informatics System
VP	(Virtue Party - Fazilet Partisi)
WMD	Weapons of Mass Destruction
WP	Welfare Party - Refah Partisi
ZEJ	Zarrab's Economic Jihad

List of Figures

Introduction

The outbreak of the Syrian Civil War, the enduring conflict in Iraq, the 2013 December 17 and 25 corruption scandals implicating President Recep Tayyip Erdogan and his inner circle, and the 2016 Turkish coup attempt have only added to the chaos in Turkey and on its borders, creating opportunities for criminal and terrorist organizations like never before. Turkey's strategic location between Asia and Europe and along the Balkan Route, as well as its proximity to the opium-producing areas of Afghanistan and Pakistan, has long assured the country a central role in the world narcotics trade. While Turkish organized crime can be discerned in some of the activities of criminal traditions dating back hundreds of years, modern transnational organized crime involving Turks and Kurds is of fairly recent vintage. No Turkish group is more prominent in organized crime circles as the Kurdish Workers Party (PKK); and for a brief time, the Islamic State in Iraq and Syria (ISIS).

This book offers a comprehensive overview of Turkey's illicit economy from the early years of the Turkish Republic to the present in terms of how criminals, Syrian refugees, and terrorists have participated in an illicit economy, facilitated by corruption. More importantly, it is distinguished by analysis of the relationship between the Turkish government and its various entities and the funding of ISIS. The authors examined reports by multinational bodies, states, and non-governmental organizations and have derived information from interviews with Turkish analysts and practitioners in the field, as well as experts on Syria, Iraq, and Turkey. Moreover, it is the most up-to-date examination of the illicit economy in Turkey. This book is structured and intended for a diverse audience, including scholars, students, and policy makers interested in the illicit global economy, conflict, and crime.

The book conflates field experience and theories used in the literature of the illicit economy as a result of broader backgrounds of the co-authors.

Also, the book uses triangulation method in most chapters, combining quantitative and qualitative data. In addition to government reports and international reports, and police statistics, the book uses ethnographic interviews with law enforcement officials and researchers with expertise on the Turkish illicit economy. Because of the current repressive atmosphere imposed by Recep Tayyip Erdogan's Justice and Development Party (AKP) governments, the respondents' identities have been kept confidential and given codes in all chapters.

The book's ten chapters are bookended by an Introduction and a Conclusion. Chapter 1 places Turkey's modern illicit economy within its historical context by chronicling various incarnations of organized criminal groups. Several case studies from the late 1990s further demonstrate the continuing intersection of politics and criminal activities. This chapter also focuses on the current crime situation, categorized as mafia-type criminal groups operating locally and criminal groups operating transnationally.

Chapter 2 focuses on factors responsible for Turkey's illicit economy, chronicling a continuum of corruption, that along with factors such as geographical location, the presence of terrorist groups, and judicial vacuums, have created a favorable environment for criminal and terrorist actors to operate within the illicit economy.

Chapters 3 through 5 survey the trafficking and smuggling activities central to Turkey's illicit economy. Chapter 3 examines drug trends in Turkey in terms of its production, use, and trafficking. Chapter 4 emphasizes the smuggling of cigarettes, oil, counterfeit pharmaceuticals, nuclear materials, and antiquities, detailing the escalation of illegal cigarette seizures, much of it taking place on the Turkish-Syrian border. What's more, this chapter presents evidence of collusion between criminal and terrorist groups. This ranges from direct involvement in the trafficking and smuggling operations to the taxation of this trade being conducted by other actors. This chapter is also distinguished by its analysis of recent data based on official statistics and research derived from semi-structured interviews with Turkish investigators by one of the authors. Moreover, Chapter 4 covers the trafficking and smuggling of antiquities by groups in Syria and Turkey. Historic sites have been plundered for centuries, but the Syrian Civil War and the rise of ISIS have brought this illicit part of the economy to global attention as a horde of valuable artifacts that has been moved through Turkey mostly destined for Western countries.

Chapter 5 focuses on the spectrum of criminal actors involved in human smuggling and trafficking operations. It examines the economic consequences of having over three million Syrian refugees sheltered in the country, as well as their potential links to the illicit economy. Moreover, it explores Turkey's strategic location as a transit country for immigrants from Asia and the Middle East attempting to get to Western Europe. This chapter is informed by the first author's law enforcement experience and findings obtained in recently conducted police operations against human traffickers.

Chapters 6 and 7 focus on endemic corruption that facilitates the illicit economy, using an in-depth examination of the December 17 and 25, 2013 graft scandals and the unprecedented purges of law enforcement officials and the judiciary members who investigated these scandals. Chapter 6 also explains how in the wake of the purges, criminal and terrorist groups have taken advantage of new opportunities in the country's illicit economy. The combined graft scandals offer a case study for examining how political corruption contributes to the expansion of the illicit economy.

Chapter 7 takes a hard look at the retaliatory attitude of the AKP government that has led to a crackdown on investigators and investigations. The purging and reassignments of police officers following the December 2013 graft scandals have impacted the illicit economy. With around 30,000 police and 4,000 judges and prosecutors forced out of their jobs in the wake of the scandals, this government strategy has only created weaknesses in public security and left a vacuum in authority that criminals and terrorist groups were quick to exploit. In this period, Turkish law enforcement has lost its institutional capacity, knowledge, and memory, confirmed by the decreasing number of smuggling, trafficking, and anti-corruption investigations. Comparing the data between 2012 and 2016, this chapter examines the ramifications of the purges on Turkish law enforcement.

Chapter 8 delves into what some researchers describe as a "nexus" between terrorists and criminals in the illicit economy. It examines how left-wing, ethnic separatist, religious, and Iranian-sponsored terrorist groups have adopted methods and strategies long employed by traditional organized crime groups to fund their operations. Different terrorist groups rely on various streams of financing. Moreover, both crime and terrorist groups play active roles in the laundering of money as well. This chapter discloses findings from recent research coming out of the eastern and southeastern regions of Turkey and demonstrates how the PKK remains active in Turkey, Iran, Iraq, and Europe.

Chapter 9 examines the impact of the Syrian Civil War in terms of how Syrian refugees in Turkey have become involved in criminal organizations and how ISIS has taken advantage of the conflict to finance its activities. It explores the creation of security vacuums that have been filled by criminals and terrorists. Particular focus is placed on the ongoing conflicts in neighboring countries, American interventions in the region, and the rise of ISIS, all of which have facilitated trafficking and smuggling operations in Turkey's southeast borderlands.

Chapter 10 explores the movement of criminal and terrorist organizations' profits through Turkey's illicit economy, explaining how both types of organizations utilize various money laundering techniques as well as the complicity of state banks in the process. This chapter is supplemented with interviews made with officials from the Turkish Financial Investigation Board. Finally, the Conclusion offers final words on the latest developments in Turkey's illicit economy.

Chapter 1

Historical Continuities of Criminals in the Illicit Economy

INTRODUCTION

Criminal groups in Turkey have historically operated in many areas of the illicit economy, ranging from extortion, smuggling, and trafficking to money laundering. Their activities are part of a continuum that dates back centuries. While criminal groups in the past were more regional and locally oriented, primarily engaged in plundering, looting, and extortion, today local mafia-type groups have expanded their operations, making their transition to transnational criminality.

Political and social conditions throughout Turkish history have determined the various characteristics of criminal groups. Some groups can trace their origins to the social bandits who operated during the Ottoman Empire and the early years of the Turkish Republic. Transnational criminal enterprises, beginning in the 1970s, have impacted criminal groups in Turkey, primarily through links to drug-trafficking organizations. This chapter chronicles the historical evolution of organized criminality from the early years of the Turkish Republic to more recent developments.

THE PERIODIC DEVELOPMENT OF TURKISH CRIMINAL GROUPS

Any examination of the evolution of organized crime can be best understood through a chronological discussion of various developmental phases that comprise the continuum of various criminal enterprises. In terms of Turkey, it is the last two developmental phases that are most critical for gaining an understanding of how the so-called "mafia paradigm" became more prominent in the late 1960s, as well as the subsequent gradual shift from the mafia paradigm to more organized incarnations of criminality since the 1980s.[1]

The activities of organized crime groups usually include three primary categories: the provision of illicit services, the provision of illicit goods, and the infiltration of legitimate business government.[2] Turkish criminal groups have traditionally been involved in all three categories. This can be best understood in their association with Turkish social, political, and economic developments. Social bandits provided services and goods during the early Republican period before morphing into more organized crime groups capable of infiltrating legitimate businesses and the national government during the era of military coups. As illustrated in Figure 1.1, the periodical development of Turkish criminal groups included their transformation from social bandits into mafia type and transnational criminal groups.

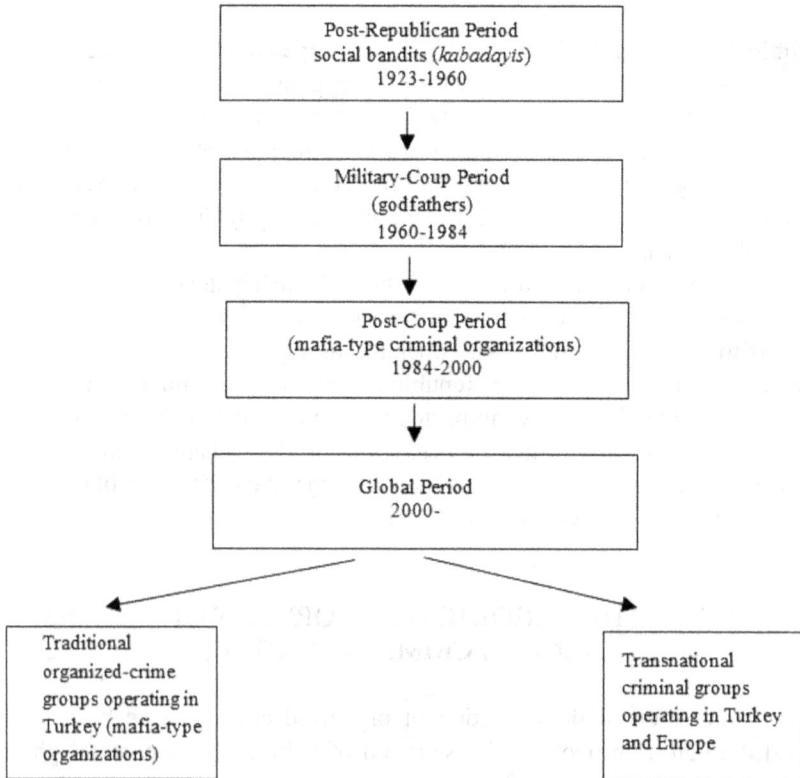

Figure 1.1 **Development of Turkish criminal groups by period.** *Source*: Cengiz, Turkiye'de Organize Suc Gercegi, 2015, 28 (Ankara: Seckin Yayinevi, 2015).

THE DEVELOPMENT OF ORGANIZED CRIME
DURING THE REPUBLICAN PERIOD (1923–1960)

Banditry is one of the oldest forms of organized social protest. It is a reality that symbolizes political resistances against oppressive regimes in peasant societies.[3] Social bandits[4] are best understood as groups of individuals who committed crimes in rural areas. Local inhabitants had a complicated relationship with the plundering bandit gangs.[5] In times of need some of the most impoverished sections of society supported these marauders who were often mythologized as the protectors of society.[6] Turkish bandits have been categorized into different groups over the years. During the Ottoman period they were called *kulhanbeyi*, while during the Republican period they were identified as *kabadayi* (in urban areas) and *efe* (in rural areas). Though identified by different names, the bandits served similar functions during the preindustrial era.[7]

The social bandit tradition is tied to the precursors to the Sicilian mafia in the nineteenth century. The activities of Sicilian bandits were often supported by the common people who felt little allegiance to a central government that was remote and unsympathetic. Nonetheless, the social bandit might have assumed the role of benefactor during times of agrarian distress, unfair taxation, and class resentment, but remained part and parcel of a common criminal milieu that banded together mostly for protection and avaricious purposes.[8] Similarly, bandits in the Turkish Republican period sold their protection, settled disputes, and protected the weak from repressive governments.[9]

In some situations, bandits supported the status quo because they were interconnected with power elites and the ruling class.[10] As a result it became difficult to differentiate between the criminal activities of society's higher echelons and the social bandits operating in Turkey. It was in this environment that social banditry underwent a structural transformation in terms of organized criminal activities. By some accounts social bandits forcefully collected food and clothing from rich people a la "Robin Hood" and distributed them to the poor. It was in this way that they became progenitors of the social bandit tradition before making the transition to mafia-type criminal organizations.[11]

To a certain extent, Turkish society accepted social banditry, but only to the extent that the bandit groups respected the social and religious values of the Turkish people. However, this did not prevent some bandit groups from degenerating over time into marauding groups. The legacy of the bandits was the tacit approval given their activities as long as they promoted public order. This heritage paved the way for the emergence of another form of social banditry, *kabadayis*, that came to prominence during the Republican period.

Many towns and cities welcomed *kabadayi*s, who were adept at resolving disputes among local people in the early years of the Turkish Republic. By most accounts *kabadayi*s refrained from committing crimes and struggled to gain the trust of people in their local environments. According to the relevant literature, *kabadayi*s can be accepted as progenitors of modern organized crime groups in Turkey.[12] *Kabadayi*s represented various ethnic groups and social classes and were as likely to come from the rich and impoverished classes as from the Muslim and Christian communities.[13]

*Kabadayi*s were most active in urban areas, while social bandits known as *efe*s, preferred rural and mountainous locales. At first, *efe*s were individuals who had rebelled against official authority before settling in the mountainous areas, where they formed gangs and engaged in smuggling and extortion activities. It did not take long for *efe*s to be regarded locally as popular heroes, considered beyond the reach of government forces. Of course, it further burnished their popular reputation when word spread that they took from the rich and distributed needed commodities to the poor. This understanding reportedly led local residents to tip off the *efe*s in advance of any police operations.[14]

*Efe*s varied regionally. In western Turkey they rebelled for individual reasons before establishing bandit gangs, while those in the southeast responded more against the general policies of the government. Both incarnations of the bandits were regarded as thugs or rebels by central authorities as they engaged in almost constant conflict with state authority. Among the push factors stimulating the development of these were government policies that inhibited traditional occupations, particularly smuggling. Their numbers proliferated in the 1960s. In the southeastern Siirt province, for example, there were at least 180 bandits.[15]

In the1950s, the *kabadayi*s rose in prominence across Turkey, thanks to the inability of official law enforcement units to provide a semblance of order and security. The *kabadayi* known as Oflu Hasan was credited, for example, with playing an active role in the resolution of a bloody feud between two families in the 1950s.[16] Beginning in the 1950s, *kabadayi*s developed close relationships with most segments of Turkish society. Their acceptance was exemplified during the 1968 funeral of the aforementioned Oflu Hasan, when famous *kabadayi*s of the era, numerous politicians, artists, and VIPs attended the funeral, and hundreds of people (including the son of the president) sent wreaths to the funeral. A similar scene unfolded at the funeral of another celebrated *kabadayi*, "Inci Baba" Mehmet Nabi İnciler, who had been murdered in 1993. The extensive interest in both funerals illustrates the enduring acceptance of *kabadayi*s by various segments of Turkish society during the second half of the twentieth century.[17]

The transformation of *kabadayis* into *babas* (godfathers) led to the diversification of activities among these groups. However, smuggling operations remained the primary activity for organized crime groups since the 1950s. To complement smuggling activities, for example, the number of illegal casinos escalated exponentially and most of the cafes in metropolitan cities were used as venues for illegal gambling. These undercover casinos, at the time, were run by the *kabadayis*.[18] During this era the procurement of contraband goods also placed high on the activities of *kabadayis*.

Restrictions on the sale of tobacco products, alcoholic beverages, and gold have shaped Turkish smuggling markets since the 1950s. In fact, smuggling was not even considered a crime until the mid-1940s. Two political factors forced the government to strengthen border controls and develop strategies to prevent smuggling: First, stronger border control was necessary to prevent the possible negative impact of the Kurdish movement in Syria, Iraq, and Iran. Secondly, the government's economic policies required that all trade activities be integrated into the national economy. Thus, free trade, or border trade, was equated with smuggling.[19]

Not surprisingly, local citizens, who were used to traveling freely across Turkey's border to visit relatives or transfer goods, did not take kindly to the new regulations, which included presenting a passport in order to cross the border into Syria, Iraq, or Iran. Thus, it took a long time for the local citizens to adapt to the new policy, resulting in unintended consequences, including several tragic incidents related to smuggling. In 1943, for example, 33 Kurdish smugglers were killed in a fusillade of bullets following a decree by Turkish Army General Mustafa Muğlalı. He would be sentenced to 20 years in prison for this atrocity.[20]

Dündar Kılıç, a well-known *kabadayi*, was extensively engaged in smuggling and, as was common among *kabadayis* in the 1950s, ran casinos. Kılıç also was a famous figure in the underground crime sector since the 1960s. He was investigated throughout his life for several murders and the wounding of dozens more but managed to elude serving long prison terms thanks to frequent general amnesties issued by governments.[21] Kılıç expanded his underground network significantly after opening a coffee house and was emboldened enough to confront local *kabadayis* who dared ask him for tributes. Kılıç became the target of several assassination attempts after he was alleged to have murdered a mafia leader called Cemali. During the 1970s, Kılıç tried to extort protection money from most bars in the Beyoglu region of Istanbul. He was arrested in an operation targeting mafia leaders but released in a short time. Similar to other *kabadayis*, Kılıç considered his social image to be extremely important. Like America's Al Capone, who attempted to burnish his image by opening soup kitchens in Chicago during the 1930s,

Kılıç went to great lengths to make a public show of helping the local poor. In 1984, Kılıç's connection with international drug trafficking groups was revealed through his relationship with heroin smugglers in Switzerland. A police investigation uncovered that Kılıç was involved in heroin smuggling in cooperation with high-level police chiefs.[22]

The image of *kabadayis* began to tarnish in the 1960s for several reasons, with the proliferation of firearms playing a major role. *Kabadayis* started to use firearms rather than brute force, their traditional way of settling conflicts. Thus, the level of violence associated with their activities increased considerably.[23]

The organized crime career of *kabadayi* Hasan Heybetli offers a blueprint for examining the inner workings of a Turkish mafia family. He virtually inherited the role of *kabadayi* from his father, Hüseyin Heybetli. The elder Heybetli was a famous *kabadayi* in the 1950s and was involved in numerous violent activities, especially in the 1970s. Yet, he owes his fame to love affairs with celebrities.[24] It should be noted that it is not uncommon for criminals to not just be accepted into certain milieus of the upper world, but to also seek social mobility for themselves. In some cases, this might take place thanks to personal contacts with celebrities or their acceptance in popular social spaces.[25] Similarly, many other *kabadayis* had similar relationships with celebrities, either to achieve fame or to feed their self-indulgent attachment to exaggerated confidence in their power.

Similarly, the life story of the Kurdish *kabadayi*, Hüseyin Uğurlu, also illustrates important codes of the criminal underworld. In one interview he admitted smuggling cigarettes and whiskey to satisfy the demand among young people but eschewed the smuggling of drugs or weapons.[26] In other cases, *kabadayis* defended their livelihoods with the caveat that they deliberately abstain from drug dealing and prostitution because these activities ran counter to the prevailing values and norms of a *kabadayi*. Likewise, they refrained from using firearms against children or women.

The inclusion of a Turkish route for the trafficking of drugs from Afghanistan in the 1970s opened up new opportunities for *kabadayis*; however, their association with drug dealing tainted their popular image. It was in this way that *kabadayis* became more identifiable as criminals rather than "Robin Hoods."[27] *Kabadayis* demonstrated a pragmatic entrepreneurial acumen, whether they were engaged in racketeering with small businesses, organizing in the gambling sector, or smuggling tobacco, alcohol, and gold. Ultimately, some *kabadayis* also transitioned to the more lucrative opportunities inherent in the smuggling of narcotics.[28]

THE DEVELOPMENT OF ORGANIZED CRIME
IN THE ERA OF MILITARY COUPS (1960-1984)

The military coups between 1960 and 1980 gave rise to new incarnations of Turkish criminal groups, as well as fundamental changes in how they operated. During this era, crime increased, due to the usual impact factors of industrialization and urbanization and the concomitant economic, political, and social problems that followed. This was especially true in the surge of smuggling cases. In 1983, at the start of the post-coup period, Turkey adopted a more liberal economy, creating a favorable environment for the circulation of dirty money. During this period, smugglers became more organized. But by 2000, fueled by the globalization process, Turkish criminal groups, like most other segments of society, underwent structural changes as they became more tied into transnational crime activities.

One important heritage of Turkey's military coups was the expansion and development of organized crime activities. The upheaval caused by the military coups left Turkey unable to form a robust rule of law, a situation that crime groups exploited. Smuggling, which was the main financing source of various factions in conflicts that plagued the country, became an irresistible activity. *Kabadayis* and mafia bosses came together to form more sophisticated organized crime groups in their overlapping areas of influence. Next, they expanded into international networks, strengthening their strategic positions and gaining prominence for arms and narcotics trafficking.

A number of factors figured into the expansion of organized crime during the 1980s, including a power vacuum in state authority in the military coup era, economic problems, judicial gaps, migration issues, and the embargo after the war with Cyprus.

Vacuum in the State System

Since the 1970s, mafia-type crimes have been among the most complicated problems Turkey has faced in terms of economic and political consequences.[29] Some people turned to organized crime to free themselves from poverty or to breach embargoes. The vacuum that arose when the state system became dysfunctional left most government institutions filled with smuggling groups. The proliferation of organized crime in Turkey in the 1970s was a corollary of weak state authority and cumbersome bureaucracy.[30]

Economic Problems

The era of coups impacted the Turkish economy in two ways: the absence of economic reforms and corruption. In the 1970s, sweeping changes occurred in the domain of world economics. Turkey, however, failed to keep up with these changes amid the military coups and found itself more or less relegated to the sidelines during this period of global economic advances. The weak coalition governments of the military-coup era put security matters at top of their agendas and ignored necessary economic reforms that would have integrated the country into the global economy. As a result, the gap between the poor and the rich widened. Smuggling became a lucrative alternative way of making money, increasing the number of people engaged in it. The flourishing of corruption under the military coup hurt the country economically, particularly from a global perspective, since global investors are more likely to shun unstable countries that are in the throes of military coups.

Judicial Gaps

Gaps in the judicial system in the 1970s also paved the way for the proliferation of criminal groups in Turkey. These gaps can be analyzed in three categories: ineffective punishments, weak law enforcement institutions, and general amnesty laws.

- *Ineffective punishments.* The judicial system especially felt the negative and chaotic consequences of the 1960 and 1971 coups and failed to make effective criminal laws. The punishments for smuggling, for example, were so meaningless that smugglers were often released soon after being sentenced by a court. Thus, laws enacted after the coups failed to deter criminals—including members of organized crime groups.
- *Weak law enforcement institutions.* Law enforcement in Turkey was weak in terms of criminal investigations. For example, primitive methods were used to collect and retain evidence of crimes. In the absence of professional law enforcement investigations, prosecutors had to depend on the statements of suspects and witnesses rather than physical evidence. Thus, paid runners often took the blame for crimes that had been committed by their bosses. This was especially true for *kabadayis* engaged in smuggling activities. In several murder cases, for example, *kabadayis* pegged their runner as the murderer.
- *General amnesty laws.* Several general amnesty laws were implemented during the military-coup era, including four general amnesty decrees and one partial amnesty decree between 1960 and 1974. The frequent amnesty declarations made it almost impossible to fight crime with a justice system

that already had no deterrent effect on criminals. That vacuum led to the release of several convicted arms and cigarette smugglers since the late 1960s.[31] This was best exemplified by the release of Abuzer Uğurlu, Bekir Çelenk, and Mehmet Cantaş, all previously convicted smugglers of arms and narcotics who were freed after the 1974 Amnesty Law was enacted.

Migration

Between the 1950s and 1980s the economic and political structure in Turkey underwent structural modifications, including large-scale migration from heavily populated rural areas to city centers. Government officials stimulated and supported the migration of villagers to urban areas because it was easier and more economic to offer services to concentrated populations in city centers rather than to those widely dispersed in rugged rural areas. The mass migration movements in the 1960s led to a rapid increase in the population of metropolitan areas. Migration had three consequences in terms of organized crime: First, *kabadayis* brought their particular culture with them, which included acting as dispensers of extralegal justice. Over time, some *kabadayis* transformed into godfathers and engaged in smuggling activities. Second, ghetto zones emerged illegally on treasury (i.e., public) lands controlled by mafia members. Those who migrated to city centers built their homes (*gecekondu*, meaning "built in night") on treasury lands in one night without regard to the law because, at the time, it was very difficult for the government to destroy such homes even though they had been built illegally. Criminal activity in the ghettos was low through the 1970s. In the years that followed, the ghettos became centers of criminal activity. The prevalence of poverty, low education levels, and the existing kinship relationships among the residents in the ghettos led to the emergence of criminal groups. As a result, those who lived in the ghettos were pushed into crimes by the circumstances. The final consequence of migration was the emergence of the land mafia, which is discussed later in this chapter.

Embargo after the Cyprus War

After the military took over the country on March 12, 1971, the entire state system was embroiled in turmoil. In addition, the embargo imposed after the 1974 Cyprus War generated considerable opportunities for criminal groups. At the behest of the United States, the United Nations imposed sanctions on Turkey after Turkish troops invaded Cyprus.

The embargo on Turkey was also imposed in response to the country's cultivation of opium. Opium is an agricultural crop, grown largely for use in the medical sector, and had a long history in Turkey. The plant, for example, was one of the country's primary export materials for many years. In the 1960s, however, the United States and European countries implemented a new strategy to curb the prevalent use of heroin by putting pressure on opium-producing countries, including Turkey.[32] The agriculture production of opium in Turkey was prohibited in 1971 by Prime Minister Nihat Erim, but that did not end the discussion.[33] The issue of opium as an agricultural crop became a central topic of debate among the political parties vying for the prime minister post, with most of the candidates promising to end the ban if elected. Finally, Bulent Ecevit ended the ban on opium cultivation as soon as he took office as prime minister in 1974. This move, however, made Turkey the target of the international community. Ecevit's repeal of the opium ban is believed to be another reason behind the UN embargo decision after the Cyprus War.[34]

As can be seen in modern geopolitical situations in places as varied as Iran, Palestine, North Korea, and so forth, sanctions can have destructive results on a targeted country's economy (and its neighbors). Not only is the international community criminalizing the state and its populace, but at the same time having the unintended consequence of creating a favorable environment for corrupt politicians and transnational smugglers.[35] In like fashion, the embargo had a detrimental effect on the Turkish economy over time, forcing the country to deplete its currency reserves. As a result, citizens were unable to meet even their basic needs. The shortage of almost everything in the country presented tremendous opportunities for crime groups to fill the void. Mafia groups that began by providing basic goods for the people during the embargo era became considerably more powerful and efficient, going as far as supplying national defense equipment to the military.

The Turkish currency deficit, by some accounts, was somewhat improved through the smuggling of arms and narcotics. Organized crime groups were in effect legalized as they became accomplices of industrialists. It is also worth noting that Turkish occupation of Northern Cyprus was not recognized as legitimate by the international community, which made Northern Cyprus a hub for money launderers. In fact, the Financial Action Task Force (FATF) in 1994 gave Turkey a very critical report regarding its efforts to combat money laundering. Two years later, the FATF report was more favorable but ignored the fact that much of the Turkish laundering activities had relocated to Northern Cyprus.

Transformation from Kabadayi to Organized Crime

The era of military coups, to a certain extent, transformed the face of Turkish organized crime. The *kabadayi* institution, which was characteristically individualistic, had evolved into organized crime networks in the 1970s. *Kabadayis* who previously focused on local problem resolution in their restricted areas, found better opportunities as organized crime groups engaged primarily in transnational smuggling activities. The 1972 academy award winning film, *The Godfather*, had significant influence on the global perceptions of organized crime. While the film depicted the activities of the Italian-American Mafia from 1945 to 1955 in the United States, following the film's release, mafia bosses in Turkey and other parts of the world either adopted the moniker of godfather or were regarded in such terms by others. In Turkey, for example, the *kabadayis* of the former era who were active in metropolitan areas were dubbed *babas* (godfathers).[36]

Trafficking of Arms and Narcotics in the Era of Military Coups

The deterioration of the socioeconomic situation in Turkey in the 1960s and 1970s led to rampant smuggling among the country's impoverished masses. At the same time, the smuggling of narcotics and weapons skyrocketed in the era of military coups. The large amount of seized narcotics indicated the active involvement of organized crime groups since the 1970s. The increase in narcotics trafficking was mainly the result of Turkey's geographical location[37] and its role as an opium producer for generations. Turkey's strategic location at the crossroads of Europe, Africa, and Asia presented opportunities for narcotics traffickers.

The fact that Afghanistan became a source country for the opium trade has impacted the Turkish narcotics trade. The ban on poppy cultivation in Iran in the 1950s and political instability and a long-lasting drought in Southeast Asia's Golden Triangle made Afghanistan a leading source country in opium trade,[38] creating new trafficking routes. One of these new routes, the Balkan route, went through Iran, Turkey, the Balkan countries, and into Western Europe. Turkey was the most important link on this route. Because the new narcotics route rendered Turkey a substantial bridge between Afghanistan and Europe, narcotics smugglers emerged in the country in the 1970s. Connections between the drug barons and politicians and high-level bureaucrats in Turkey were revealed during this period.

According to research by the U.S. Drug Enforcement Administration, 150 tons of opium were harvested in Turkey during the early 1970s, with between 35 and 50 tons of the harvest used in the production of illegal drugs. Police uncovered heroin processing laboratories in Van province in 1979; all contained large amounts of opium. The precursor, acetic anhydrate, known to originate in European countries, was seized from seven of the laboratories, suggesting that the Turkish mafia was an important link in the international narcotics trafficking network between Europe and the United States.[39]

Turkish criminal groups enhanced their dominance in the drug trafficking sector during the era of military coups. There was little doubt of their prominence after revelations chronicled a meeting of drug barons held in Bulgaria in 1980. At the meeting were Turkish, Albanian, and Bulgarian drug kingpins. It was chaired by a Turkish drug lord, İsmail Hacı Süleymanoğlu, also known as Oflu Ismail, who controlled the heroin market in the Netherlands. Three decisions were made at the meeting: first, the need to be wary about trafficking drugs because the number of checkpoints would be increased after the military coup in Turkey; second, the need for smuggling precursor chemicals for the manufacture of drugs; and third, the need to find new markets in Iraq and Iran. Whether these decisions were put into practice is unknown; however, it has been acknowledged that the number of Turkish organized crime groups dealing in the heroin trade rose in the 1980s.[40]

The famous Turkish arms and drug smuggler Behçet Cantürk lent credence to the notion of government involvement in drug trafficking, commenting, "… such large amounts of drugs cannot be trafficked without the protection of the state officials…." By the same token, the seizure of 15 tons of acetic anhydride from a truck en route to Turkey from Germany in November 1988 hinted at the volume of narcotics turnover in Turkey in the 1980s.[41]

Armed clashes that resulted in military coups also caused a spike in the volume of arms smuggling in Turkey. The internal turmoil and clashes in the 1970s raised security concerns among the Turkish people, leading more and more people to attempt to acquire firearms for self-protection. Smugglers were more than happy to supply all sides with the necessary volume of firearms. More than 800,000 automatic and semiautomatic firearms and 5 million rounds of ammunition were imported into Turkey while the embargo was in effect.[42]

State-Organized Crime Group Nexus in the Era of Coups

The collaboration of the political establishment with criminal groups is considered to be one of the most dangerous challenges to the rule of law, human rights, and economic development. This relationship is chronic in Turkey because of the fact that the balance and forms of power among players are constantly in flux.[43]

A political-criminal nexus often emerges in situations where the state is unitary or weak. Moreover, unitary and noncompetitive states lack a robust system of checks and balances,[44] presenting opportunities for politicians to enter into relationships with criminals. On the other hand, weak states tend to become hospitable to a political-criminal nexus as a result of existing inefficient and patronage systems as well as inability of government to establish an effective rule of law system.[45] In both unitary and weak states, criminal groups take advantage of zones of impunity or sanctuary to operate more effectively.[46] The latter one is more applicable to Turkish cases. The weak states in the 1960s and 1970s paved the way for a political-criminal nexus.

Politicians, in their relationship with criminals, are driven by a variety of motives, ranging from financing their lavish lifestyles to winning elections, or maintaining their leadership status.[47] In the case of Turkey, money was the primary motivation for the linkage between politicians and criminal conspirators. For example, after gaining considerable power at the end of the 1970s, Turkish organized crime groups began making connections with politicians and bureaucrats, offering them bribes in exchange for protecting their smuggling activities. One striking example involves Minister of Customs and Trade, Tuncay Mataracı, who was sentenced to life imprisonment for accepting bribes from smugglers in 1978. Mataracı had appointed certain customs officers upon the demand of arms and drug smuggler Abuzer Uğurlu. Uğurlu confessed his crimes in 1982, saying that he imported the smuggled goods into Turkey via the İpsala Customs Bureau by paying bribes to the customs chief. Uğurlu also admitted that he convinced Mataracı to appoint the customs chiefs affiliated with his criminal organization.[48]

Myriad examples of the politician-mafia nexus appeared in the late 1960s and in the 1970s. A Turkish senator and a parliament member, for example, who had been arrested in France while trying to dispatch 146 kilos of morphine base, were sentenced to prison in 1968. In a different case, a Turkish parliament member was arrested with heroin in Germany in 1978. Similarly, a police chief was arrested with 40 packs of heroin in Istanbul in 1979. This police chief was a member of a crime group processing heroin in a laboratory in the southeastern Diyarbakır province and trafficking to Germany. Corrupt politicians and bureaucrats also became involved in arms smuggling. The name of a Turkish minister, for example, was mentioned frequently in one of the arms smuggling cases that occurred in Italy.[49]

The nexus between politicians and smugglers continued after the 1980 military coup. In 1983, several high-rank military staff members were convicted by the martial law courts for their close relationship with smugglers. The military staff members allegedly had been working with smugglers of electronic goods from Lebanon and Syria into Turkey.[50] In a different case, although Şükrü Balcı, a high-level police chief, was linked to arms smuggling he was still promoted and appointed as the chief of Istanbul Police Department.[51]

The 1983 MIT (Milli Istihbarat Teskilati - National Intelligence Agency of Turkey) report unveiled the dimensions of the complex relationships and cooperation among organized crime groups, politicians, and bureaucrats during the era of military coups. Internal accountability and transparency were nonexistent in this era. Some of the details mentioned in the report are as follows:[52]

- Because the ongoing terrorist activities in Turkey had been financed by organized crime, an anti-smuggling department was established within the MIT in 1983. Mehmet Eymür was appointed as the chief of the department.
- Loan shark Baki Cengiz Aygün, also known as "Banker Bako," went bankrupt and found shelter with the previously mentioned *kabadayi*, Dundar Kılıç, after the1980 coup. By doing so, he shielded himself from his clients while getting Kılıç's henchmen to collect debts owed to Banker Bako Kılıç.
- Political parties of all ideological affiliations had demonstrated connections with organized crime groups.
- One of the generals who had been a member of the 1980 coup council had close connections with Dündar Kılıç and drug barons such as Sarı Avni and Behçet Cantürk.
- Another army general had connections with Kılıç, and that general's son was Kılıç's business partner.
- The governor of Istanbul officially rewarded a mafia member who publicly promoted the governor's image.
- The MIT Istanbul bureau chief had close connections with Kılıç in 1981 and 1982. The MIT chief allocated a storeroom at the harbor for smugglers. Moreover, Kılıç stated at his interrogation that the governor and police chief of Istanbul had extorted money from religious minorities.
- Organized crime groups flourished in the era of Mehmet Ağar while he was working as a police chief in Istanbul. He took an active role in bringing together mafia members and high-level bureaucrats of Ankara. Mafia members used these bureaucratic connections to appear as if they were legitimate.
- Police chiefs in the Istanbul Police Department facilitated the connection between mafia leaders and bureaucrats in Ankara. The contacts usually included procuring gifts, entertainment, and women.
- Famous figures of the underground world also ramped up political tensions by providing financial support to Leftist terrorist groups. A member of the Revolutionist-Left terrorist organization, for example, stated in his interrogation that he had met occasionally with Kılıç, who donated money to the organization

ORGANIZED CRIMES IN THE POST-COUP ERA (1984–2000)

Former Turkish President Turgut Özal took office after the 1983 post-coup elections and modified the country's economic system from a statist economy to a free-market economy. This substantial shift triggered structural transformations within Turkish organized crime groups as well. Three main development areas are salient for this period:

- Developments within organized crime groups between 1984 and 1994, particularly the operation of godfathers, policies on the financing of terrorist activities, and the strengthening of the nationalist mafia.
- Organized crime used as leverage to design the political domain, particularly dirty relationships unveiled after the attempted assassination of former president Özal and the Susurluk scandal.
- Crime groups procuring services from citizens, particularly the emergence of mafia-type organized crime groups in areas with the potential for high profits.

Organized Crime Developments between 1984 and 1994

Military coups paralyzed the entire state system in Turkey. The economic and social vacuums that emerged after the coup helped the augmentation of organized crime groups. Some of the more noteworthy police operations in the post-coup are described below.

Godfathers Operation

After the 1980 military coup, the impact of sophisticated organized-crime networks wreaked havoc on the weak Turkish economy. In reaction to that situation, the Özal government took serious measures to mitigate the impact of organized crime on the economy. One of them was a 1984 police operation against prominent godfathers. Several famous mafia leaders were arrested in the operation, making it a milestone in efforts to stem the development of organized crime in Turkey. After the operation, crime groups were forced underground to conduct their activities more covertly.[53]

Ülkücü (gray wolves) mafia

The concept of an *ülkücü* (conservative-nationalist political group) *mafia* emerged in Turkey in the 1980s. Many members of the *ülkücü* movement had been jailed after the 1980 coup. The imprisoned *ülkücüs* became involved in organized crime after being released from jail because of their strong connections with the state bureaucracy and politics, strong kinship relations, and familiarity with firearms. These groups were called *ülkücü* mafia because their former identity fit well with their nationalist ideology. For example, Alaattin Çakıcı was a mafia leader from the *ülkücü* tradition and community. Çakıcı was adjudicated in the 1980 coup era and sentenced to one and one-half years in jail for the murder of 41 people. Soon, he was covertly employed by the state against the Armenian terrorist organization known as ASALA. He joined the operations against ASALA in Lebanon. Çakıcı was a publicly well-known mafia leader in the 1990s.[54]

Termination of the financers of terrorism

In the post-coup era, government officials acknowledged that some prominent underground figures were financing terrorist activities. A striking example is Behçet Cantürk, a drug trafficker from Diyarbakir province's Lice region. The region was highly associated with the manufacturing of drugs. Cantürk once claimed that for those who are from Lice, dealing with the narcotics business is inevitable. Cantürk was one of the most powerful drug barons in the country. In addition, he was added to the blacklist of financiers of terrorism in the 1990s. In 1994, Cantürk's vehicle had been stopped by someone clad in police attire while Cantürk was on his way home with his private driver. A couple of days later, Cantürk's corpse was discovered in Kocaeli. Several other Kurdish businessmen/smugglers who were on the same blacklist were assassinated in the 1990s.[55] The government at the time tried to dry up the main revenue sources of the PKK terrorist organization by targeting their financiers who also were engaged in organized crime; however, killing Kurdish smugglers to cut off the terrorist organization's revenue was a provisional, palliative, and flawed strategy. The chances of success would have been higher had the government adopted a more legitimate and long-range strategy that included legal regulations against revenue from crimes and enhancement of the intelligence and operational capacity of law enforcement units.

Organized crime-political nexus

The connection between crime groups, politicians, and bureaucrats contributed significantly to the development of organized crime in Turkey. The deficiencies in the state system in the post-coup era paved the way for the maintenance of former nefarious relationships between criminals and politicians. The involvement of the criminal-bureaucrat-politician nexus in operations of the state in the 1990s is illustrated by two cases: the assassination attempt against Turgut Özal and the Susurluk scandal.

Assassination Attempt against Turgut Özal

Turgut Özal, who dominated Turkish politics between 1983 and 1993, gave the coup-ridden country new hope for integrating Turkey into the developed world through his liberal economic policies. As president, Özal took substantial steps to shift the semi-socialist closed economic system into an open and free-market economy. His liberal policies hurt the interests of organized-crime groups and entrenched state actors; as a result, they targeted Özal for assassination on two occasions during his period in office. His sudden death in 1993 while serving as president of the country aroused strong suspicions of poisoning. Twenty-one years later, in 2013, Özal's grave was reopened to investigate the claims of poisoning. Any doubts about poisoning as the cause of death were dispelled when the autopsy found two types of toxic materials in his remains.[56]

The Özal era can be considered a turning point in terms of the development of both deep-state actors[57] and organized-crime groups. The deep-state structure viewed Özal as a great threat because the democratization movement he introduced diminished the entrenched impact of the deep-state actors on state institutions. According to one theory, Özal was killed by the deep state because he was about to permanently solve the enduring Kurdish problem. After Özal's death, the theory holds, deep-state structures enhanced their power and efficiency in the state structure, corruption became prevalent in the public sector, and chaotic unsolved assassinations increased considerably in Turkey.

The plot against Özal also affected the development of organized crime in Turkey. The imposition of martial law between 1980 and 1983 had weakened the previous government's efforts to combat organized-crime groups. Meanwhile, the smuggling of gold and cigarettes remained prevalent across the country. Özal introduced a strategy that targeted the smugglers' main revenue sources. The importation of gold was forbidden, and the gap was filled mostly by smugglers. Özal then legalized the importation of gold and announced amnesty for the acts of early smugglers if they gave their inventory to the state. Although many gold retailers obeyed the law, smugglers continued their activities. A similar strategy was used against the smuggling of cigarettes. The gold and cigarette smugglers apparently were not satisfied, as both groups allegedly supported the Özal assassination attempts.[58]

Susurluk Scandal

The relationship between organized-crime groups and politicians has existed for many years in Turkey—only the balance of power between the actors has changed over time.[59] By most accounts the tentacles of the Turkish underground world reach into the government itself. The Susurluk car accident on November 3, 1996, is regarded as one of the most significant demonstrations of the close network between the mafia and the state and is considered to be a milestone in terms of the development of organized crime in Turkey. Of particular note were the individuals involved. These included Hüseyin Kocadağ, former deputy police chief of the Istanbul Police Department; Abdullah Çatlı, issued a red notice for murder and narcotics smuggling; and Çatlı's girlfriend Gonca Us, who died at the crash scene. The only person who survived the accident was Sedat Bucak who was a parliamentarian and tribe leader in the southeastern Siverek province. In the trunk of the crashed Mercedes Benz, investigators found assault rifles and ammunition and a brown bag of narcotics materials.[60] The assault rifles had been registered to the inventory of the General Police Directorate.[61]

Abdullah Çatlı had been trained by special military forces known as the Gladio in the 1970s.[62] He was hunted by the police for taking part in the assassination of journalist Abdi İpekçi and the jailbreak of İpekçi's assassin Mehmet Ali Ağca. Interpol had issued a red bulletin on Çatlı after he escaped from a Swedish prison and for his drug smuggling activities.

Former deputy police chief Kocadağ was one of the founders of Turkey's Police Special Forces unit in 1985, operating under the General Police Directorate. It was comprised of nationalist police officers. Its main focus was the PKK terrorist organization.[63] The minister of interior, however, had to resign after it was discovered that he had met with Kocadağ, Çatlı, and Bucak in a hotel lobby a couple of days before the traffic accident.[64] Afterward, the minister of interior revealed that he was involved in certain covert operations that he could not disclose for the well-being of the state and those operations.[65]

After the traffic accident, a parliament commission report and several investigations conducted by the media found robust evidence linking politicians with the criminal underworld. The Susurluk accident unveiled intermingled relationships among drug barons and cabinet ministers, forcing a few cabinet ministers to resign in 1998.[66] According to the results of the investigation, the members of the special police unit founded to combat the PKK and similar organizations were trained by Gladio, which had contacts within the *ülkücü* group, and was involved in international drug trafficking. The unit included 80 police officers and 30 smugglers. Some important members of the unit were Abdullah Çatlı, Haluk Kırcı, Sami Hoştan, Sedat Peker, Sedat Bucak, Tarık Ümit, Savaş Buldan, and Ali Yasak. These individuals were provided with several legal passports with various aliases. The officers were in charge of protecting the smugglers and politicians and extorting businessmen. The smugglers engaged in drug trafficking between Azerbaijan and Western Europe. Over time, some of the police officers in the unit started to act as independent bandits. For example, several police officers from this unit made attempts to extort the murdered king of casinos, Ömer Lütfi Topal.[67]

The Susurluk investigation report acknowledged that the special unit was concocted by the state to combat the PKK terrorist organization but noted that some members of the unit took an active role in the assassination of some Kurdish businessmen who had been providing financial support to the PKK. The special unit spun out of control over time and started to commit crimes such as black-market operations and drug trafficking for their own interests.[68]

Mafia-type organized crime

Several post-coup developments transformed Turkish organized crime syndicates. In the 1990s some adopted a family-type of structure and engaged in more lucrative operations. By the early 2000s, extensive efforts by the police brought these mafia-type groups under control. Two factors were the hallmarks of the mafia-type organizations: group structure and group rules.

Group Structure

Criminal groups have different group structures varying from bureaucracy to a group made up of members sharing the same friendship, kinship, culture, and ethnicity that enabled group members to have emotional ties and reciprocal trust.[69] Mafia-type crime groups in Turkey are organized hierarchically like a family, where all of the members are connected to one another. Members of the group are either immediate family members or have some other kinship ties. Because of the family structure of these groups, mafia-type organized-crime groups are identified by ethnicity or the geographic region where the organization operates. Two examples from Turkey are the Karadenizliler group and the Diyarbakir gang.[70]

Group Rules

The term *mafia* is most often associated to the organizational culture identified with certain Italian organized crime groups. The mafia culture includes rules and norms, ranging from *partito* (i.e., the organization's relations with the state) to *omerta* (i.e., secretness). Turkish mafia-type organized-crime groups have a similar culture. Group members act in secrecy, emphasize the development of close relationships with the state, and never give any information to police when arrested. These are the rules of the game, and members who broke the rules were strictly punished.[71]

Activities of Mafia-type Organized Crime Groups

Mafia-type crime groups generally carried out their activities within the country where they lived and in areas with high profit potential. Such crime groups relied on the extensive use of violence and frequently shifted their areas of activity as the government closed legal gaps and police operations increased. The primary areas of activity for Turkish mafia groups in the 1990s and early 2000s were extortion, check clearing, land regulations, and "snatching" mafia.[72]

Extortion

Turkish mafia groups were involved in extortion, especially in the 1990s. They systematically extorted nightclubs and shared such venues among themselves based on geographical regions. According to one police chief, a well-known mafia leader was so adept at extortion that he had been sending torture videos to those who refused to pay him. The police chief also stressed that many mafia leaders made considerable amounts of money by this method.[73]

The check-clearance mafia

Economic crises in the 1990s negatively affected citizens' balance of payments, and most debts could not be paid on time. Creditors faced lengthy lawsuits when they followed regulations and applied to the courts for relief. Creditors were further victimized by the devaluation of the Turkish lira during the economic crises. Seeing the urgent need for a solution, organized-crime groups seized the opportunity and became heavily involved in the check-clearance business.[74]

The land mafia

Most developing countries faced the land mafia, which took advantage of urbanization policies. Such policies in Turkey stimulated migration from rural areas to city centers in the 1950s. The number of houses built on public lands in remote areas of city centers mushroomed almost overnight. The houses were called *gecekondu* (i.e., a squatter's house; shanty or shack). *Gecekondus* (i.e., neighborhoods) sprang up and turned into ghettos. The public lands in city centers were plundered by the use of force in this period. Crime groups did not hesitate to seize the opportunity to claim public lands and sold the property to immigrants at astronomical prices.[75]

The snatching mafia

Especially at the beginning of the 2000s, snatching was one of the most formidable crimes in metropolitan areas. Lenient punishments and a high profit margin for snatching attracted many crime groups, and several snatching cases occurred every day. The crime groups systematically exploited children because the risk of punishment was so low. One snatching group, which was soon taken out by the police, had abducted tens of children from their families in the southeastern Diyarbakır province. The group had promised the families that their children would work in Istanbul; however, the children actually were forced to commit snatchings.[76]

From extortion to snatchings, mafia-type organized-crime groups were active in Turkey on the local scale, and they easily shifted areas of activity when their income channels were blocked. It should be noted that the weak police force created a favorable environment to operate in the late 1990s,[77] when the police were grappling with inadequate training, poor pay and onerous working conditions and endemic corruption.[78] Statistics from the

Anti-Smuggling and Organized Crime Unit show that the number of mafia-type crime groups has dwindled in Turkey, especially after the enactment of Law 4442 in 1999, which provided police with more sophisticated investigation techniques such as wiretapping and surveillance with technical devices. The proliferation of police operations after the enactment of the law forced crime groups to shift their areas of activity to smuggling, which is less risky. A considerable number of organized-crime groups in Turkey, however, now are engaged in transnational smuggling activities.

ORGANIZED CRIME IN THE ERA OF GLOBALIZATION (2000-2018)

The global era in Turkey began in 2000 and was marked by the operation of traditional and transnational criminal groups. Police investigations have shown that mafia-type criminal groups are active in Turkey, leading to the investigation of 86 crime groups in 2015. These groups primarily were engaged in coercion, usury, robbery, murder, and kidnapping.[79]

Increasing globalization has influenced criminal activities. Currently, more crimes have some type of transnational dimension, with groups more likely to operate outside their traditional boundaries.[80] New transnational crime groups, thriving in shadow economies, have taken advantage of the decline of border control, increased mobility, well-developed forms of communication, and expanded international transportation.[81] More specifically, globalization has led to modifications in group structures and the modus operandi of organized crime groups. Many have shifted their criminal enterprises from more traditional forms of crimes such as extortion to newer activities.[82]

The cooperation and collaboration of crime groups across several national borders is recognized as transnational organized crime (TOC).[83] Self-perpetuating criminal organizations are capable of operating beyond national borders. Their structures are variegated as well, ranging from hierarchies and clans to networks.[84] Transnational crime groups have a tendency to be more fluid, better networked, and less hierarchical in structure than traditional criminal groups.[85] As opposed to mafia-type criminal groups comprising family-type kinship relations, many TOC groups operate with a structure based on clans. With this type of network, relationships are more elastic and looser.

Turkish Transnational Crime Groups Abroad

Crime groups comprised of Turks living in Europe also exhibit transnational characteristics. In the 1980s, Turkish crime groups in Europe were merely providing contact points and markets for their counterparts in Turkey; however, as these groups gained enough strength over time, they started to build their own global networks independently. For example, Dutch police found a criminal group comprised of Turkish immigrants engaged in exchanging cocaine and heroin in the Netherlands.[86]

Diaspora communities in developed countries have occupied a critical role in linking transnational crime groups. Suffering from unemployment and marginalization in their new countries, it has not been uncommon for Turkish immigrants to take part in some capacity in illicit networks.[87] It should be noted that the emigration of people from a number of countries facilitated drug trade in Europe in the 1960s and 1970s, including heroin transferred from Turkey.[88] Although Turks had lived in Europe for several generations as of the 1980s, many had difficulties assimilating into the culture of Western Europe. Worse still, the Turks remained uneducated and poor. These factors led considerable numbers of Turks to participate in organized crime.[89] According to a comprehensive and scientifically based annual report from Germany's BKA (Bundeskriminalamt, or Federal Criminal Police Office), the country initiated criminal investigations of 107,000 Turks in 2008, who comprised the second largest ethnic group in terms of organized crime arrests that year.[90]

In addition to linkages in Europe, Turkish crime groups have operated in the Caucasus, Central Asia, and the Middle East with a focus on drug and human trafficking.[91] In Europe, Turkish organized crime is one of the most active groups in the heroin sector. For example, 64.2 percent of Turkish groups engaged in heroin trafficking in Germany in 2007.[92] In the Netherlands, 26 out of 29 Turkish crime groups became involved in drug trafficking, and 18 of these groups dealt only in heroin.[93] According to the *2016 EU Drug Markets Report*, Turkish crime groups play an active role in the distribution of heroin in key regions of Europe.[94] They have established connections in South America. For example, two Turkish traffickers were arrested in Paraguay in 2017 because of their linkages to cocaine trafficking in that country. These drug traffickers also had relationships with human traffickers who excelled at luring female couriers to target countries where they are exploited for purposes of commercial sex.[95]

Transnational Crime Groups in Turkey

The transformation of organized crime groups as a consequence of globalization also affected Turkish organized-crime groups in terms of their areas of activity. Since the 1970s, Turkish organized crime groups had focused on the smuggling of gold, cigarettes, and narcotics mostly in neighboring regions. At the end of the 1990s, these groups were established transnationally, and expanded operations on a global scale. In recent years, a considerable number of foreign criminals was arrested while affiliated with Turkish crime syndicates. Most of the alliances were formed around narcotics trafficking, human trafficking, and human smuggling. A report from the Turkish National Police Department of Anti-Smuggling and Organized Crime (ASOD) emphasized that many foreign criminals had been arrested in Turkey in relation to narcotics trafficking. For example, drug traffickers from 47 countries were arrested in 307 cases in Turkey in 2010. Of these 35 percent were from Iran, 9 percent from Turkmenistan, 5 percent from Georgia, 5 percent from Bulgaria, 5 percent from Nigeria, 3 percent from Bolivia, 3 percent from Syria, 2 percent from South Africa, and 2 percent from the U.K.[96] In these cases, 39 percent of foreign nationals were involved in drug trafficking, including 21 percent in cocaine and 21 percent in methamphetamine trafficking.[97] On the other hand, 186 Turkish drug traffickers mostly connected to the transnational drug trafficking organizations in Turkey, were arrested in 17 countries, including 51 percent of Turkish drug traffickers in Germany, followed by 21 percent in Cyprus, 9 percent in France, 3 percent in the U.K., and 3 percent in Austria.[98] Turkish crime groups have at the same time expanded their areas of activity to include human trafficking and human smuggling.[99]

Several cases recorded in 2008 testify to the transnational nature of Turkish crime groups. In one case, British and Ukrainian traffickers were members of a transnational Turkish drug-trafficking group operating in Istanbul. The British trafficker was a broker connecting the Turkish group to opportunities in Europe and China. The British trafficker, under the leadership of a Turkish trafficker, assigned two Ukrainian traffickers to transfer eight kilograms of heroin from Istanbul to Beijing. In a second case, Turkish, Nigerian, and Italian drug trafficking groups collaborated in the trafficking of heroin from Istanbul to Rome. The Nigerian group in Rome hired an Italian courier to complete the operation. In a third case, traffickers from Turkey, Iran, and Western European countries cooperated in the exchange of heroin and synthetics drugs. In a fourth case, Turkish, Bulgarian, and Iranian crime groups trafficked heroin from Iran to Spain through a Malaysian courier. Drug money was carried in cash by a Bulgarian criminal who was arrested in Turkey.[100] Chapters 3, 4, and 5 further chronicle the activities of transnational criminal groups.

NOTES

1. Klaus Von Lampe, *Organized Crime: Analyzing Illegal Activities, Criminal Structures* (Los Angeles: SAGE, 2015).

2. Jay Albanese, *Organized Crime in Our Times* (New York: Routledge, 2014).

3. Eric Hobsbawn, *Bandits* (New York: New Press, 2000).

4. No one has contributed more to the discussion of this phenomenon than British historian Eric Hobsbawm, who coined the term "social bandit" in 1959. By

most accounts the social bandit, as initially conceptualized, is basically a European-American construct and does not fit every historical experience. Over the following half century his concept has been increasingly debated. His book, *Social Bandits and Primitive Rebels*, Glencoe, Il., 1960 was originally published as *Primitive Rebels: Studies in Archaic Forms of Social Movements in the 19th and 20th Centuries*, Manchester, 1959.

5. Karen Barkey, *Bandits and Bureaucrats: The Ottoman Route to State Centralization* (New York: Cornell University Press, 1994).

6. Eric Hobsbawm, *Primitive Rebels* (New York: Norton & Company, 1965).

7. Yucel Yesilgoz and Frank Bovenkerk, "Urban Knights and Rebels in the Ottoman Empire" in Organized Crime in Europe, eds Cyrille Fijnaut and Letzia Paoli (New York: Springer, 2006), pp. 203-224, 223-224.

8. Mitchel P. Roth, *An Eye for An Eye: A Global History of Crime and Punishment* (London: Reaktion Books, 2015).

9. Mitchel P. Roth, *Global Organized Crime: A 21st Century Approach* (London: Routledge, 2017), 345.

10. Anton Blok, "The Peasant and the Brigand: Social Banditry Reconsidered." *Comparative Studies in Society and History* 1972, 1/4:494-503.

11. Murat Çulcu, *Türkiye 'de MAFIA 'laşmanın Kökenleri 1: Her Sakaldan bir Kıl* (istanbul: e Yay., 2001).

12. Çulcu, *Türkiye 'de MAFIA 'laşmanın Kökenleri.*

13. Roger Deal, *The Kabadayis of Istanbul* (Istanbul: Istanbul Press, 2000).

14. Yucel Yeşilgöz and Frank Bovenkerk, *Türkiye'nin Mafyası* (İstanbul: İletisim Yayınları, 2000).

15. Yeşilgöz and Bovenkerk, *Türkiye'nin Mafyası.*

16. Engin Bilginer, *Babalar Senfonisi* (İstanbul: Cep Kitapları, 1990).

17. Yeşilgöz and Frank Bovenkerk, *Türkiye'nin Mafyası.*

18. Yeşilgöz and Frank Bovenkerk, *Türkiye'nin Mafyası.*

19. Yeşilgöz and Frank Bovenkerk, *Türkiye'nin Mafyası.*

20. İsmail Beşikçi, *Orgeneral Muğlalı Olayı Otuzüç Kurşun* (İstanbul:Bilim Dizisi, 1991).

21. Halit Çapın, *Bir Kabadayının Anatomisi* (İstanbul: Parantez Yayınevi, 1995).

22. Ugur Mumcu, *Silah Kaçakçılığı ve Terör* (İstanbul: Tekin Yayınevi, 1995).

23. Yeşilgöz and Bovenkerk, *Türkiye'nin Mafyası.*

24. Bilginer, *Babalar Senfonisi.*

25. Roy Godson, *Menace to Society: Political-Criminal Collaboration* (New York: Transaction Publishers, 2003), 9.

26. Mumcu, *Silah Kaçakçılığı ve Terör.*

27. Refi Cevdet Ulunay, *Sayılı Fırtınalar, Eski İstanbul Kabadayıları.* (İstanbul: Arba Yayınları, 1994).

28. Yeşilgöz and Bovenkerk, "Urban Knights and Rebels in the Ottoman Empire."

29. Çulcu, *Her Sakaldan Bir Kıl.*

30. Mahmut Cengiz, *Turkiye'de Organize Suc Gercegi ve Terorun Finansmani* (Ankara: Seckin Yayinevi, 2015).

31. Mumcu, *Silah Kaçakçılığı ve Terör.*
32. Roth, *Global Organized Crime: A 21st Century Approach,* 345.
33. Ryan Gingeras, *Heroin, Organized Crime, The Making of Modern Turkey* (London: Oxford University Press).
34. "Haşhaş Belgeseli Gerekçe/Documentary Justification," accessed on March 3, 2018 from http://hashasbelgeseli.blogspot.com/2012/01/hashas-ve-abd.html.
35. Peter Andreas, "Criminalizing Consequences of Sanctions: Embargo Busting and Its Legacy," *International Studies Quarterly* 49 (2) (2005): 335-360.
36. Bilginer, *Babalar Senfonisi.*
37. Cengiz, *Turkiye'de Organize Suc Gercegi ve Terorun Finansmani.*
38. Vanda Felbab-Brown, *Shooting up Counterinsurgency and the War on Drugs* (Washington DC: Brookings Institution Press, 2010), 114.
39. Mumcu, *Silah Kaçakçılığı ve Terör.*
40. Yeşilgöz and F. Bovenkerk, *Türkiye'nin Mafyası.*
41. Suat Parlar, *Kirli İşler İmparatorluğu* (İstanbul: Bibliotek Yayınları, 1998).
42. Mumcu, *Silah Kaçakçılığı ve Terör.*
43. Godson, *Menace to Society,* 1.
44. Godson, *Menace to Society,* 9.
45. Godson, *Menace to Society,* 10.
46. Godson, *Menace to Society,* 5.
47. Godson, *Menace to Society,* 9.
48. Mumcu, *Silah Kaçakçılığı ve Terör.*
49. Mumcu, *Silah Kaçakçılığı ve Terör.*
50. Mumcu, *Silah Kaçakçılığı ve Terör.*
51. Yeşilgöz and Bovenkerk, *Türkiye'nin Mafyası.*
52. "MİT Raporu (Banker Bako)."
53. Ferhat Unlu, *Susurluk Gümrüğü* (Istanbul: Birey Yayınları, 2000).
54. Yeşilgöz and Bovenkerk, *Türkiye'nin Mafyası.*
55. Soner Yalçın, *Beco Behçet Cantürk'ün Anıları* (İstanbul: Su Yayınevi, 1999).
56. Idris Gursoy, *Suikast ve Zehir Özal'ın Ölümündeki Sır* (Istanbul: Z Kitap, 2013).
57. Deep state is used to define criminalized elite groups who hold sway on the governments through paramilitary organizations and loyal bureaucrats and politicians to the ideology of these elites. According to speculations, these people are believed to be behind the 1960, 1971, and 1980 coups in Turkey. The police investigations conducted in 2007, 2008, and 2009, known also as Ergenekon investigations, proved that a group of elites infiltrated to the government and became involved in criminal organizations and employed terrorist strategies to control governments. Whenever they felt that they could lose the power from their hands, they resorted to violence.
58. Gursoy, *Suikast ve Zehir Özal'ın Ölümündeki Sır.*
59. Godson, *Menace to Society.*
60. Mark Galeotti, "Turkish Organized Crime: Where State, Crime, and Rebellion Conspire," 25-42.
61. Yeşilgöz and Bovenkerk, *Türkiye'nin Mafyası.*

62. Daniele Ganser, *NATO's Secret Armies: Operation Gladio and Terrorism in Western Europe* (London: Frank Cass, 2005).

63. Yeşilgöz and Bovenkerk, "Urban Knights and Rebels in the Ottoman Empire."

64. Mark Galeotti, "Turkish Organized Crime: Where State, Crime, and Rebellion Conspire," *Transnational Organized Crime*, 4, 1, Spring, (1998): 25-42.

65. Michael M. Gunter, "Susurluk: The Connection between Turkey's Intelligence Community and Organized Crime," *International Journal of Intelligence and Counter Intelligence*, 11, 2, Summer, (1998): 119-141.

66. Galeotti, "Turkish Organized Crime: Where State, Crime, and Rebellion Conspire."

67. Yeşilgöz and Bovenkerk, *Türkiye'nin Mafyası*.

68. M.R. Haberfeld and Ibrahim Cerrah, *Comparative Policing: The Struggle for Democratization* (California: SAGE, 2008).

69. Howard Abadinsky, *Organized Crime*, 11th Edition, (Boston, Cengage Learning, 2017), 4 and 5.

70. Cengiz, *Turkiye'de Organize Suc Gercegi ve Terorun Finansmani,* 61.

71. Cengiz, *Turkiye'de Organize Suc Gercegi ve Terorun Finansmani,* 61 and 62.

72. Cengiz, *Turkiye'de Organize Suc Gercegi ve Terorun Finansmani,* 62.

73. Cengiz, *Turkiye'de Organize Suc Gercegi ve Terorun Finansmani,* 62.

74. Cengiz, *Turkiye'de Organize Suc Gercegi ve Terorun Finansmani,* 62.

75. Cengiz, *Turkiye'de Organize Suc Gercegi ve Terorun Finansmani,* 63.

76. Cengiz, *Turkiye'de Organize Suc Gercegi ve Terorun Finansmani.*

77. Ozkan, Okan, Interview by Mahmut Cengiz, Personal Interview, Istanbul, July 25, 2014.

78. Gareth Jenkins, "Power and unaccountability in the *Turkish* security forces," *Conflict, Security and Development*, 1, (2002):83–91.

79. *2015 Turkish Report of Anti-Smuggling and Organized Crime (ASOD)* (Ankara: ASOD Publications), 53-54.

80. Jan V. Dijk and Toine Spapens, "Transnational Organized Crime Networks Across the World." In *Transnational Organized Crime An Overview from Six Continents,* eds. Jay Albanese and Philip Reichel, (Los Angeles: Sage, 2014): 7-28, 20.

81. Louise Shelley, *Dirty Entanglements* (New York: Cambridge University Press, 2014), 103.

82. Michael D. Lyman and Gary W. Potter, *Organized Crime* (Hoboken, NJ: Pearson, 2015), 12.

83. Lyman and Potter, *Organized Crime,* 240.

84. Abadinsky, *Organized Crime,* 8.

85. Shelley, *Dirty Entanglements,* 104.

86. Cengiz, *Turkish Organized Crime from Local to Global,* 67.

87. Shelley, *Dirty Entanglements*, 104.

88. Roth, *Global Organized Crime,* 315.

89. Cengiz, *Turkish Organized Crime from Local to Global,* 50.

90. Cengiz, *Turkish Organized Crime from Local to Global,* 61.

91. Cengiz, *Turkish Organized Crime from Local to Global,* 66, 81, 86, and 91.

92. Cengiz, *Turkish Organized Crime from Local to Global*, 66.

93. Cengiz, *Turkish Organized Crime from Local to Global*, 68.

94. "2016 EU Drug Markets Report." Accessed on March 2, 2018 from http://www.emcdda.europa.eu/system/files/publications/2374/TD0416161ENN_1.PDF, 20.

95. Ottolenghi, Emmanuel, Interview by Mahmut Cengiz, Personal Interview, Washington DC, March 13, 2017.

96. *2010 Turkish Report of Anti-Smuggling and Organized Crime*, (Ankara: ASOD Publications), 40-42.

97. *2010 Turkish Report of ASOD*, 39.

98. *2010 Turkish Report of ASOD*, 45.

99. S. Janssens and J. Arsovska, "People Carriers: Human Trafficking Networks Thrive in Turkey," *Jane's Intelligence Review* December, (2008): 44-47.

100. Cengiz, *Turkish Organized Crime from Local to Global*, 26-28.

Chapter 2

Explaining the Illicit Economy in Turkey

INTRODUCTION

The expansion of illicit economies throughout the world has influenced geopolitics and global financial systems. According to some estimates, which are for the most part conjecture, the total amount of illicit money in financial markets each year is anywhere between 1.0 and 1.6 trillion USD with half of it originating in developing and transnational economies.[1] Turkey's illicit economy ranks it among the most prominent countries. Its value in the country has been estimated to be in the billions of dollars. This dark economy is a variegated one, including the trafficking and smuggling of drugs, cigarettes, pharmaceuticals, contraband, antiquities, oil, and humans. Most of these activities could not flourish without rampant corruption. In 2010, the Istanbul Accountants Association valued Turkey's underground economy at around 5.2 billion USD.[2]

Due to a lack of legitimate opportunities as far as jobs and education, it should not be surprising that many Turks have found some form of sustenance and livelihood by working in various sectors of the illicit economy. Criminal and terrorist organizations, whose distinctions are often blurred, are major players in transnational networks. Moreover, Turkey has become an epicenter for money laundering activities. The rise of the AKP (Justice and Development Party) in 2002, has been accompanied by endemic, almost insurmountable corruption.

THE ILLICIT ECONOMY: CAUSATION
AND DETERMINANTS

Turkey's propensity for attracting criminal and terrorist groups can be explained by several factors. In order to understand the current underground economy, it is necessary to examine the crucial factors underpinning it. The factors for the most part, involve the national economy, Turkey's strategic location, and the particulars of Turkish society and the judicial system.

Economic Factors

Economic factors are critical to the development of an illicit economy. As the economy of a country develops, crime groups are quick to identify potential opportunities. Developed countries offer especially attractive environments for criminal groups seeking to siphon from more sophisticated economies. The Turkish economy is among the more developed economies in the world. In 2016, Turkey was ranked 18th in the world in terms of GDP per capita,[3] making Turkey a particularly seductive environment for criminal gangs versed in human trafficking and smuggling as well as the trafficking in drugs, cigarettes, and antiquities.

The supply-and-demand economic model can explain the emergence of crime groups, particularly in the realm of drug trafficking. According to the World Drug Report 2017, 29.5 million people suffered drug use disorders, with opioids the most dangerous and accounting for 70 percent of drug disorders.[4] The number of countries that prohibit the use of illegal drugs has grown concomitantly with the increase in drug users. For example, the number of people using cannabis worldwide increased by 8.5 percent, cocaine by 27 percent, and opiates by 34.5 percent in 2008. Prohibition has brought many short-term gains in the fight against the use of illegal drugs, but these have been fleeting.[5] What's more, the legalization of certain types of drugs has done little to curb the appetite for illegal drugs. According to some studies, ecstasy and cannabis users are particularly unconcerned about laws that prohibit the use of illegal drugs.[6] If the demand for illegal drugs is high, then suppliers of those drugs will step in to meet the demand by whatever means available. The exact number of drug addicts in Turkey is unknown, but it is in such high numbers that it has created a high demand, inevitably providing motivation for crime groups to enter the illicit drug trade. Case data for drug trafficking is a good indicator of the number of addicts in Turkey. In 2015, for example, the police recorded around 108,000 drug trafficking cases.[7]

Another example of the supply-and-demand effect on criminal activity comes from human trafficking. In countries where prostitution is either legal or at least tolerated, the demand is high for human trafficking victims who can be exploited in the sex sector.[8] A sizeable number of victims of human trafficking have been deported each year from Turkey where prostitution is tolerated. The demand for workers in the sex sector provides areas of opportunity for crime groups serving as suppliers. The tightening of borders, the prosecution of human traffickers, and the imposition of sanctions have failed to stop human trafficking.[9] In Turkey, for example, the closure of entertainment venues (such as discos, bars, and nightclubs) where victims were once sold, the deportation of victims, and the incarceration of human traffickers have done little to stem the human trafficking problem.[10] As long as the demand for victims continues, deported women will simply be brought back into the country by human smugglers, and new trafficking groups will replace those groups that have been incarcerated.

Tariffs and taxes are also important drivers of smuggling and shadow economies.[11] It should be noted that in a supply-and-demand scenario higher taxes on the goods directly affects the demand side. For example, in Turkey, higher taxes on and prices for cigarettes, oil, pharmaceuticals, and cell phones create opportunities for smugglers on the supply side.

Furthermore, GDP per capita and unemployment rates influence some to turn to smuggling and trafficking in order to make ends meet.[12] With its high unemployment rate, Turkey's eastern and southeastern regions are economically poorer than its western regions. For example, in research conducted by Turkonfed in 2013, the GDP per capita averaged 15,800 USD in western cities including Istanbul and Izmir. Conversely, it is only around 3,800 USD in far eastern and southeastern cities located on Turkish borders.[13]

In the poorer regions, coca or opium poppy cultivation offer better employment opportunities, leading many inhabitants to be drawn to the jobs intrinsic to the trafficking of illicit substances or the manual production of synthetic drugs.[14] Police reports on smuggling cases by region confirm the prevalence of smuggling and trafficking in the eastern and southeastern regions of Turkey.[15]

Geographical Factors

The geographical position of a country is crucial to an analysis of the illicit economy. The terrain, traditions, and domestic control in a given country can make the territory attractive for illicit trade.[16] Countries located on a smuggling route are more likely to feel the effects of the illicit economy. Examples include Mexico, which is affected by cocaine trafficking taking place in the Central American corridor between Colombia and the United States,[17] and Western Africa, which has become a nexus for cocaine trafficking between South America and European countries.[18]

Crime groups have emerged in Turkey on a regular basis as a consequence of the country's geographical proximity to prominent smuggling routes.

The Balkans route is probably the best known of these. The Turkish land-scape has played an increasingly important role in connecting opium prod-ucts coming from Afghanistan with destinations in European countries. The Balkan route has also served as an alternative route for transporting nuclear materials from ex-Soviet countries to Europe in the 1990s. Likewise, ciga-rette smugglers take advantage of the Turkish route to evade taxation and tariffs on cigarettes destined for Europe from Iran, Iraq, and Syria.[19]

Crime and terrorism thrive in conflict regions in no small part due to the lack of the rule of law. In this type of troubled environment, there is no effective employment system since conflict destroys the economy and repels investors.[20] Black markets rapidly emerge in the aftermath of conflicts, such as in the cases of Somalia, Syria, Iraq, and so forth.[21] As a result, it is not uncommon for post-conflict countries to be plagued by a recrudescence of crime groups when the conflict ends, as gangs take advantage of the social and political dislocation to use the fledgling country as both a source and transit for various types of smuggling and trafficking activities. The impacts of previous conflicts in Iraq and the ongoing civil war in Syria have further transformed both countries into smuggling hubs. For criminal groups operat-ing on the borders of these conflict zones with Turkey, the wars have opti-mized their abilities to operate at home and abroad. For instance, while Iraq was a source country for Turkey in the 1990s—especially for the smuggling of weapons—it has also morphed into both a transit route and a source coun-try for human trafficking smuggling and drug trafficking in subsequent years. This continuum is especially noticeable along Turkey's border with Syria, where the smuggling of cigarettes, oil, goods, and narcotics skyrocketed after the conflict intensified (see Chapter 9).

Corruption in neighboring countries further facilitates the development of the illicit economy. International smuggling routes more and more venture into regions plagued by political and civil corruption, further enabling the activities of criminal groups. For example, stricter Turkish law enforcement between 2005 and 2013 led criminal actors to select alternative routes in lieu of the traditional Balkan route. Heroin smugglers took advantage of routes that passed through mostly corrupt countries. The prevalence of corruption in neighboring states has placed Turkey in a perilous position in terms of illicit trade because law enforcement and customs, paralyzed by the effects of endemic corruption, have been stymied in their ability to suppress smug-gling and trafficking. In the 2017 Corruption Perception Index, published by Transparency International, Iran was ranked 130, Iraq 169, and Syria 178 among 180 countries,[22] confirming the prevalence of corruption in the region. The higher level of corruption in these countries also diminishes the ability of law enforcement agencies in Turkey to cooperate with neighboring police entities.

Social Factors

In countries with a legacy of organized crime, illicit trade, which would be regarded as deviant behavior elsewhere, has become a lifeline for many Turkish people just trying to keep bread on their tables. This is perhaps best exemplified by a cigarette smuggler, operating in Turkey, who refused to accept the notion that what he did was criminal, stating that "...what I have done is not a theft. It is just smuggling inherited from my father. There is nothing wrong with this job. This is a traditional way of making money."[23]

For decades, smuggling has been conducted as a daily occupation by residents in Turkey's eastern and southeastern border areas. Locals rarely question the illegality of smuggling; rather, they regard their smuggling activities with more neutral nomenclature such as "border trade." Not surprisingly any government measures directed at suppressing the daily "border trade," are perceived as acts of aggression, leading to various forms of social protest. In the town of Lice in Diyarbakır province, for example, police and military forces seized 6 tons of cannabis in December 2014 after taking high level security measures. To protest government intervention and the seizure of the contraband, local residents set fires in protest,[24] claiming that the state was infringing on their ability to earn a living.[25]

Similarly, oil smugglers have also engaged in demonstrations against attempts by police to suppress oil smuggling on the borders. Like the aforementioned Turk who claimed he was merely carrying on a family tradition, one of the demonstrators commented, "...I have been a smuggler since my grandfather's era. This is my job, and nobody can stop me doing this."[26] These types of statements testify to the fact that smuggling is deemed more acceptable when it has been conducted across generations in the region.

Confirming the argument above, throughout Turkish history, many well-known smugglers originated in the eastern and southeastern regions of the country. Subsequent generations carried on the smuggling traditions in these same territories. Police statistics from 2013, for example, show that most smugglings cases occurred in Turkey's southern and eastern border cities.[27] By most accounts, the smuggling of cigarettes and drugs is overwhelmingly controlled by the local population.

Unfortunately, perceptions of smuggling as a daily job or a relatively benign activity has also negatively affected the development of the cities in these regions. Regions exposed to prominent levels of smuggling activity frequently remain underdeveloped. High-volume smuggling provinces such as Hakkari, Iğdır, Ağrı, Van, Şırnak, and Mardin and the cities within those provinces have little chance of developing legitimate economies. According to the Social and Economic Development Index of 2015, Turkey's eastern and southeastern regions are the most underdeveloped areas[28] that function as entry points for many kinds of smuggling and trafficking. A prime example is Iğdır province, home to some of Turkey's most fertile lands. Several types of agriculture can flourish in the province's fertile terrain and favorable climate. Cultivated land, however, is limited in Iğdır. The local population of Iğdır points to the prevalence of smuggling as the reason why farming and livestock breeding in the province has not developed further.

Another example is the district of Doğubayazıt in Ağrı province, situated along Turkey's border with Iran. Smugglers engage in illicit trade when its benefits exceed its potential costs.[29] People in Doğubayazıt find cigarette smuggling lucrative, with the price of a package of cigarettes costing 1.2 Turkish liras compared to 4.5 Turkish liras if purchased in Istanbul. Thus, criminal groups earn 3.3 Turkish liras for each package of cigarettes they sell.[30] Many types of smuggled items are sold in open markets in Doğubayazıt, an area where smuggling is consistently one of the primary ways of making a living.

Local residents in Doğubayazıt for whom smuggling has become second nature, protest any police operations aimed at shutting down the markets, hoping to send authorities the message that smuggling is an economic lifeline in the district. When police raid these open markets, such as the one in December 2014, at least three protesters were hospitalized, and the police seized 710,000 packages of cigarettes.[31]

A similar case took place in Iğdır province in April 2013. In this instance, police raided an open market selling smuggled cell phones and seized 2,317 phones that had been smuggled through neighboring Iran. During the raid, locals attacked to the police, and one of the police officers was taken to the hospital. In response to the raid, residents sought assistance from an Iğdır parliament member from the Nationalist Movement Party (MHP). The parliament member accompanied by a band of local residents raided the police department, excoriating the police, emphasizing that while "Kurds are free to smuggle everything in this region... you persecute and extort the money of these Turks in Iğdır. Selling smuggled cell phones is a way of living in here."[32] In this case, the parliament member was more concerned with the local black market than any Turkish statute book, even when constituents break the law. This episode further illustrates the peculiar relationship between some politicians and the law.

Another explanation for the acceptance of smuggling in the region is linked to Turkish counter-terrorism policies implemented in Doğubayazıt and other areas suspected of supporting terrorist activities. Some observers suggest that smuggling activities are also facilitated by the governments' somewhat laissez-faire approach.[33] It is not uncommon for government officials to apply a hands-off approach, preferring to refrain from certain aspects of prohibition enforcement against the illicit economy.[34] The Turkish government has surreptitiously condoned illegal smuggling by the local population as long as they stayed away from terrorist activities. Such a policy has encouraged people living in the eastern and southeastern parts of the country to break the rules and engage in smuggling.[35]

Factors Related to the Judicial System

The competence of the Turkish judicial system and its accompanying criminal justice process can also impact smuggling and trafficking activities. Weak judiciary systems with less punitive lower penalties create opportunities for smugglers.[36] Turkey's judicial system, lacking deterrence, has contributed to creating a favorable environment for those involved in the illicit economy. Crime groups rapidly shift to safer and less risky areas when faced with more retributive penalties. For example, 122 suspects who had previously been convicted of trading 50 grams or more of heroin between 2010 and 2012 shifted to cigarette smuggling in Turkey, probably because it was less risky than drug smuggling, and the probability of getting released, when arrested, was higher.[37]

Another factor related to the ineffectiveness of the Turkish judicial system is the conflict between general laws (laws that regulate a main topic, such as smuggling) and special laws (codes that regulate thematic categories, such as oil smuggling and cigarette smuggling), which provides ample opportunities for crime groups to operate within the country. For example, the regulations related to oil smuggling in the Anti-Smuggling Act (#5607) comes under the general law, while the regulation in the Petroleum Market Law (#5015) is considered a special law. Similarly, the regulations related to cigarette smuggling in the 5607 law can be considered general regulations, while the Tobacco and Alcohol Market Law numbered 4733 is a special law. To better understand the conflict between the two types of laws, consider the following example: In 2012, the police were told to apply law 4733 (special law) to the investigation of cigarette smuggling because the punishments were more severe. The police, however, preferred to use law 5607 (general law), which offered less severe penalties. What cinched the choice for police was the fact that the law allowed them to use wiretapping and surveillance to apprehend the smugglers. The contradictions between general and special laws lead to weaknesses and vacuums that smugglers and traffickers are eager to fill.[38]

Gaps stemming from the interpretation of laws based on special interests also help create a climate favorable to the illicit economy. For example, the ninth article of the 5015 Petroleum Market Law states that "except for facilities such as factories, construction sites, transportation fleets and the like which have the capacity to host storage units for gasoline to distribute their own vehicles, only the licensed oil distribution stations can sell oil products to vehicles." The law provides the transportation fleets with the opportunity to store copious amounts of oil and derivatives; however, transportation companies in the border areas rely on this article to justify the stockpiling of smuggled oil in their storage units. The result is a stronger oil-smuggling sector and the growth of crime groups dealing with that sector in the border areas of the country.[39]

The final factor related to the judicial system's weakness is that police lack the capacity to confiscate criminal assets. Turkey is a haven for money launderers. That is why Turkish crime groups operating in Europe generally transfer their income to Turkey, where few investigations aimed at the financial resources of crime groups and terrorist groups have ended successfully. The Financial Investigation Crimes Investigation Board (MASAK) in charge of money laundering investigations has been handed thousands of cases over the past few years. Out of these the only cases that went forward in the judicial process were 14 related to terrorist financing and 13 drug trafficking cases in 2012;[40] and 6 drug trafficking and 6 terrorist financing cases the following year.[41] The failure arises because law enforcement officials in Turkey—rather than the suspects—are responsible for proving whether or not a source of income was gained through criminal activity. As a result, those who are arrested and convicted are able to return immediately to their routine criminal activities as soon as they are released from prison.[42]

In addition to the aforementioned factors, corruption, the Syrian refugee crisis, and the impact of corruption scandals have created a favorable environment for criminals and terrorists in Turkey. Corruption is endemic in Turkey, and a significant amount of government investments end up in the pockets of politicians and bureaucrats. Furthermore, corruption is entrenched in the customs, facilitating illicit trade (see Chapter 6). The other factor is the impacts of anti-corruption police investigations, implicating President Recep Tayyip Erdogan, his inner circle, and his political party. After these investigations, Erdogan started a crackdown to make over the government, purging entire organized crime, intelligence, and anti-terror units. This situation has created loopholes filled by criminal and terrorist organizations (see Chapter 7).

Syrian Refugees

The last factor that deserves special attention is the increasing role played by Syrian refugees in various criminal activities. After the Syrian civil war started in 2011, Turkey opened its doors to Syrian refugees with little thought given to how they would be integrated and assimilated into Turkish society. Currently, Syrians have become active in smuggling and trafficking in Turkey and in the region. These factors are closely examined in subsequent chapters.

NOTES

1. Fredrich Schneider, "The Hidden Financial Flows of Organized Crime: A Literature Review and Some Preliminary Empirical Results" in Illicit Trade and Global Economy, eds C. Storti and P. Grauwe (London: The MIT Press, 2012): 31-48.

2. "İllegal Türkiye: 5.2 milyar dolar!", *Haberturk,* accessed on March 12, 2018 from http://www.haberturk.com/ekonomi/makro-ekonomi/haber/653555-illegal-turkiye-52-milyar-dolar.

3. "Projected GDP Ranking (2016-2020)" *Statistics Times,* accessed on March 10, 2018 from http://statisticstimes.com/economy/projected-world-gdp-ranking.php.

4. "World Drug Report", *2017UNODC Press Release*, accessed on March 3, 2018 from https://www.unodc.org/unodc/en/press/releases/2017/June/world-drug-report-2017_-29-5-million-people-globally-suffer-from-drug-use-disorders--opioids-the-most-harmful.html.

5. "International Supply and Demand: Drug Policy" *The Economist*, London 399.8736 (June 4, 2011): 70-71.

6. "Supply Always Comes On The Heels Of Demand: What Effects Do control strategies have on drug users themselves?," *Addiction*, (November 1, 2012), Vol. 107, No. 11, p. 1903.

7. *2017 Turkiye Uyusturucu Raporu* (Ankara: Narkotik Suclarla Mucadele Daire Baskanligi), 6.

8. David A. Feingold, "Human Trafficking," *Foreign Policy*, No. 150 (September/October 2005): 26-30.

9. Feingold, "Human Trafficking," 27, 30.

10. Mahmut Cengiz's field experience, 2011-2013, Iğdır.

11. Mohammad Reza Farzanegan "Dark Side of Trade in Iran: Evidence from a Structural Equation Model" in Illicit Trade and Global Economy, eds C. Storti and P. Grauwe, (London: The MIT Press, 2012): 73-118.

12. G. Frechette, "A Panel Data Analysis of the Time-Varying Determinants of Corruption," Working Paper 28, Montreal, p 2006.

13. Erdinc Yeldan and Kamil Tasci, "Orta Gelir Tuzağından Çıkış: Hangi Türkiye" Turkonfed, accessed on March 8, 2018 from http://www.turkonfed.org/Files/ContentFile/ogt-raporu-ii-cilt.pdf.

14. Vanda Felbab-Brown, *Shooting Up Counterinsurgency and the War on Drugs*, (Washington DC: Brookings Institution, 2010), 21.

15. *2016 Turkish Report of ASOD,* 42.

16. James Dallis Medler, "The Smugglers' Landscape: Geography, Route Selection and the Global Heroin Trade," unpublished dissertation, (George Mason University: 2004), p. 5.

17. Paul Rexton Kan, "What We're Getting Wrong about Mexico," *Parameters*, (Summer 2011), pp. 37–48, p. 43.

18. Ashley Neese Bybee, "The Twenty-First Century Expansion of the Transnational Drug Trade in Africa." *Journal of International Affairs*, Vol. 66, No. 1, (Fall/Winter, 2012): 69-84.

19. Cengiz, *Turkiye'de Organize Suc Gercegi ve Terorun Finansmani*, 106.

20. Louise Shelley, *Dirty Entanglements* (New York: Cambridge University Press, 2014), 153.

21. Phil Williams, "Lawlessness and Disorder: An Emerging Paradigm for the 21st Century" in *Convergence,* eds Michael Miklancic and Jacquline Brewer, (Washington DC: NDU Press, 2013):13-36, 26.

22. "Corruption Perception Index 2017" *Transparency International,* accessed on March 7, 2018 from https://www.transparency.org/news/feature/corruption_percept ions_index_2017.

23. Mahmut Cengiz's field experience, February 12, 2014, Iğdır.

24. "Dile kolay! 6 ton esrar ele geçirildi" *Sabah Gazetesi,* accessed on March 12, 2018 from https://www.sabah.com.tr/yasam/2014/12/23/dile-kolay-6-ton-esrar-ele-gecirildi.

25. "Erdoğan Lice olaylarının ESRAR'ını anlattı," *Haber Vitrini,* accessed on April 6, 2017, from http://www.habervitrini.com/gundem/erdogan-lice-olaylarinin-esrarini-anlatti-349317.

26. Mahmut Cengiz's field experience, February 18, 2014, Iğdır.

27. *2013 Turkish Report of Anti-Smuggling and Organized Crime*, 57.

28. "The 2015 Turkish Election: The Unclear Economic Dimension" *Geo-Currrents,* accessed on March 12, 2018 from http://www.geocurrents.info/geopoli tics/elections/the-2015-turkish-election-the-unclear-economic-dimension#ixzz59VP Cx1Rr".

29. Farzanegan, "Dark Side of Trade in Iran: Evidence from a Structural Equation Model," 94.

30. Mahmut Cengiz's field experience, September 12, 2013, Doğubayazıt.

31. "Doğubayazıt'ta 5 kamyon kaçak sigara ele geçirildi" *Diyadinnet,* accessed on March 12, 2018 from https://www.diyadinnet.com/haberi-106157-doğubayazıtta-5-kamyon-kaçak-sigara-ele-geçirildi.

32. Mahmut Cengiz's field experience, April 11, 2013, Iğdır.

33. Mahmut Cengiz's field experience, September 12, 2013, Doğubayazıt.

34. Felbab-Brown, *Shooting Up Counterinsurgency and the War on Drugs*, 27.

35. Mahmut Cengiz's, the author, field experience, September 12, 2013, Doğubayazıt.

36. Norton, 1988.

37. Mahmut Cengiz, *Orta Dogu'da Kuresel Tehditler* (Ankara: Adalet Yayinevi, 2016), 96.

38. Mahmut Cengiz, *Turkiye'de Organize Suc Gercegi ve Terorun Finansmani* (Ankara: Seckin Yayincilik, 2015), 112.

39. Cengiz, *Turkiye'de Organize Suc Gercegi ve Terorun Finansmani*, 113.

40. "The Financial Crimes Investigation Board (MASAK) Activity Report 2012," *Ministry of Finance MASAK,* accessed on March 12, 2018 from http://www.masak .gov.tr/media/portals/masak2/files/faalrap_2012.pdf, 28.

41. The Financial Crimes Investigation Board (MASAK) Activity Report 2012, *Ministry of Finance MASAK,* accessed on March 12, 2018 from http://www.masak .gov.tr/media/portals/masak2/files/faalrap_2013.pdf, 32.

42. Cengiz, *Turkiye'de Organize Suc Gercegi ve Terorun Finansmani,* 112 and 113.

Chapter 3

Drug Trends

Abuse, Production, and Trafficking

INTRODUCTION

Few illicit businesses are as lucrative as the drug trade. With a customer base teeming with addicts and recreational users, drug trafficking provides a consistent funding source for criminals, terrorists, and corrupt officials.[1] Drug trafficking makes up a significant portion of Turkey's illicit economy. The expansion of the drug trade in Turkey totaled an estimated 1.2 billion USD as far back as 2010.[2] The number of traffickers and drug trafficking cases increases every year, peddling an ever-changing array of substances ranging from heroin, cocaine, and synthetic cannabis to acetic anhydrite, methamphetamine, and captagon. Transnational networks throughout Europe and beyond transport the drugs through Turkey. Not surprisingly, more of the illicit products remain in Turkey to feed the needs of a growing user base there. With Turkey playing an increasingly prominent role in the drug trafficking pipeline a number of Turks have taken leadership positions in some of the most dominant drug trafficking groups.

Important Turkish drug cases in 2016 and 2017 revealed the country to be an important player in the drug-processing sector as well. Additionally, drug use in Turkey has reached an alarming level. This chapter utilizes official reports, police statistics, international reports as well as interviews[3] with drug trafficking experts to present a clearer picture of drug abuse, trafficking, and processing in Turkey.

Drug Trends

Turkey fills a key role in the international illicit drug trade, both as a transit location and as a target country. To some extent, it also is a source country for captagon, cannabis,[4] heroin and methamphetamine. Turkey's location along the Balkans route has facilitated its transition to a key drug smuggling hub (Figure 3.1).[5] The civil wars in Iraq in the early 2000s and Syria in the early 2010s have only heightened Turkey's susceptibility to major drug smuggling activities. On the other hand, domestic drug abuse continues to grow unabated as drugs flood the country, while the government pays attention elsewhere. Making matters worse is the fact that treatment facilities are inadequate to meet the needs of the growing addict population. The Turkish drug trade has harmed most sectors of the country's social, economic, political, and security structure. Meanwhile, the government turns a blind eye on the drug crisis, particularly on the demand side. Law enforcement prioritizes the supply side of the drug problem, measuring its success by the number of large seizures, while ignoring a steady rise in drug use and addiction.[6]

Figure 3.1 The main Balkans drug trafficking route passing over Turkey. *Source*: "Narcotic Superhighways: The Top 5 Routes for Drug Trafficking," HETQ Investigative Journalists, accessed on March 7, 2018 from http://hetq.am/eng/news/23813/narcotic-superhighways-the-top-5-routes-for-drug-trafficking.html.

Many crime groups have entered the illicit economy through the drug trade. Many diversify into other illicit activities over time, including the lucrative opportunities presented by human trafficking or cigarette smuggling. By most accounts, the global drug market is valued in the billions of dollars. In 2011 alone, it was estimated to be more than 320 billion USD.[7] In 2014 estimates placed it at somewhere between $426 and $652 billion.[8] According to the UNODC World Drug Report 2017, revenues from drug trafficking were close to 27.7 billion Euros in European Union (EU) countries.[9]

Turkish organized crime groups involved in drug trafficking share the heroin, cannabis, and cocaine market along with their counterparts in some European countries, such as Germany.[10] The variety of drugs seized in Turkey[11] offer insight into the types of drugs consumed in the country.

For more than a half century, drug traffickers have taken advantage of Turkey's strategic location between Europe and Asia, transporting narcotics produced in Afghanistan to Western Europe via Turkey. After gaining experience and competency by cooperating with their Iranian counterparts, Turkish drug traffickers became the most active runners in the drug trade along the Balkans route,[12] as seen in the map of Balkans Route below. According to estimates, the market value for heroin that follows this route is roughly 20 billion USD.[13]

Drug trafficking in Turkey has resulted in a huge increase in the volume of drugs available for the rising domestic demand. According to police reports, in 2014, around 60,000 drug traffickers were detained in the country,[14] increasing to 170,000 in 2017.[15] The number of inmates sentenced for drug crimes in Turkey was around 50,300 in 2017.[16] Current drug trends revolve around the increasingly widespread use of cannabis,[17] the rising number of heroin addicts, and the proliferation of synthetic drugs, such as methamphetamine[18] or so-called bonsai (synthetic cannabinoids).[19]

Why Is Drug Abuse Increasing in Turkey?

Similar to the rise and expansion of opioid use in EU countries with an estimated 1.6 million heroin addicts taking treatment in 2015, Turkey is now suffering the same scourge.[20] There are myriad explanations for the sharp rise of drug use in Turkey. Most focus on easy access to drugs, ease of cannabis cultivation, lack of inspections in schools, media messages about drugs and drug use, the large number of addict celebrities regarded as role models by the country's youth, and problems arising from the treatment processes for drug abuse.[21]

Easy access to drugs in Turkey has facilitated the rise in substance abuse. According to media reports, virtually any illicit drug can be accessed cheaply, especially in metropolitan areas of the country. Because drugs are so easy to obtain, drug users often begin taking drugs at an early age.[22] In contrast with the official U.S. approach to the use of illegal drugs, which vacillates on whether cannabis/marijuana use leads to the use other illegal drugs,[23] Turkish experts continue to underscore the role of cannabis as a gateway drug on the downward path to a predicted heroin habit. For many years, the cultivation of cannabis was tacitly allowed in Turkey. The cannabis plant, which needs only sunshine and water to grow, is cultivated across Turkey, especially in the southeastern region of the country. Because the cultivation of cannabis was punished—until 2014—only with a fine, the substance was cultivated and used widely in Turkey. In 2014, for example, more than 1 million people used cannabis. Meanwhile, social workers and law enforcement officials still insist that cannabis users are more prone to shifting to heroin or other hard drugs.[24]

Drug use is widespread in Turkish schools, with recorded cases involving children still in elementary school. The lack of adequate inspections in schools contributes significantly to the problem. Guidance counselors at schools are so overwhelmed with routine workloads that they cannot pursue specific activities to detect and guide students who use drugs. In addition, school principals and other directors are not eager to cooperate with the police and inform them about drug dealers operating near schools.[25] The results of a study by the Turkish Monitoring Centre for Drugs and Drug Addiction indicate that 1.5 percent of students had tried at least one kind of illegal drug. Such usage, however, is not entirely benign. In 2014, for example, a 13-year-old student died from using illegal drugs.[26] According to one media release in 2016, there were drug abuse cases of children as young as ten years old.[27]

The media also shares some blame for the prevalence of drug use in Turkey. Some television shows geared toward young people, for example, portray drugs as an alternative strategy to relieve stress and other problems. Celebrities who have been tied to drug use can also influence the attitudes and actions of young people. The Istanbul Police Department, for example, arrested several celebrities—including movie actors and pop-music stars—who are regarded as role models by young people. The abundance of police investigations of celebrities[28] has come close to creating the perception that drug use accompanies professional success, wealth accumulation, and societal popularity.[29]

Turkish health policy is lacking and ineffective when it comes to drug addiction and treatment. Rehabilitation and treatment programs are limited, despite an increase in the number of addicts seeking treatment.[30] In 2011, around 155,000 addicts applied to the Alcohol and Substance Treatment Center for treatment, but only 2,117 of them received in-patient treatment. Other applications were rejected because treatment facilities were not available. Treatment centers exist in only 15 of Turkey's 81 provinces, which means that drug users must queue up for months to get accepted into a treatment program. Of the 25 treatment centers nationwide, only 35 beds are available for teenagers. All of these numbers are far below the norm in Western countries.[31] Furthermore, rehabilitation programs in Turkey underperform, and appropriate reintegration programs do not exist. Recidivism is quite common among drug users. In 2013, for example, 48.5 percent of the drug users treated in centers had previously received treatment. This high percentage indicates that government rehabilitation services are alarmingly inadequate.[32]

Drug Production

An examination of acetic anhydride (AA) cases reveals the evolving nature of Turkey's transition into a drug processing country. Turkey has been exposed to AA trafficking for decades, with the exact characteristics varying by historical period. Drug trafficking cases in Turkey during the 1990s revealed Turkey's role as a transit country, tracking heroin and morphine transported from east to west and AA carried from west to east. In some cases, heroin laboratories seized in Turkey indicated that the country was also a heroin processing country.[33]

A large number of AA seizures occurred in Turkey during the 1990s,[34] a clear indication that the country probably hosted illicit heroin laboratories. According to media reports from this era, in the 1990s Turkey had become one of the largest heroin processing countries, producing an estimated 30 to 40 percent of the heroin consumed in Europe.[35] This was a period when police were poorly-educated and –equipped to deal with the problem. What's more, corruption was endemic in the country's police departments. The police used torture as an investigation tool, due to the absence of traditional investigation tools—such as wiretapping, surveillance, undercover agents, and witness protection units. Those tools were not provided until the early 2000s when Turkey began the negotiation process that allowed it to join the EU. The 1990s also saw increased cooperation between Kurdish groups operating in EU countries and traffickers operating in Turkey. Behcet Canturk and Urfi Cetinkaya were some of the well-known Kurdish traffickers who helped traffickers in Turkey to open illicit laboratories to process heroin. As a result, large amounts of AA were seized during the 1990s.[36]

The high availability of AA continued into the early 2000s. In 2000 alone, Turkey seized a total of 23.6 tons of AA. While Western Europe was linked to the smuggling of AA, shipments that originated in Romania, Russia,[37] Bulgaria, Georgia, Saudi Arabia, and Syria were seized.[38] In 2000, other AA seizures were confiscated from primitive kitchen-type laboratories scattered in the eastern and northwestern regions of the country.[39]

In 2001, Turkey seized a total of 40.4 tons of AA. The countries of origin were Russia, Yugoslavia, and Italy. In a 2001 case, traffickers used a route from Italy through Bosnia Herzegovina and into Turkey.[40] The quantity of AA seizures decreased after peaking in 2002. According to the Anti-Smuggling and Organized Crime Department (ASOD), AA seizures decreased because demand for the chemical coincided with an increase in heroin production in Afghanistan.[41] For example, Turkish police seized almost 10.1 tons of AA in 2003,[42] dropping to only 1.6 tons in 2005.[43] Intensive law enforcement efforts in 2005 led to an important impact in AA seizures in following years, forcing traffickers to use other routes that did not pass through Turkey.[44]

Formal negotiations between Turkey and the EU aimed at priming its
admission into the organization prompted Turkey to enact new laws in 2004
that offered police more effective and strategic tools to fight drug trafficking
groups in the country. A new crime-fighting model introduced in 2006 sought
to prevent corruption among law enforcement officials, provided training programs to help officers improve their tactical skills, and to teach officers how
to use crime-fighting strategies such as surveillance, wiretapping, undercover
agents, and confidential informants. Turkish police officers cooperated more
closely with their European counterparts, leading to an increased capacity
to conduct controlled delivery investigations. The mentality among Turkish
police officers changed as they focused on large drug trafficking organizations in order to identify the traffickers' networks, group leaders, and criminal
connections. The police also were better able to collect and analyze data. The
new model was successful and enabled the police to seize large amounts of
drugs. For example, the amount of heroin seized in Turkey was almost double
the amount of heroin seized in all EU countries combined. In addition, traffickers began to use routes that did not pass through Turkey because they
were aware of Turkey's concerted effort to thwart traffickers and smugglers.
Primitive kitchen-type heroin laboratories were relocated from the eastern
part of Turkey to the border provinces of Iran.[45]

As shown in Figure 3.2, the amounts of AA seized between 2006 and 2013
fluctuated greatly,[46] primarily because the police were under the political
pressure to shift their focus from the seizure of AA to the seizure of illegal
drugs—including huge amounts of heroin and cannabis. The government's
action was based on the belief that the seizure of large amounts of AA
would flag the country as a heroin processor. Government reports echoed the

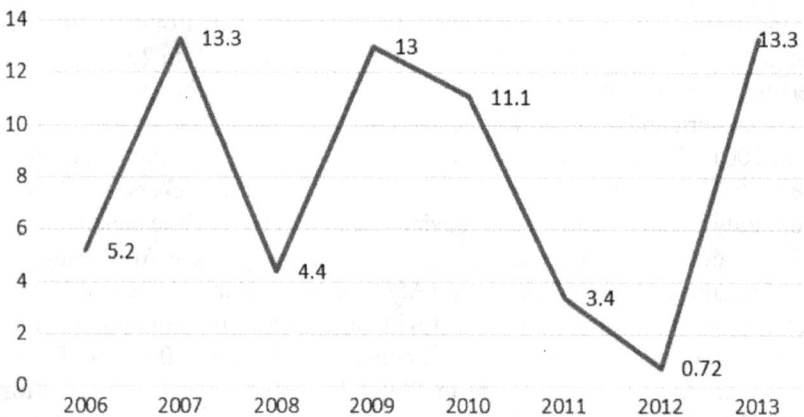

Figure 3.2 AA seizures, in tons, between 2006 and 2013. *Source: Turkish ASOD Reports, 2010: 24 and 2013: 8.*

sentiment with statements, for example, that only a limited amount of seized AA was destined for Iran or Afghanistan. What the government failed to realize, or chose to ignore, was that drug traffickers seldom used Turkey to process heroin because of intensive police efforts to combat AA trafficking between 2006 and 2013.[47]

The corruption scandals of December 2013 implicating President Recep Tayyip Erdogan, his inner circle, family members, and some ministers and high-level bureaucrats resulted in a destructive crackdown on the activities of entire police units (see Chapter 6). As a result of purging, almost entire drug trafficking units, police counter-drug trafficking efforts suffered dramatically (see Chapter 7). An examination of recorded drug cases from this era further supports the contention that Turkey was indeed a drug processing country. However, unfortunately, unlike past years, which offered detailed crime statistics, in this new environment police shared limited information about drug cases. For example, the police drug reports for 2015 and 2016 made no mention of AA seizures. The International Narcotics Control Board's Precursors and Chemicals 2016 Report indicated that Turkey seized 4,400 liters of AA in 2015.[48] Further media research revealed that after 2013, it was mostly customs officials who made random AA seizures, indicating two categories of seizures: those that transit from Turkey and those that are destined for Turkey.

AA Transiting Turkey

Turkey has maintained its position as a transit country for the trafficking of AA on the Balkans route. According to the Ministry of Customs and Trade, customs officials seized 14 tons of AA in a truck at the Kapikule border gate in December 2013.[49] The year 2017 saw a number of large AA seizures. In January customs officials seized 810 liters of AA and arrested four suspects in Istanbul. The truck, like an earlier case, entered Turkey through the Kapikule border gate from Bulgaria.[50] In another case, customs officials seized 1,554 liters of AA at the Kapikule border gate later. Although the driver of the truck was Turkish, customs officials did not share any more information about the source and destination of the AA.[51] Later in 2017, customs officials seized 6,773 liters of AA—enough to produce 3.5 tons of heroin. After completing their investigation, customs officials arrested seven traffickers, including one of Dutch nativity. As of June 22, 2017, customs officials had seized 11.6 tons of AA. They gave no destination information for the AA but noted that the source country was the Netherlands (which probably explains the involvement of the Dutch trafficker).[52] The customs seizures indicate strategy of utilizing Turkish trucks for illicit AA transportation. Therefore, both the transporters and receivers were linked to Turkish traffickers.

AA Targeting Turkey

The police have found an increasing number of heroin laboratories since 2014. All were stocked with AA and other materials needed to process heroin. In a February 2015 case, the police raided a heroin laboratory on a farm in Şanliurfa province and found 15.2 kg of heroin as well as morphine base and AA materials. This investigation resulted in the arrest of five traffickers.[53] In a May 2015 case in Van province, the police found a heroin laboratory with 123 kg of heroin, 1.5 tons of AA, and 112 kg of morphine base, and arrested nine traffickers.[54]

The police continued to discover heroin laboratories in 2016 and 2017. In an October 2016 case, for example, the police found a laboratory with 42 kilos of heroin and some AA and arrested one trafficker.[55] In a July 2017 case in Sakarya, the police raided a poultry farm. They found almost 1 ton of processed heroin and arrested five traffickers.[56] Considering that heroin processers need double the amount of AA, observers speculated that the traffickers transferred almost 2 tons of AA to Sakarya, almost 150 km distant from eastern Istanbul.

Police continued to seize traffickers and product in the second half of 2017. In October, police in Van province seized heroin precursors along with 200 liters of AA, arresting one trafficker.[57] In a December case, the police located a heroin laboratory in the aforementioned province stocked with 172 liters of AA, heroin precursors, as well as 1 kg of methamphetamine and some Sudafed pills. The police arrested three traffickers, including one Afghani.[58]

In a case recorded in the last days of 2017, the police busted a heroin laboratory in Yuksekova, a town in Hakkari province along the Iranian border, seizing 200 kg of heroin, 125 kg of opium, and 50 liters of AA, arresting three Kurdish traffickers in the process.[59] Lastly, in the early days of 2018, police seized 550 liters of AA in Hakkari province, on the border with Iran and Iraq.[60]

All of these AA seizure cases were related to the processing of heroin. AA, however, also has been used as a compound substance to produce methamphetamine (MA).[61] Recently discovered MA laboratories in Turkey indicate that Turkish traffickers use AA in the production of MA.[62] After 2014, MA laboratories began to spread across Turkey.[63] Media news reports confirmed the increasing number of MA laboratories. In 2015, for example, Istanbul police arrested eight Turkish and Iranian traffickers in Istanbul, all linked with the transportation of precursor substances from Iran to Istanbul in order to produce MA. In this case, 900 liters of chemical substances were confiscated.[64] Police continued to target MA production throughout 2017, particularly in Istanbul, where police seized 23.4 kg of MA from a laboratory run by two Turkish traffickers who were tied to MA precursors brought in from Iran.[65] Several months later, Istanbul police raided two houses, uncovering more MA precursor materials including 50 liters of chemical substances. Four Iranian traffickers and one Afghani trafficker were arrested in this case, confirming Iranian involvement to the transfer of this substance from Iran to Turkey.[66] Finally, in a January 2018 case, the police seized small amounts of MA, heroin, and cannabis as well as chemicals in processing drugs in a house in Denizli province and arrested four traffickers.[67]

AA seizures in Turkey indicate that heroin laboratories are scattered across Istanbul and can be found in some eastern Turkish provinces as well—such as Hakkari, Van, and Şanlıurfa—each bordering Iraq, Iran, and Syria. At one time, Van had been the traffickers' preferred location for processing heroin, but more recently has fallen out of favor among these criminal groups. Demonstrating that closing one factory at a time is like a game of "whack-a-mole," at this writing, Van has once again emerged as a heroin-processing center. The broader geography of heroin laboratories demonstrated that AA materials can be easily transferred to different provinces after entering the country. However, there is still little information on how AA is transferred once inside Turkish borders.

Drug Trafficking

Turkey has long been a key transshipment country for the trafficking of illegal drugs.[68] This phenomenon predates the 1960s, when Turkey played a significant role as an opium source country for the Marseilles heroin processors[69] of the so-called "French Connection."[70] The cultivation of opium in Turkey dates back as far as the first half of the nineteenth century, when the poppy trade and production flourished as one of the country's primary exports.[71] Seizures in the 1950s and 1960s put Turkey's involvement in the opium trade on the radar of international law enforcement agencies. American sources put the amount of narcotics seized in Turkey between 1952 and 1962 at 6,662 kilos.[72] By the 1970s, opium production led to a spike in drug trafficking in Turkey, prompting the United States and some European countries to ramp up pressure on Turkey and other opiate- and heroin-producing countries to end the illegal production of the drug.[73] In this period, Turkey's successful transition mainly stemmed from its use of the *poppy straw*[74] method,[75] while the production of government-controlled opium remained constant.[76]

Over the past couple of years, drug trafficking activities have become increasingly diversified. In 2016, for example, police handled roughly 81,200 drug-trafficking cases, resulting in the detention of 114,300 traffickers and 5.6 tons of heroin, 1,480 kg cocaine, 12.9 million captagon pills, and 147 tons of cannabis.[77] The types of drugs captured are a microcosm of Turkey's domestic drug consumption.

Heroin is one of the most widely consumed drugs in the world. Its retail value was 68 billion USD in 2009.[78] Turkey has been exposed to broader trade of heroin due to mainly its geographical proximity to the Balkan drug-trafficking route. That strategic location also means that fluctuations in the manufacture of opium in Afghanistan affect the volume of seizures by the police in Turkey. The amount of opium produced in Afghanistan and the amount of heroin seized in Turkey was highly correlated, meaning that any decrease or increase in the amount of opium produced in Afghanistan directly affected the amount of heroin seized in Turkey.[79] For instance, in response to a 38 percent decrease in opium production in Afghanistan, Turkish heroin seizures decreased 32.7 percent in 2015.[80] Similarly, shifting routes for Afghan heroin resonated in Turkish seizures. When traffickers began to use Iraqi and Syrian routes for Afghan heroin,[81] Turkish police made seizures on the country's borders with Syria and Iraq. For example, the police seized 600 kg of heroin transferred from Iraq in 2012 and 2013.[82]

Drug traffickers use various routes inside Turkey. In 2012, they began to favor sea routes to transfer their goods.[83] For example, drug traffickers who attempted to transport 250 kg of heroin stashed in a container ship at Turkey's Gemlik harbor and destined for Germany were arrested in a joint operation with the German police in 2012.[84] Always wary of detection, Turkish drug traffickers closely followed the operational capabilities of law enforcement units, shifting their routes or areas of activity as needed. As shown in Figure 3.3,

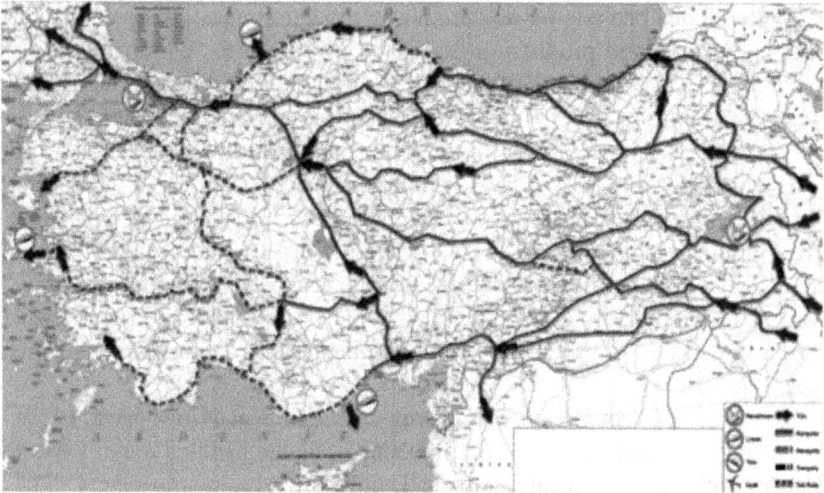

Figure 3.3 Heroin routes within Turkey. *Source*: Cengiz, Turkiye'de Organize Suc Gercegi ve Terorun Finansmani, 130.

the locations of heroin seizures are indicative of the various routes taken by the traffickers. One of these alternative routes is the Black Sea coast route. A considerable increase in heroin seizures along this route occurred in 2012 and 2013. In 2012 and 2013, for example, 779 kg of heroin were seized on the Black Sea coast route.[85]

Drug traffickers in Turkey tend to deal in more than one type of drug. Police investigations have revealed that some crime groups smuggled cannabis and methamphetamine in addition to heroin. On the other hand, most of the heroin seizures were made in the provinces situated on the trafficking route.[86] In 2013, for example, 30 percent of all heroin seizures in Turkey occurred in Istanbul.[87] Other provinces where large amounts of heroin were seized include Ağrı, Van, and Hakkari, all of which are border cities and entrance points for bringing heroin into Turkey from Iran.[88]

Turkish crime groups, however, have not operated in a vacuum. Since the 1990s, Turkish crime groups—including drug traffickers—have worked in collaboration with various transnational crime groups to funnel heroin into European countries. Turkish crime groups have since come to dominate the heroin-trafficking business by building strong relationships with European crime groups and continue to play a significant role in the global organized crime network.[89] For example, in 2012, international crime connections were uncovered in 317 heroin investigations. These investigations found that the target countries for heroin traffickers were Great Britain, Canada, Holland, and Germany. The Canadian connection was identified in six operations,[90] further demonstrating that Turkish crime groups have moved their spheres of influence and business networks overseas,[91] beyond the boundaries of their known operations in European countries.

Cannabis is perhaps the most commonly used and produced illicit drug in the world today and is the most popular drug in Turkey. Every country has some type of cannabis market. Its retail value was 142 billion USD in 2005.[92] According to a 2017 Turkish Drug Report, almost 50 percent of Turkish drug cases involved cannabis seizures.[93] The cannabis produced within Turkey generally is intended to meet domestic demand. Domestic smuggling activities are substantial, as exemplified by the arrest of 148,860 Turkish cannabis smugglers from all regions of the country between 2008 and 2012.[94] Cannabis popularity has only increased in the following years; around 74,200 cannabis traffickers were arrested in 2017 alone.[95] Moreover, countries such as Iran, Iraq, and Syria, have been linked to global crime networks trafficking cannabis into Turkey.[96]

Cocaine is another illicit drug that accounts for a significant share of drug activity. In 2009, its retail value in the world was estimated at 85 billion USD.[97] In recent years, Turkey has become a transit and target country for cocaine traffickers.[98] In 2013, 430 kg of cocaine were seized.[99] Seizures increased to 1,485 kg in 2017.[100] Cocaine is trafficked into Turkey by couriers or in containers.[101] Couriers transport small amounts of cocaine at a time, mostly by putting it in small plastic bags and swallowing it.[102] Investigations revealed that cocaine traffickers used 45 different routes in 2012. West African smugglers are the most prominent outside actors. Over a five-year period in the 2010s, 122 Nigerian smugglers were arrested in Turkey for cocaine smuggling.[103] If the increasing amounts of cocaine seized in the Mersin harbor is any indicator, shipping containers are being utilized to smuggle in a substantial amount of cocaine.[104]

Historically, ecstasy was manufactured primarily in Belgium and the Netherlands; by around 2012, however, the source of production had shifted to Asia and the United States, as the production of ecstasy in other parts of Europe declined substantially.[105] Despite the drastic change in the global scale of ecstasy production, Europe remains the primary supplier of the drug seized in Turkey. In 2013, for example, 77 percent of all ecstasy seized in the country was transported from Belgium and the Netherlands.[106] A smaller percentage (around 19 thousand pills in 2012) is smuggled into Turkey via war-torn Syria.[107] The police seized around 8.6 million ecstasy pills in 2017.[108]

Captagon is manufactured primarily in European countries before being transported to target destinations in the Middle East via Turkey. By 2012, however, Turkey had become a stand-alone target country for captagon.[109] Beginning in 2013, captagon and other types of drugs were being trafficked into Turkey using a Syrian route. The overwhelming majority of captagon seizures in 2013 were made in Turkish cities near the Syrian border, including Hatay, which accounted for 95 percent of seizures, and Gaziantep, which accounted for 3 percent of the seizures. The seizure of captagon transferred from Iran and Armenia to Turkey suggests that the drug is also probably being manufactured by Turkey's eastern neighbors.[110] In 2017, police seized 26.3 million captagon pills.[111]

The synthetic drug, methamphetamine (MA), has grown in popularity in Turkey in recent years. Since Iran is a source country for MA, traffickers typically use a route running through Turkey to transport the drug to target countries in the Far East.[112] The MA typically was brought to Istanbul and then trafficked through flights destined for East Asian countries.[113] In 2013, for example, most of the MA traffickers arrested in Turkey were from Iran.[114] A year earlier, a significant amount of MA was seized in Turkish cities located on the Turkish-Iranian trafficking route.[115] For example, in 2012 and 2013, police in the province of Iğdır on the Turkish-Iranian border seized a combined total of 54 kg of MA. Police investigators determined that Iranian and Turkish traffickers cooperated to transfer MA in 0.5-kg packages to Istanbul. From there, the MA packages would be trafficked on Turkish airlines to

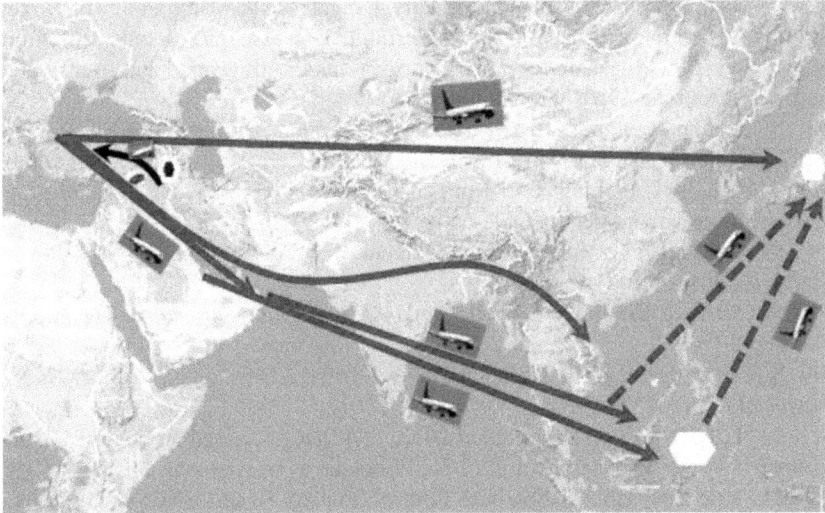

Figure 3.4 Smuggling routes for transporting methamphetamine from Iran through Turkey and on to target countries. *Source*: Cengiz, Turkiye Organize Suc Gercegi, 146.

Malaysia and Japan.[116] Figure 3.4 illustrates how MA originating in Iran is trafficked to target countries. According to the map, the MA is transported to Istanbul by plane or trucks and then moved from Istanbul to target countries using air routes.

NOTES

1. Louise Shelley, *Dirty Entanglements* (New York: Cambridge University Press, 2014), 244.

2. "İllegal Türkiye: 5.2 milyar dolar!", *Haberturk,* accessed on March 12, 2018 from http://www.haberturk.com/ekonomi/makro-ekonomi/haber/653555-illegal-turkiye-52-milyar-dolar.

3. This chapter used qualitative data obtained in open-ended ethnographic interviews. The dataset is comprised of 17 interviews conducted with 4 social workers and 13 law enforcement officials in Turkey. The respondents were experts on drug trafficking and drug use in Turkey. They were selected through a snowballing technique because it was the best way to find experts on the topic. The respondents voluntarily participated in the research, and each interview lasted two hours. Each respondent stipulated to keep his/her identity confidential. Therefore, each respondent was codified to anonymize his/her identity, using letters and numbers. For instance, DrLe1 symbolizes the first law enforcement official and DrLe13 is the last law enforcement official, whereas Sw1 is the first social worker and Sw4 is the last one.

4. Mahmut Cengiz, "Amped in Ankara: Drug Trade and Drug Policy in Turkey from the 1950s through Today," *Brookings Institution*, accessed on September 2017 from https://www.brookings.edu/research/amped-in-ankara-drug-trade-and-drug-policy-in-turkey-from-the-1950s-through-today/.

5. Mahmut Cengiz, "Turkey Has a Major Drug Problem: Here's How to Get a Handle on It," *Brookings Institution*, accessed on April 6, 2017, from https://www.brookings.edu/blog/order-from-chaos/2017/04/05/turkey-has-a-major-drug-problem-heres-how-to-get-a-handle-on-it/.

6. Sw1 and Sw2, Interview by Mahmut Cengiz, Personal Interview-Skype, March 26, 2017.

7. "State of the Illicit Economy," *World Economic Forum Briefing Papers*, October 2015, 6.

8. Channing May, "Transnational Crime and the Developing World," *Global Financial Integrity* (Washington D.C., March 2017).

9. "UNODC World Drug Report 2017," *UNODC*, accessed on March 12, 2018 from https://www.unodc.org/wdr2017/field/Booklet_5_NEXUS.pdf, 24.

10. "2015 International Narcotics Control Strategy Report (INCSR)-Germany," U.S. Department of State, accessed on March 27, 2017, from https://www.state.gov/j/inl/rls/nrcrpt/2015/vol1/238971.htm.

11. *2014 Turkish Report of Anti-Smuggling and Organized Crime Department (ASOD)*, (Ankara: ASOD Publications, 2014), 28.

12. Cengiz, *Turkiye'de Organize Suc Gercegi ve Terorun Finansmani*, 136.

13. Shelley, *Dirty Entanglements*, 218.

14. *2014 Turkish Report of Anti-Smuggling and Organized Crime*, 28.

15. "2018 Türkiye Uyuşturucu Raporu," Narkotik Suclarla Mucadele Daire Baskanligi, (Ankara: 2018), 15.

16. "2018 Türkiye Uyuşturucu Raporu," 44.

17. "Cannabis in Turkey," *Sensi Seeds*, accessed on March 27, 2017, from https://sensiseeds.com/en/blog/cannabis-turkey/.

18. Cengiz, *Turkiye'de Organize Suc Gercegi ve Terorun Finansmani*, 136.

19. *2014 Turkish Report of ASOD*, 15.

20. "Avrupa Uyusuturuc Raporu Trendler ve Gelismeler 2017," Avrupa Uyusturucu ve Uyusturucu Bagimliligi Izleme Merkezi (EMMCDA), accessed on February 28, 2018 from http://www.emcdda.europa.eu/system/files/publications/4541/TDAT17001TRN.pdf, 66.

21. Sw2 and Sw4, Interview by Mahmut Cengiz, Personal Interview-Skype, March 29, 2017.

22. Sw1 and Sw2, Interview by Mahmut Cengiz, Personal Interview-Skype, March 26, 2017.

23. A research study in the United States found that cannabis users were the least likely group of drug users to develop substance dependence. Transition from use to dependence was highest for nicotine users, followed by users of cocaine and alcohol. Catalina Lopez-Quintero, José Pérez de los Cobos, Deborah S. Hasin, "Probability and Predictors of Transition from First Use to Dependence on Nicotine, Alcohol, Cannabis, and Cocaine: Results of the National Epidemiologic Survey on

Alcohol and Related Conditions (NESARC)," *Drug and Alcohol Dependence*, May 1, 2011; 115(1-2): 120-130. Some studies, however, have found that marijuana use in the United States is a gateway for the use of other illegal drugs such as cocaine and methamphetamine. These studies also found that people who have used marijuana are more likely to use other illegal drugs than those who have not used marijuana. Robert L. DuPont, "Marijuana Has Proven to Be a Gateway Drug," *New York Times*, April 26, 2016, accessed on March 30, 2017, from https://www.nytimes.com/roomfo rdebate/2016/04/26/is-marijuana-a-gateway-drug/marijuana-has-proven-to-be-a-gate way-drug. In another study, researchers found that marijuana is the first drug for 70 percent of all consumers of illegal drugs and that half of marijuana users transition to other drugs. "Nearly Half of Marijuana Users Transition to Other Drugs, Study Finds," Promises Treatment Centre, accessed on March 30, 2017, from https:// www.promises.com/articles/drug-addiction/nearly-half-of-marijuana-users-transition -to-other-drugs-study-finds/.

24. Sw1 and Sw2, Interview by Mahmut Cengiz, Personal Interview-Skype, March 26, 2017.

25. Sw2 and Sw4, Interview by Mahmut Cengiz, Personal Interview-Skype, March 29, 2017.

26. "Uyuşturucu Kullanımında Tehlikeli Artış," *Bengu Turk*, accessed on March 30, 2017, from http://www.benguturk.com/uyusturucu-kullaniminda-tehlikeli-artis_ d14023.html.

27. "Türkiye'de uyuşturucu kullanımı 10 yaşına kadar düştü," *Ahaber,* accessed on March 1, 2018 from https://www.ahaber.com.tr/saglik/2016/11/14/turkiyede-uyusturucu-kullanimi-10-yasina-kadar-dustu.

28. "One of them was Tarkan, the pop singer, who was detained with charges of possessing some amount of hashish in Istanbul." Philip Robbins, *Middle East Drugs Bazaar* (New York: Oxford University Press, 2016), p. 159.

29. DrLe1, DrLe5, DrLe8, and DrLe11, Interview by Mahmut Cengiz, Personal Interview, April 7, 2015.

30. *2015 International Narcotics Control Strategy Report*, Turkey.

31. Ali Unlu, "Sosyo-Ekolojik Model Bakış Açısıyla Dünya'da ve Türkiye'de Madde Kullanım Problemi ve önlemler," *Uyuşturucu Gerçeği*, (Ankara: Atılım Üniversityesi Yayınları, 2013).

32. *2014 Turkish Drug Report.*

33. "1996 An Overall Assessment of Illicit Traffic in Use", *Anti-Smuggling and Organized Crime Department,* accessed on February 25, 2018 from http://www.kom. pol.tr/Documents/Raporlar/1996eng.pdf, 10.

34. Turkish police seized AA in 34 cases in 1994 and 1995. Most of these seizures were made in the northwestern part of Turkey at the country's border gate with Bulgaria, a common entry point for traffickers. In some cases where large amounts of AA were seized, Germany was the source country. From there, the AA was transferred to Dubai, Saudi Arabia, and to Syria and Turkey (1995 An Overall Assessment of Illicit Traffic in Use, 33). Given that 11 of the 34 cases occurred along the Turkish-Bulgarian border, it is clear that the source countries for AA were European countries (1995 An Overall Assessment of Illicit Traffic in Use, 36).

In 1996, the police seized AA in six cases. One of those cases occurred in Izmir where the police seized around 22 tons of AA. The source country was Belgium, and the materials were transferred by ferry through Italy to Izmir on the western cost of Turkey. One of the traffickers in his statement said that almost half of the AA was targeted for transfer to Iran (1996 An Overall Assessment of Illicit Traffic in Use, 8). In 1999, Turkish traffickers became involved in drug trafficking cases abroad, mostly in European countries. For example, 80.9 percent of 131 Turkish traffickers arrested in 1999 were apprehended in Germany. Some of these traffickers became involved in transporting almost 3 tons of AA that year (1999 Turkish Drug Report 1999, 25).

35. Kadri Gursel, "Türkiye uyuşturucu laboratuvarı," *Milliyet,* (January 2, 1999), accessed on December 31, 2017, from http://www.milliyet.com.tr/1999/01/02/haber/hab02.html.

36. DrLe2, DrLe3, DrLe5, Interview by Mahmut Cengiz, Personal Interview-Skype, July 29, 2017.

37. Among these countries, Russia was the most prominent; 5.5 tons out of 23.6 seized in 2000 from the Turkish port Samsun had been transferred from Russia (2000 ASOD, 23-24).

38. *2000 Turkish Report of ASOD*, 23 and 24.

39. *2000 Turkish Report of ASOD*, 23.

40. *2001 Turkish Report of ASOD*, 30.

41. *2003 Turkish Report of ASOD*, 28

42. *2003 Turkish Report of ASOD*, 60.

43. *2004 Turkish Report of ASOD*, 85.

44. *2005 Turkish Report of ASOD*, 34.

45. DrLe8, DrLe9, DrLe10, Interview by Mahmut Cengiz, Personal Interview-Skype, July 21, 2017.

46. In 2010, the police seized 11.1 tons of AA in four cases involving four traffickers per case. It is important to emphasize that AA cases in Turkey arrested only a few traffickers and were mainly committed by either individuals or small-scale criminal groups. For example, 10 traffickers were arrested in 7 cases in 2016, 13 traffickers in 5 cases in 2007, 25 traffickers in 8 cases in 2008, and 18 traffickers in 5 cases in 2009 (2010 ASOD, 26). The traffickers in these cases were foreigners. Most of them were drivers and came primarily from the Balkans and from Central European countries. No final destinations for the AA were identified, and no connections were found between the supply of the chemical precursor and major drug organizations. In most cases, AA traffickers used a shell company name for the consignor and shipped the AA to legal companies that had no connection to drug trafficking. AA networks, however, were much more careful about concealing the real identity of consignors and receivers of the substance (2010 ASOD Report, 27). Police seizures of AA fluctuated between 2011 and 2013, with 3.4 tons seized in 2011, 72 liters seized in 2012, and 13 tons seized in 2013 (2013 ASOD, 8).

47. DrLe1, DrLe4, DrLe6, Interview by Mahmut Cengiz, Personal Interview-Skype, July 25, 2017.

48. "2016 Precursors and chemicals frequently used in the illicit manufacture of narcotic drugs and psychotropic substances," *International Narcotics Control Board,*

accessed on January 2, 2018, from file:///E:/EMCCDD%20DRUG/PRE-AR_E_ ebook_r%202016.pdf, 25.

49. "Kapıkule'ye Gelen Tırda 14 Ton Asit Anhidrit Ele Geçirildi," *Ministry of Customs and Trade,* accessed on February 20, 2018 from https://www.gtb.gov.tr/ kurumsal-haberler/Kapıkuleye-gelen-tirda-14-ton-asit-anhidrit-ele-gecirildi.

50. "Eroin yapımında kullanılan kimyasal ele geçirildi," *Ministry of Customs and Trade,* accessed on March 3, 2018 from https://www.gtb.gov.tr/yakalama-haberleri/ eroin-yapiminda-kullanilan-kimyasal-ele-gecirildi

51. "Kapıkule'de uyuşturucu yapımında kullanılan madde ele geçirildi," *Ministry of Customs and Trade,* accessed on November 22, 2017, from https://www.gtb .gov.tr/yakalama-haberleri/Kapikulede-uyusturucu-yapiminda-kullanilan-madde-ele-gecirildi

52. "Pendik Limanı Ro-Ro Sahası'nda 6 ton 773 kilo kimyasal madde ele geçirdi," *Ministry of Customs and Trade*, accessed on February 17, 2018 from https ://www.gtb.gov.tr/yakalama-haberleri/pendik-limani-roro-sahasinda-6-ton-773-kilo -kimyasal-madde-ele-gecirdi

53. "Şanlıurfa'da eroin imalathanesi," *Haber7*, accessed on March 2, 2018, from http://www.haber7.com/guncel/haber/78316-Şanlıurfada-eroin-imalathanesi

54. "Baskale'de Eroin Imlathanesi Bulundu," *Haberler*, accessed on March 18, 2018 from https://www.haberler.com/baskale-de-eroin-imalathanesi-bulundu-73 22394-haberi/

55. "Mezradaki uyuşturucu imalathanesinde 42 kilo eroin," *Gazetevatan,* accessed on February 19, 2018 from http://www.gazetevatan.com/mezradaki-uyu sturucu-imalathanesinde-42-kilo-eroin-89283-gundem/

56. "Sakarya'da uyuşturucu operasyonu," *Hurriyet*, accessed on December 25, 2017, from http://www.hurriyet.com.tr/sakaryada-uyusturucu-operasyonu-37041414

57. "Jandarmadan Uyuşturucu Tacirlerine Operasyon," *Milliyet,* accessed on January 1, 2018 from http://www.milliyet.com.tr/jandarmadan-uyusturucu-tacirlerine -operasyon-van-yerelhaber-2336827/

58. "Van'da Eroin Imalathanesi Bulundu!," Sehrivan Gazetesi, accessed on March 1, 2018, from http://www.sehrivangazetesi.com/haber-van-da-eroin-imalathan esi-bulundu-46336.html

59. "Yüksekova'da uyuşturucu imalathanesine operasyon," *Haberturk*, accessed on September 18, 2017 from http://www.haberturk.com/yerel-haberler/57565228-yuksekovada-uyusturucu-imalathanesine-operasyon

60. "Hakkari'de Uyusturucu Operasyonu," *Milliyet*, accessed on March 13, 2018 from http://www.milliyet.com.tr/hakkari-de-uyusturucu-operasyonu-hakkari-yerelha ber-2548273/.

61. 2017 International Narcotics Control Strategy Report, United States Department of State, accessed on March 3, 2018 from https://www.state.gov/documents/org anization/268025.pdf, 52.

62. According to the Precursors and Chemicals 2016 Report, Turkey also seized 200 kg of ephedrine and 26,500 kg of pseudoephedrine in 2016, 51.

63. DrLe6, DrLe12, DrLe13, Interview by Mahmut Cengiz, Personal Interview-Skype, July 27, 2017.

64. "'Meth' çetesi çöktü," *Hurriyet,* accessed on November 23, 2017, from http: //www.hurriyet.com.tr/meth-cetesi-coktu-40029325

65. "Uyuşturucu polisi rezidansı bastı! 15 milyon dolarlık metamfetaminin ele geçirildi," *Aksam,* accessed on March 12, 2018 from http://www.aksam.com.tr/ yasam/uyusturucu-polisi-rezidansi-basti-15-milyon-dolarlik-metamfetaminin-ele-gecirildi/haber-606949

66. "Uyuşturucu imalathanesine narkotik baskını," *Sozcu,* accessed on February 24, 2018 from http://www.sozcu.com.tr/2017/gundem/uyusturucu-imalathanesine -narkotik-baskini-1982502/

67. "Nazilli'de uyuşturucu imalathanesi çökertildi," *Ses Gazetesi,* accessed on March 4, 2018 from http://www.sesgazetesi.com.tr/asayis/nazillide-uyusturucu -imalathanesi-cokertildi/13457.

68. Vanda Felbab-Brown, *Shooting Up Counterinsurgency and the War on Drugs*, (Washington DC: Brookings Institution, 2010), 2.

69. The French Connection gained serious attention in American popular media in the 1950s. Iran was a source for "French Connection" opium smuggling. Then American pressure on Iran produced results and Iran prohibited opium cultivation in the country in 1955. However, opium cultivation continued in Turkey (Gingeras, *Heroin, Organized Crime, and the Making of Modern Turkey,* 83).

70. Philip Robbins, *Middle East Drugs Bazaar*, (New York: Oxford University Press, 2016) 160.

71. Ibrahim Ihsan Toroy, "Expansion of Opium Production in Turkey and the State Monopoly of 1828–1839." *International Journal of Middle East Studies.* 13 (02), (1981): 191–211.

72. Ryan Gingeras, *Heroin, Organized Crime, and the Making of Modern Turkey,* (New York: Oxford University Press, 2014), 98.

73. Gingeras, *Heroin, Organized Crime, and the Making of Modern Turkey,* 199.

74. The poppy straw method was introduced in Turkey in the 1970s. The farmer is allowed to cultivate poppy plants similar to other countries. Nonetheless, the farmer is banned to incise the poppy pods to collect the poppy gums during the harvest. The state puts a strict scrutiny to make sure that no pods have been incised. Farmers cut and crush poppies that represent the poppy straw and sell it to the state (David Mansfield "An Analysis of Licit Opium Poppy Cultivation: India and Turkey," accessed on March 15, 2018 from https://www.researchgate.net/publication/266277621_AN_A NALYSIS_OF_LICIT_OPIUM_POPPY_CULTIVATION_INDIA_AND_TURK EY).

75. James Windle "Poppies for Medicine in Afghanistan: Lessons from India and Turkey." *Journal of Asian and African Studies* (Leiden). 46 (6), (12/2011): 663 - 677."

76. Roth, *Global Organized Crime,* 170.

77. *2017 Türkiye Uyuşturucu Raporu,* 6,7,8, and 9.

78. Justin Picard, "Can We Estimate the Global Scale and Impact of Illicit Trade." in *Convergence,* eds Michael Miklancic and Jacquline Brewer, (Washington DC: NDU Press, 2013), pp. 37-62, 40.

79. Behsat Ekici and Adem Coban, "Afghan Heroin and Turkey: Ramifications of an International Security Threat," *Turkish Studies,* (New York: Routledge: 2014), pp. 1-24.

80. *2017 Türkiye Uyuşturucu Raporu,* 6.

81. *Avrupa Uyusuturuc Raporu Trendler ve Gelismeler 2017,* 25.

82. *2012 Turkish Report of Anti-Smuggling and Organized Crime,* p. 30; *2013 Turkish Report of Anti-Smuggling and Organized Crime,* 6.

83. "Drug Smugglers Take to the High Seas to Avoid Border Patrol," *New York Post,* February 24, 2014, accessed on April 7, 2017, from http://nypost.com/2014/02 /24/drug-smugglers-take-to-the-high-seas-to-avoid-border-patrol/.

84. *2012 Turkish Report of Anti-Smuggling and Organized Crime,* 60.

85. *2012 Turkish Report of Anti-Smuggling and Organized Crime,* 61; *2013 Turkish Report of Anti-Smuggling and Organized Crime,* 6.

86. Cengiz, *Turkiye' de Organize Suc Gercegi ve Terorun Finansmani,* 141.

87. *2013 Turkish Report of ASOD,* 9.

88. *2013 Turkish Report of ASOD,* 9.

89. Cengiz, *Turkiye' de Organize Suc Gercegi ve Terorun Finansmani,* 141.

90. *2012 Turkish Report of ASOD,* 62-63.

91. Cengiz, *Turkiye' de Organize Suc Gercegi ve Terorun Finansmani,* 141.

92. Justin Picard, "Can We Estimate the Global Scale and Impact of Illicit Trade," 40.

93. *2017 Türkiye Uyuşturucu Raporu,* 8.

94. *2012 Turkish Report of ASOD,* 65.

95. *2018 Türkiye Uyuşturucu Raporu,* 17.

96. *2012 Turkish Report of ASOD,* 56.

97. Justin Picard, "Can We Estimate the Global Scale and Impact of Illicit Trade," 40.

98. *2013 Turkish Report of ASOD,* 15.

99. *2013 Turkish Report of ASOD,* 15.

100. *2018 Türkiye Uyuşturucu Raporu,* 18.

101. *2012 Turkish Report of ASOD,* 68.

102. Cengiz, *Turkiye' de Organize Suc Gercegi ve Terorun Finansmani,* 144-145.

103. *2012 Turkish Report of ASOD,* 68.

104. *2013 Turkish Report of ASOD,* 16

105. Cengiz, *Turkiye' de Organize Suc Gercegi ve Terorun Finansmani,* 145.

106. *2013 Turkish Report of ASOD,* 15.

107. *2012 Turkish Report of ASOD,* 37.

108. *2018 Türkiye Uyuşturucu Raporu,* 19.

109. *2012 Turkish Report of ASOD,* 39.

110. *2012 Turkish Report of ASOD,* 40.

111. *2018 Türkiye Uyuşturucu Raporu,* 20.

112. Behsat Ekici and Salim Ozbay, "Iranian Methamphetamine and Turkey: An Emerging Transnational Threat," *Trends in Organized Crime,* Vol. 16, (2013): 286-305.

113. DrLe6, DrLe12, DrLe13, Interview by Mahmut Cengiz, Personal Interview-Skype, July 27, 2017.

114. *2013 Turkish Report of ASOD*, 20.

115. *2012 Turkish Report of ASOD*, 41.

116. DrLe2, DrLe3, DrLe5, Interview by Mahmut Cengiz, Personal Interview-Skype, July 29, 2017.

Chapter 4

Illicit Markets

Cigarettes, Oil, Pharmaceuticals, Antiquities, and Nuclear Materials

INTRODUCTION

Smuggling is central to the Turkish illicit economy. Pervasive smuggling activity in Turkey has threatened the country's legitimate economy for years. Meanwhile, the value of the illegal market for cigarettes, oil, and pharmaceuticals totals in the billions of dollars. Demand for cheaper goods and the relative acceptance of smuggling as a legitimate activity have presented a plethora of opportunities for criminals. Take the impact of oil smuggling. Turkey pays considerably more for the oil it consumes compared to its neighbors Iran, Iraq, and Syria. Illustrating the age-old solution to exorbitant prices, criminals smuggle oil from these countries and sell the commodity much cheaper on the domestic market.

Criminal groups also benefit from the favorable environment in Turkey for the smuggling of counterfeit pharmaceuticals and antiquities, though the process for doing so is more complicated. The threat of nuclear smuggling persists, although the police have not detected any nuclear smuggling activity since 2006. Indications are that smuggling will increasingly threaten Turkey's legal economy and be a source of revenue for the country's illicit economy. This chapter analyzes the smuggling of oil, cigarettes, antiquities, pharmaceuticals, and nuclear materials.

Cigarette Smuggling

Cigarette smuggling in Turkey facilitates the ready availability of a product that endangers human health, provides a lucrative funding source for terrorist organizations and criminal groups, fosters unfair competition in the legal cigarette market, and causes a serious loss of tax revenue for the government.

Substantial price discrepancies across different regions and the low probability of apprehension are among the incentives that induce people and groups to become involved in cigarette smuggling.[1] Other incentives for cigarette smuggling, especially in Turkey, include taxation issues, weak regulations and laws, the fractioning of guardianship, the existence of corruption, the social acceptance of smuggling, the underdevelopment of the country's southeastern and eastern regions, and the country's culture, history, and geography.[2]

The tax levied on cigarettes in 2014 was 82.2 percent, making Turkey the sixth most highly taxed cigarette-consuming country in the world.[3] That tax, however, has not been a deterrent for Turkish residents who choose to smoke. The demand for cigarettes coupled with an extremely low likelihood of apprehension has only emboldened smugglers to meet that demand. According to the chief of a Turkish National Police Anti-Smuggling Unit, one cigarette smuggler was arrested 168 times, but never served any jail time. Given the weak or unenforced penalties against cigarette smuggling in Turkey and the high profit margin, some traffickers of other goods shifted their focus to cigarette smuggling in 2012.[4]

Cigarette smuggling has proven to be a lucrative cross-border criminal business.[5] As far back as 1999, 3.4 percent of the cigarettes consumed in Turkey had been smuggled, with global tax revenue loss 7.3 percent.[6] Billions of cigarettes were legally produced in and exported from Turkey, but they never appeared in Turkish government statistics because the cigarettes were smuggled into their final market.[7] Cigarette smuggling also is a profitable activity for criminal groups in Turkey. According to Turkish government statistics, 23 million people (60 percent men and 15 percent women) in the country smoke cigarettes. Around 100,000 of those people die from tobacco-related health problems each year.[8]

Paying one of the highest cigarette taxes in the world,[9] it should be no surprise that smokers go to great lengths to avoid paying the tax. Consider this scenario: If each smoker smokes half a package of cigarettes a day, that comes to 11.5 million packages per day, 345 million packages per month, and 4,150 billion packages per year. Because these cigarettes has been purchased from smugglers, only a tiny fraction of them is taxed. In 2015, for example, the police seized 143 million packages of smuggled cigarettes,[10] which means that one-twenty-ninth of each cigarette is taxed in Turkey. Cigarette smuggling remains among the leading and most lucrative revenue streams in the illicit economy. A box of cigarettes, for example, can sell for 13 Turkish liras at an entry point in the eastern part of the country, but by the time it reaches Istanbul the price is almost tripled to 35 Turkish liras. In total, criminal groups earn around 13 billion Turkish liras (3 billion USD) a year if smokers smoke half a package a day. If consumption rises to one package a day,

Figure 4.1   Amount (packages) of contraband cigarettes seized in 2016 by provinces. *Source: Turkish Report of Anti-Smuggling and Organized Crime Department (ASOD)*, 2016: 29.

the total income doubles to 26 billion Turkish liras. Figure 4.1 illustrates the widespread use of smuggled cigarettes, indicating police seizures in 79 out of the country's 81 provinces.

Turkish police have been seizing untaxed cigarettes since the 1970s. By the 1990s seizures had increased to levels matching seizures in European Union (EU) countries. Cigarette seizures were the highest in EU countries (around 6 billion) between 1990 and 2000, at a time when international tobacco companies were accused of complicity in cigarette smuggling.[11] In the 1990s, the two main sources for cigarettes smuggled into Turkey were Bulgarian traffickers and passengers on various modes of transportation who smuggled into the country more than the legally permitted number of cigarettes. Police seized 1.2 million packages of cigarettes in 1993, but that number plummeted to around 450,000 in 1994 and 1995. All of the seizures were in western Turkish cities, confirming that the Balkans route was used to bring the goods into Turkey.[12] The number of cigarettes packages seized by the police increased to 903,000 in 1996 and 1.8 million in 1997. Almost all Turkish cities were exposed to cigarette trafficking, though demand for smuggled cigarettes was greatest in metropolitan cities. Given that smuggled cigarettes were found in all Turkish border cities close to Bulgaria, Iran, Iraq, and Syria, the cigarettes most likely came from these neighboring states.[13] By 1999, Turkey's southern and eastern borders had become prominent and significant transit points for cigarettes smuggled from Iran, Iraq, and Syria. That same year, Turkish police seized 1.4 million packages of cigarettes throughout the country.[14]

In 2004, law enforcement began to focus on the tax loss from smuggled cigarettes. Asian and European countries were the sources of most smuggled cigarettes, with were transferred across Turkey's border with Iran and Syria or brought in through the port of Mersin in southern Turkey using a sea route. The number of cigarettes seized in 2004 totaled 4.3 million packages.[15]

Taxation revenue from cigarettes decreased 5 percent in 2005 compared with the previous year, creating a vacuum filled by cigarette smugglers. For example, legal cigarette sales dropped 40 percent in southeastern cities close to Turkey's border with Iran and Iraq. That decrease followed a spike in the number of cigarettes trafficked in these cities between 2002 and 2004. In one such border city, Şırnak, residents consumed 163 tons of cigarettes in 2002 but only 20 tons in 2004. The following year Şırnak was ranked third among Turkish cities with the most cigarette seizures.[16] Of the 11.7 million packages of cigarettes seized throughout Turkey in 2007, 9.8 million packages came from cities bordering Syria, Iran, and Iraq.[17] An increased demand for cigarettes in Turkey led smugglers to diversify their routes in 2009. In addition to routes linked to the three border countries, smugglers began using the port of Sinop in the Black Sea region that year.[18]

Turkish law enforcement began to see positive results against smuggling and trafficking after it implemented an improved crime-fighting model, including intensive training programs designed to professionalize law enforcement and offering police officers better strategies for fighting organized crime groups. Officers learned effective ways to apply the law that prohibits smuggling and trafficking and how to implement effective police tactics. The most essential element of this model was to give priority to countering endemic corruption. In this period, few police officers were fired for corruption. Nonetheless, police seizures increased steadily after 2006.

The effort against cigarette smuggling peaked in 2010 when the number of smuggling suspects arrested rose from 4,300 in 2009 to 14,700 in 2010. Likewise, the number of packages of cigarettes seized rose from 10.1 million in 2009 to 43.6 million in 2010.[19] That same year, the police seizures of cigarette packages reached an all-time high as a result of the government's increase in tobacco excise taxes. The government labelled cigarettes more dangerous than terrorism and increased its excise 30 percent.[20] This increase continued in following years.

As a result of deepening investigations of cigarette smuggling groups, the police discovered that cigarettes produced in Bulgaria, China, and Dubai were stockpiled in Iran, Iraq, Romania, Georgia, and Northern Cyprus and then transferred to Turkey via sea and land routes.[21] A pair of investigations in 2011 uncovered two transnational criminal groups engaged in smuggling cigarettes from countries along the Black Sea. Forty-four smugglers were arrested with 4 million packages of cigarettes and 44,000 bottles of liquors. From the two investigations combined, the police confiscated one ship, one container, two vessels, and seven trucks.[22] For all of 2011, the police seized 69.7 million packages of smuggled cigarettes—an increase of 60% compared with 2010.[23] The exponential increase continued the following year when 99.1 million packages of cigarettes were seized.[24]

Figure 4.2 illustrates the routes used by cigarette smugglers who targeted Turkey in 2012. According to the map, cigarettes were smuggled into Turkey from its eastern and southeastern neighbors as well as from Romania and Georgia. Cigarettes originating in the United Arab Emirates and China were first transported into and then stockpiled in Iran, Iraq, and Syria, before being smuggled into Turkey by automobiles, backpackers, and other methods of conveyance. An alternative sea route has also been used to move cigarettes originating in China into Turkey. Mersin harbor in southern Turkey is widely used.

Eighty percent of the cigarettes smuggled into Turkey in 2013 entered the country along its eastern and southeastern borders after being stockpiled in Libya, Egypt, Syria, Iran, and Iraq. By the end of the year, the police had seized 108 million packages of cigarettes. The ongoing conflict in Syria has created opportunities for cigarette smugglers, leading to an increase in

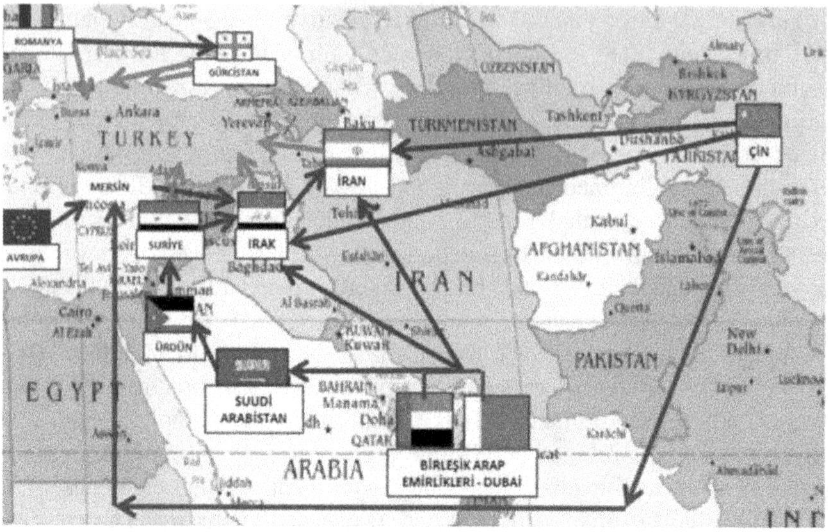

Figure 4.2 Cigarette smuggling routes targeting Turkey. *Source*: Cengiz, Turkiye'de Organize Suc Gercegi, 159.

the number of cigarettes smuggled from Syria.[25] For example, police seized 1.63 million packages of cigarettes and 1.2 million respectively in the cities of Hatay and Şanlıurfa on the border with Syria. A significant amount of these cigarettes originated in Romania, Bulgaria, and Georgia but were exported or ostensibly exported from these countries to Middle Eastern countries.[26] Cigarettes from Syria accounted for almost 25 percent of the cigarettes seized in 2013.[27]

The origins of smuggled cigarettes were almost the same in 2015 as they were the previous year. While the percentage of cigarettes from Bulgaria dropped slightly to 45 percent, cigarettes from China (brands: J&J, Ashima, Marble, Empire, and Dubai) constituted 20 percent. Turkish cigarettes that had been exported and then illegally brought back into Turkey (brands: Vigor, Toros 2005, Swisse, President, Kent, and Viceroy Black Galleon) stayed at 10%. The remaining 25% of smuggled cigarettes came from Indonesia (brand: United), United Arab Emirates (brand: Capital), South Korea (brands: Esse, Vigor, and Pine), Armenia (brand: Akhdamar), Jordan (brand: Mikado 2010), Poland (brand: Brillant), Georgia (brands: Winston and Pırvelli), Russia (brand: Jinling), France (brand: Glauses), and Germany (brand: Glauses).[28]

The tax revenue loss was 9.5 billion USD between 2009 and 2014.[29] In 2015 alone, tax losses reached 500 million USD. Smugglers have adopted a variety of strategies for evading cigarette taxes and beating the customs

practices of the National Turkish Transit Regime. It is common for international passengers on various modes of transportation to purposely exceed
the government's legal limit on the number of cigarettes brought into the
country. Other methods include concealing cigarettes in vehicles and trucks,
abusing mail-order companies, and crossing the Turkish border illegally.[30]
For example, cigarettes that originated in Bulgaria, China, Indonesia, and the
United Arab Emirates have been first transferred to the port of Jebel Ali in
Dubai and then to the port of Bandar Abbas in Iran. From there, cigarettes
are stockpiled along the borders with Iraq, Iran, and Syria.[31] Smugglers then
bring the cigarettes into Turkey, using one of the aforementioned tax-evasion
strategies.

On the face of it, compared to narcotics and humans, the illicit cigarette
trade might seem like a more benign form of organized trafficking. But as
demonstrated above, it can wreak havoc on the Turkish treasury. Many countries lack adequate law enforcement attention and smugglers are quick to take
advantage of this situation.[32] Cigarette smugglers are resourceful and adap-
tive. In one seizure, for instance, the police discovered that smugglers stashed
cigarettes in a coffin. In another seizure, police discovered that a smuggler
used the façade of taking his son to the hospital emergency room, going as far
as setting up an intravenous infusion device connected to his son's arm. The
smuggler had clandestinely stashed cigarettes under his son's bed. Another
smuggler used a washer and dryer to carry smuggled cigarettes. After taking
out the motor and other parts, they loaded them with cigarettes. Even though
the police arrested the smuggler in this case, the criminal attempted this sub-
terfuge on several more occasions, adding a bathroom boiler to his smuggling
strategy. Smugglers have hidden cigarettes in tea trays and prayer mats.[33] One
resourceful malefactor scooped out the inner part of watermelons, stashing
the cigarettes inside instead. One of the better-thought-out ruses was to hire a
police officer to drive from Iran to Turkey in a vehicle stockpiled with cigarettes. This rarely failed since police officers are not required to present travel
documents, thus preventing their cars from being searched.[34]

Illicit cigarette traffickers typically diversify their criminal activities,
engaging contemporaneously in other illicit activities, including crimes
related to drug, wildlife, counterfeit goods, and many others. The cigarette
trade is just another method of raising venture capital for other enterprises.
In one European case, a Czech police officer, for example, investigated the
concomitant smuggling of rhino horns and cigarettes.[35] Most cigarette smugglers in Turkey have a history of smuggling other goods or have simultaneously become part of ongoing smuggling operations. It is common for human
smuggling, oil smuggling, and arms trafficking groups to concurrently engage
in cigarette smuggling. In a case recorded in an eastern Turkish city on the

border with Iran, a human smuggling group was engaged in drug trafficking, oil smuggling, and cigarette trafficking. When attempts at human smuggling failed, the group turned to cigarettes. The group's linkage with smugglers across the Iranian border allowed the group to engage in many types of smuggling.[36]

Corruption also facilitates cigarette smuggling in Turkey. Hardened cigarette smugglers exploit the customs practices at the National Turkish Transit Regime. According to Turkish law, only customs officials can frisk loaded trucks under the jurisdiction of the transit regime. In a case recorded in 2013, the police learned that a cigarette smuggling group had prepared counterfeit documents. With the connivance of customs officials, the truck was identified as being under the auspices of transit regime's jurisdiction. Once this was done the door of the truck was sealed shut. The police seized 3 million packages of cigarettes from this group after using wiretaps to discover the group's smuggling technique.[37]

Oil Smuggling

Oil smuggling is one of the more profitable sources of income for organized crime and terrorist groups, exploiting a demand for cheaper oil and the opportunities to earn tax revenue from the sale of smuggled oil. Illicit oil is easily sold in Turkey. In fact, it is common knowledge that cheaper illicit oil is available.[38] The main facilitators for Turkish oil smuggling networks include the country's high taxes, its proximity to countries with lower oil prices, and the insurmountable challenges of controlling its borders and harbors.[39] In 2012, for example, the price of oil in Turkey was the second highest in the world at 2.72 USD per liter. That compares with Turkey's eastern neighbor Iran, which had the second lowest price at 10 cents per liter. Turkey's other neighbors include Iraq, where it sells for 78 cents per gallon, and Syria, where it sells for 96 cents.[40]

Syria, Iran, and Iraq are main source countries for cross-border oil smuggling, stemming from substantial price differences. The Syrian civil war that started in 2011 presented opportunities for criminal and terrorist organizations. In the provinces bordering Syria, the recorded cases of oil smuggling have continued to increase (see Chapter 9). Iran has been a traditional source for Turkish oil smugglers. In 2007, the market value of trafficked Iranian oil was estimated in the range of 4 billion USD.[41] According to some accounts, 68 percent of smuggled exports are under the control of mafia networks. The Iranian government has also been heavily involved in the smuggling economy. For instance, The Islamic Revolutionary Guards Corps (IRGC) generates 12 billion USD revenue from smuggling. They have also been tied to the illegal selling of subsidized gasoline out of Iran.[42] According to

2013 records, each day 7-10 million liters of petrol and diesel are smuggled out of the country, mainly from the border region. Iran, with an unemployment rate of 28.1 percent, has only increased the participation of the region's unemployed youth in smuggling activities connected with Turkey.[43] Kurdish families on both sides of the Turkish/Iranian border have collaborated in oil smuggling and other smuggling ventures. In a case recorded in 2012, the police found that oil smugglers simultaneously operate in arms smuggling, human trafficking, and oil smuggling with their counterparts on the Iranian side of the Turkish border.[44]

Iraq is an oil-rich country with the world's second largest reserves.[45] The illicit oil trade came to the attention of international authorities in the 1990s when Saddam Hussein violated UN sanctions. The post-Saddam regime (after 2003) has also been implicated in oil smuggling networks.[46] Since 2003, Iraq has by some accounts exported 33 billion USD in oil. However, this revenue stream is mostly exploited by corrupt Iraqi officials, rather than spending it on the reconstruction of the country.[47] Not surprisingly, Turkey's geographic proximity makes it a destination for Iraqi oil smuggled on the northern route.[48] According to Turkish Customs officials, each year almost 200,000 Turkish trucks travel to Iraq, bringing back up to one million tons of smuggled oil.[49] A smuggler can make 7,450 USD for each truck smuggling oil to Turkey.[50] The intensive flow of truck passages from the Habur Border Gate at Turkish and Iraqi border makes it impossible to thoroughly check these trucks. After the establishment of new government in 2003 in Iraq, only one percent of these trucks were checked by the United Nations.[51] Confirming the post-2013 trends in Iraq, Turkey increasingly began to seize oil after 2003.

By most accounts, the number of motor vehicles registered in Turkey each year negatively correlates with the consumption of legitimate oil products. Although many vehicles are registered each year, the amount of oil consumed has steadily decreased, prompting criminal and terrorist groups to fill the gap with smuggled oil. In 2004, for example, oil consumption increased 24 percent, while the number of vehicles registered increased 70 percent. That same year, Turkey generated 20 percent to 25 percent of its tax revenue from the purchase of oil products.[52] In 2013, oil tax revenue accounted for 51 percent of total private consumption taxes collected.[53] The revenue loss was almost $2 billion in 2004,[54] increasing to $5 billion in 2017.[55] Each year, 2.5 million tons of smuggled oil is transferred into Turkey, representing one-fifth of the oil consumed in the entire country. According to a study by Turkey's Parliamentary Oil Smuggling Examination Board, 7.8 million tons of smuggled oil entered the country in 2015 and 2016.[56] Turkish police, however, seized only 18,000 tons in the same period,[57] which equates to police seizing only one liter of every 434 liters of smuggled oil.

Despite the extent of oil smuggling in Turkey, the government has done little to stop the activity or even acknowledge it. The yearly reports from the Anti-Smuggling Unit of the Turkish National Police in the 1990s contained no information on oil smuggling. Since the early 2000s, data about oil smuggling have been sparse. The government's superficial approach to the problem and its apparent lack of concern can be in part attributed to corruption among some government officials. There is little reason to believe that officials are not aware of the prevailing oil smuggling, but in the current political climate the tendency is to look the other way, or at least demonstrate some complicity in the illicit enterprise.

Smuggled oil reaches Turkey from multiple sources. While massive amounts of oil have been smuggled on ships through sea routes, as noted previously, some oil is smuggled in from neighboring countries with lower oil prices.[58] In 2014, for example, most of the oil seized by the police came from the provinces of Izmir and Mersin and the province of Kocaeli, smuggled by criminals using sea routes. Police seizures of oil in Turkish cities located along the Syrian border confirm the impact of the Syrian war on oil smuggling. Most of the oil seized from cities along the Syrian border came from Hatay, followed closely by Gaziantep, Adana, and Şanlıurfa.[59]

The acumen of professional criminals has only perpetuated the oil smuggling problem. When the police became concerned about oil smuggling in the early 2000s,[60] criminals developed new techniques such as using hidden tanks and remote-control tank systems.[61] The amount of oil seized in Turkey increased steadily between 2011 and 2013, but it plummeted[62] over the next two years (2014-2016).[63]

Criminals groups are typically involved in one of three levels of oil smuggling, breaking down roughly to small-volume, medium-volume, and large-volume operations. Corruption plays a pivotal role at each level. Not only does corruption enable small-volume actors to cross the country's borders, it also provides opportunities for medium-volume smugglers to bribe customs officials and for large-volume smugglers to forge counterfeit documents.

Small-Volume Smuggling

Small-volume oil smuggling has occurred in Turkish cities on its borders with Iran, Iraq, and Syria. The smugglers in this category generally operate in small groups. Familial and kinship relations provide opportunities for these smugglers to operate. They typically run low-tech operations. In many cases mules are used to transport oil; conversely, they are quite capable of building short-distanced primitive pipelines into the borderlands. In a case recorded in 2012, military investigators found that smugglers used hundreds of mules to transport oil from Iran and Turkey. The military seized 15 tons of oil in that case. The smugglers also had built two short pipelines to transfer oil from Iran to Turkey.[64] In another case, border officials detected a 3-kilometer impromptu pipeline between Turkey and Iran in addition to five storage tanks with a capacity of 5,000 liters each.[65]

Villagers purchase mules for a variety of purposes, including the smuggling of oil and cigarettes. For some residents living in villages in the borderlands, oil smuggling has become an occupation. Each mule can carry at least 140 liters of oil. Smugglers transport oil into city centers after retrieving it from stockpiles held in village oil tanks. It takes two hours for operatives to collect the oil and bring it to the villages by mule. In some cases, these beasts of burden have been forced to transport oil three times in a single night. Turkish and Iranian border officials are aware of the ongoing smuggling; however, bribes of five Turkish liras per mule go a long way toward clearing troublesome security checkpoints. By some accounts, oil smugglers can earn almost 20,000 Turkish liras in a good month.[66]

Medium-Volume Smuggling

Medium-volume oil smugglers typically own transportation companies and oil stations. Turkish law allows transportation companies to stockpile; however, transportation companies in cities closer to the country's eastern and southern borders are more likely to store oil smuggled from abroad. In a case recorded in the province of Iğdır, the police found that almost all transportation companies stockpiled smuggled oil. These transportation companies also violated load and trip limits for trucks. Turkish law mandates a load limit of 550 liters of oil per truck coming into Turkey from abroad. The law also has a limit of four trips per truck each day. The police found that the trucks belonging to companies in Iğdır made more than four trips per month and each truck exceeded the load limit for oil, carrying an average of almost 2,000 liters of oil. When the police began seizing the oil, the companies developed new techniques. For example, some companies attached hidden compartments inside the tanks, which meant that customs officials were measuring only the oil outside the hidden compartment, making the measurable amount of oil under the load limit. The tactic, however, was not failsafe. Witnesses who cooperated with the police helped investigators uncover the scheme. Undeterred, the oil-smuggling companies changed their routes, entering the country through another border gate.[67]

One Iğdır oil smuggling investigation in particular confirmed diverse actors in oil smuggling.[68] In this case, police discovered that the Iğdır criminal group consisted of some consortium such as oil providers in the Nakchivan Autonomous Region, Turkish and Nakchivanian customs officials, Turkish border military officials, drivers, and the owners of Iğdır transportation companies.

Customs and military officials allowed trucks that violated the load limit to cross the border without checking whether the trucks were exceeding the limit of four trips per month. The companies stockpiled the oil and sold it for 2.9 Turkish liras (almost 1.5 USD in September 2013 currency rate) per liter after having purchased it for 1.3 (almost 60 cents) Turkish liras per liter. According to police calculations, the monthly revenue for each company was around 200,000 USD. When the police raided the houses of customs officials on December 16, 2013 as part of the investigation, they found vast amounts of cash. The police estimated that the customs officials involved in the crime group received around 20,000 Turkish liras (around 10,000 USD) in bribe money each month. By contrast, the typical monthly salary for a customs official is around 2,500 Turkish liras (around 1,200 USD).[69]

Some avaricious Turkish customs officials hired trucks in the Nakchivan Autonomous Region to smuggle oil into Turkey. The police found similar evidence when they investigated military personnel. The truck drivers bribed military personnel with a prearranged amount of cash. This was settled en route to the delivery destination after being processed at customs checkpoints. In return for bribes, the military personnel informed drivers of the scheduled cargo check times. The military personnel who participated were given a list of companies that were in the scheme, further illustrating corruption among the military personnel.[70]

In another investigation, police found that oil stations were trading smuggled oil. The smugglers set up hidden tanks that were operated by remote control during unexpected police raids. Police wiretaps revealed how the system worked. According to the police, the stations sold oil between 2008 and 2012 valued at 4 million USD. One of the owners of the stations was part of a human smuggling network operating between Turkey and Iran. Another owner was a loan shark working for an organized crime group. This operative used his money exchange office to launder money using the hawala technique. He was responsible for transferring the laundered money of human traffickers operating in Azerbaijan. This case demonstrates how oil smugglers will often move into different areas of criminal activity to generate additional revenue.[71]

Large-Volume Smuggling

Large-volume oil smuggling has not been studied scientifically, and investigations of the crime are rare. What researchers do know about it is based primarily on anecdotal information that suggests the involvement of media bosses and wealthy businesspersons. In one investigation, the prosecutor indicted a criminal group comprised of Aydin Dogan, founder of Dogan Holding and Media (one of Turkey's largest conglomerates), and 46 suspects on charges of importing oil from Russia and Belarus. These two countries are not members of the European Union Customs Union (EUCU), so instead, the crime group listed the United Kingdom as the source of the oil. The group used counterfeit documents in an attempt to avoid paying taxes on the imported oil. According to the indictment, the group evaded 6.3 million USD in taxes for 64 oil transfers.[72]

There are anecdotal reports that President Erdogan has used the investigation for leverage over the aforementioned Dogan, who has a strong influence on the media sector. Relations between President Erdogan and Dogan's media company were tense when the AKP began to rule the country in 2002. To protect himself and his political party, President Erdogan ordered prosecutors and treasury inspectors to fire Dogan. Inspectors from the Ministry of Treasury carried out the mandate by assessing Dogan's oil company a fee of 2 billion Turkish liras. Dogan was forced to sell the company to pay the fee, losing one-third of his fortune.[73] This case is considered an example of the dark relations between Erdogan and Dogan. The only way for Dogan to operate, legally or illegally, was to obey President Erdogan and support his regime.

In another investigation, the police found that one of the big oil companies in Turkey smuggled oil using counterfeit documents. The company opened a front company in the Cayman Islands to appear to be the company purchasing oil abroad. The real oil company in Turkey then transferred a vast amount of oil from countries with lower oil prices, using the front company to make it appear that the oil was being transferred from EUCU countries.

Counterfeit Pharmaceuticals

The prescription pharmaceutical market is vast and expanding globally, with an estimated market value of between 800 and 900 billion USD. In some countries, up to 50 percent of pharmaceuticals are counterfeit. Criminals are attracted to the counterfeit pharmaceuticals market because fake drugs are easier to make than other forms of product counterfeiting, such as phony designer clothing.[74] Global statistics underline the serious threat posed by counterfeit pharmaceuticals. For example, the value of the counterfeit drug market is around 200 billion USD.[75] An estimated 80 percent of counterfeit drugs consumed in the United States have been transferred from overseas. The consumption of counterfeit pharmaceuticals has spiked in European countries.[76] As one of the source countries, China detained 1,332 counterfeiters and confiscated 362 million drugs in 2013.[77] Around 10,000 websites that sold counterfeit pharmaceuticals were shut down in 2014.[78] Some experts proclaim that the widespread counterfeiting of pharmaceuticals is one of the more serious problems related to global drug trafficking networks.[79]

A number of explanations have been offered for the availability of counterfeit drugs in Turkey. Among the conditions cited are poverty, illiteracy and lack of awareness, lack of an official supply chain and the growth of the internet, the entanglement of crime and corruption, lack of adequate legislation and regulation, the failure of agencies to cooperate with each other, the excessive cost of many popular pharmaceuticals, the scarcity and inconsistent supply of drugs and devices, and the expansion of free trade.[80] In the case of Turkey, all of these apply at one level or another. In addition to having been both a target and transit country in the past, Turkey is now also a source country for some types of pharmaceuticals. Counterfeit pharmaceutical cases in Turkey are grouped in two categories: 1) Turkey as a source country and 2) Turkey as a target country.

Turkey as a Source Country for Counterfeit Pharmaceuticals

Before delivering counterfeit pharmaceuticals outside Turkey, criminals are able to obtain them either through corrupt business transactions or from other criminal actors. Police investigations have uncovered consortiums of doctors, pharmacists, and pharmacy company dealers who operate in the fashion of an organized crime group. Upon the receipt of bribes, members of the crime group forge the documents needed to acquire the drugs and then market them in other countries.[81] In 2013, the police determined that the health sector was the leader for linkages to corruption; almost 35 percent of corruption suspects that year worked in the health sector. These suspects were indicted on charges of conspiracy to rig bids on treatment services and purchasing pharmaceuticals for the hospitals.[82]

The lack of hospital inspections increases the likelihood of corrupt transactions occurring in state and private hospitals and other medical facilities. In a case recorded in the Iğdır province, police found that the owner of the hospital generated revenue from corrupt treatment services and medicines obtained illegally through bribery transactions. The owner's bribery relationships with Ministry of Health inspectors helped him make a large haul. In return for receiving bribes, the inspectors ignored inappropriate transactions at the hospital. This case also uncovered the transfer of some medicines to the PKK terrorist organization.[83]

Although the Ministry of Health introduced strategies in the early 2010s to prevent corruption, criminals have responded by finding new ways to continue obtaining pharmaceuticals from the legal health sector. For example, when the Ministry of Health began to use bar codes on drug boxes, the criminals used counterfeit doctor reports and prescriptions to fraudulently obtain drugs. This meant that the government would end up paying for medicines obtained through fraud. The criminals then began to smuggle the illegally obtained drugs out of the country because they knew that with the bar codes still attached, they could not resell the drugs within the country.[84] Transnational networks in the region were used to smuggle the drugs out of the country. In one police investigation, the police arrested 28 criminals from Turkey and Syria who had been involved in forging counterfeit prescriptions, obtaining medicines with the phony documents, and then smuggling the drugs into Iraq, Egypt, Syria, and Azerbaijan.[85]

Iran is another target country for pharmaceuticals smuggled from Turkey. In 2016, for instance, Turkish police seized around 400,000 pharmaceuticals in the province of Van, which borders Iran. Criminals aimed to transfer these drugs to Iran.[86] In the same year, the police arrested 13 Iranian pharmaceutical smugglers in a case recorded in Van province, which was ranked as the third province in terms of pharmaceutical seizures. Another province, Ağrı, bordering Iran was the first to seize the most pharmaceuticals.[87] It should be noted that the demand for counterfeit drugs flourished in Iran in the early 2010s because of embargoes imposed by the United States, the United Nations, and the European Union because of Iran's stubborn insistence on developing nuclear weapons. These sanctions affected the drug market in Iran. Drugs were scarce, smuggling groups stepped in to fill the vacuum, and counterfeit pharmaceuticals flowed across the border between Turkey and Iran.[88] Turkish seizures of illegally obtained pharmaceuticals in areas close to the Iranian border confirmed that smuggled pharmaceuticals were brought into Iran.

Pharmaceuticals counterfeiters are flexible in their abilities to use different methods in order to mimic a genuine product in order to evade detection. They are more prone to manipulating raw materials and packaging to imitate original products.[89] Police investigations have uncovered the flexibility of methods used by Turkish counterfeiters. One scheme involves transferring raw materials from abroad and printing counterfeit empty boxes and prospectuses in Turkish printing houses. Seizures of counterfeit pharmaceuticals abroad have confirmed that Turkey is a source country. For example, Viagra made in Turkey was transferred to the U.S. with Turkish instructions via Singapore in 2015.[90] The seizure of other counterfeit drugs in the U.S. shed light on how Turkey has continued to be a source country for such drugs. In one case, a Canadian company imported counterfeit drugs from Turkey and sold them to doctors in the U.S. at low prices.[91] On another occasion, the owner of a Turkish pharmaceutical company was sentenced to 30 months in prison after being implicated in an operation that traded counterfeit cancer drugs in the U.S. Later, another Turkish counterfeiter engaged in the same operation was arrested and pled guilty.[92] These cases prompted U.S. authorities in 2016 to express concern about the lack of efficiency and fairness regarding inspections of the pharmaceutical manufacturing process in Turkey.[93]

In 2013, Turkish police arrested an organized crime group comprised of 60 individuals who manufactured counterfeit pharmaceuticals in Turkey. The police seized 20,000 pharmaceuticals, one-third of which were cancer drugs. The criminals marketed the cancer drugs for much less than the actual price.[94] In a case recorded in 2016, the police arrested two Turkish individuals and one Syrian individual for being in possession of 250 kg of menthol, 6,400 empty medicine boxes, 5,000 medicine box lids, and 35,000 medicine prospectuses. The market value of the seized materials was around 2 million Turkish liras (600,000 USD).[95] Criminals also have been known to transfer abroad the raw materials used in producing counterfeit pharmaceuticals. In a 2017 investigation, the police arrested 17 individuals for possession of 42,000 pharmaceutical capsules, 144,000 empty pharmaceutical boxes, 100 liters of liquid raw material, and 100 prospectuses in the Russian language.[96] In another 2007 investigation recorded in Izmir, the police seized raw materials and tools used to produce counterfeit drugs, revealing that raw materials were brought from abroad and marketed online.[97] In a 2018 investigation, the police detained 14 counterfeiters who attempted to produce counterfeit drugs in Istanbul.[98]

In addition to smuggling pharmaceuticals into other countries from Turkey, criminals have been known to market the drugs domestically. The domestic market for counterfeit pharmaceuticals operates through websites or on the black market by relatives of the counterfeiters.[99] In 2016, for example, 570 buyers of pharmaceuticals complained to the Board of Pharmacists.[100] One out of every five medicines produced and sold in Turkey is counterfeit. Examiners found that around 40,000 kinds of pharmaceuticals are at risk of being produced by ineligible and inappropriate companies—double the number in the previous year. The Ministry of Health responded by shutting down 5,300 websites after charging the site owners with selling counterfeit pharmaceuticals.[101]

Turkey as a Target Country for Counterfeit Pharmaceuticals

Turkey is a target country for smuggled counterfeit pharmaceuticals. In 2010, the number of pharmaceuticals seized in Turkey increased almost 400 percent compared to the previous year. Most of the drugs had originated in China and were seized in cities close to the Iranian border.[102] In one study based on Counterfeit Incident System (CIS) reports, China was reported as the source country in most cases.[103] In 2011, around 7 million pills were seized in Turkey, representing a 447 percent increase over the previous year. A sizeable number of the seized pills were fake sex and weight-loss drugs that had also originated in China. Almost one-tenth of the aforementioned pills were seized in cities bordering Syria, one-tenth in cities bordering Iran, and a small amount in cities bordering Iraq. These seizures confirmed the extent of pharmaceutical trafficking along Turkey's eastern and southern borders. In two target cities, Istanbul and Ankara, police seized almost 5 million smuggled pharmaceuticals.[104] These smugglers developed new techniques in 2013, transferring some drugs in freighters along sea routes. That same year, 9.2 million counterfeit pills were seized.[105]

Syria has emerged as a focal point in the distribution of counterfeit pharmaceuticals sourced in India and China. It should be noted that the Hezbollah terrorist organization also is active in this kind of trafficking, producing drugs in laboratories in the Lebanon's Beqaa valley.[106] Syrian refugees in Turkey have become major couriers for transferring pharmaceuticals from Syria to Turkey, as seizures from 2015 confirm. For example, almost 65 percent of all counterfeit pharmaceuticals seized in Turkey came from cities on the Syrian border. Police in the Turkish province of Kilis on the Syrian border seized more counterfeit pharmaceuticals than any other province on the border with Syria. Moreover, animal medicines that are prohibited from being produced in Turkey were smuggled from Iran into Turkey, and weight-loss medicines of Chinese origin were stockpiled in Istanbul and sold on the Internet in nearly the same way that sex medicines were sold.[107] The Syrian route remains popular for the smuggling of pharmaceuticals. For example, the police in 2016 seized 492,000 packages of medicines in Gaziantep near the Syrian border that had been stashed in a truck coming from Syria.[108]

Antiquities Trafficking

Trafficking in antiquities, art objects, and other forms of cultural property is lucrative for criminals and terrorists. Its market value has been estimated at several billion dollars each year.[109] Antiquities trafficking is not a victimless crime. Whereas it has not been considered as a serious crime, it deserves to be, due to its connection to terrorism, drug and human trafficking, and violent insurgencies.[110]

Turkey has been hit hard by the trafficking of antiquities for at least several decades. These years can be divided roughly into three distinct eras. The first period, in the 1990s, was marked by the significant increase in stolen antiquities, mostly stolen from museum collections.[111] During these years, the most prominent destination countries for Turkish art traffickers included the United States,[112] Germany, Russia, Austria, Denmark, and the United Kingdom.[113] By the late 1990s, the trafficking of antiquities had morphed into a nationwide phenomenon, as exemplified by police reports of 55 seizures out of Turkey's 81 provinces.[114] Analyses of these cases revealed that antiquities traffickers were mostly tomb robbers and illegal excavators who operated individually and locally. Most dealers were in urban centers, facilitating better contacts with international traffickers who eased the sale of these antiquities abroad, mainly to the U.S.[115]

The trafficking of antiquities became increasingly dominated by organized crime groups in the early 2000s. During this period, Turkish traffickers introduced websites in order to acquire and market antiquities. In the most recent period, Turkey has become embroiled in antiquities trafficking coming out of Iraq and Syria, where cultural relics are plundered with impunity by criminals and terrorists. Now considered a transit country for antiquities for this lucre, the trafficking of Turkish antiquities has expanded with the assistance of transnational criminal groups.

The trafficking of antiquities requires well-established networks capable of cooperating with each other in Turkey. As opposed to other types of trafficked commodities, such as cigarettes and arms, the trafficking of antiquities takes longer and necessitates higher levels of trust. For example, while it takes on average two weeks to successfully market cigarettes after transferring them to Turkey, it may take several months to find an appropriate customer for antiquities and conclude a sale.[116]

Additionally, people involved in this kind of trafficking must also have at least some expertise in antiquities, as it is very common to encounter counterfeit objects in this area. Consequently, people who are active in this kind of trafficking tend to be international dealers having close linkages in Turkey or the Turkish diaspora in European countries and the U.S. These groups contact each other confidentially and prefer meeting in smaller cells, gathering in clandestine locations around the Grand Bazaar in Istanbul, in order to locate customers or connect with dealers in Turkey and abroad. They frequently change their meeting locations and are careful to avoid the scrutiny of the law enforcement.[117]

The legal collectors and wealthy families interested in collecting antiquities, have a partial impact on the trafficking of antiquities in Turkey, thus are complicit in the sordid process. For instance, whereas a wealthy family may be mostly interested in antiquities that belong to Islamic heritage, another family may be interested in antiquities that have roots in the Byzantium Empire. When these families make contact with dealers in Istanbul to complete one or two pieces of a private collection, the price of the antiquities market increases.[118]

The Impact of Conflicts on the Trafficking of Cultural Relics in Iraq

The second period of antiquities trafficking in Turkey included cases related to the impact of the 2003 U.S. invasion in Iraq, during which a considerable number of antiquities were looted by criminal groups and marketed in

Western countries. Also, antiquities trafficking was used as a source to fund insurgency in Iraq.[119] Turkey was one of the transit countries for these items during this period.

Smuggling and trafficking syndicates continue to plague the Turkish-Iraqi border. It has always been challenging for the Turkish and Iraqi governments to curb ongoing smuggling across their shared border, in no small part because smuggling is a common economic source for many families in these areas. Similar to the 1990s, when the Turkish-Iraqi border was used to smuggle other merchandise, during the following years this region continued as a corridor for the trafficking of cigarettes, drugs, arms, and oil. Additionally, this area was used by traffickers of antiquities in the 1990s[120] and 2000s. There were seizures of antiquities in the cities bordering Iraq or en route to these cities from Iraq in the 1990s. The density in terms of the number of suspects and cases may be an indication of organized crime groups that operated on the Turkish and Iraqi border.[121]

The U.S. intervention in Iraq produced many unintended consequences, including the plundering of Iraqi's cultural heritage. Subsequent to the collapse of the Iraqi government, the looting of the museums increased at an unprecedented rate.[122] Turkish statistics from the early 2000s affirm that Turkey was used as an alternative transit country for the transfer of many Iraqi antiquities. In fact, the number of antiquities trafficking cases doubled from 252 in 2003 to 525 in 2004. There was also a sharp rise in the number of historical artifacts and coins seized and suspects detained by law enforcement during this period.[123] This increase continued in the years after 2004. For example, the number of antiquities seized in Turkey reached 17,936 in 2007.[124]

The Iraqi route has been popular with antiquities traffickers. In a February 2018 case, two traffickers were seized attempting to smuggle 13 million USD worth of ancient artifacts from Kirkuk-Iraq to Turkey. Investigation revealed that Iraqi traffickers were going to hand over the artifacts to their Turkish counterparts at the Turkish-Iraqi border.[125]

The Impact of Conflict on Antiquities Trafficking in Syria

The third period of antiquities trafficking in Turkey is defined by the impact of the Syrian conflict on this illegal trade. Syria is one of the largest source countries in the world, hosting 4,500 recorded and catalogued archaeological sites.[126] However, these sites were subject to be looted by criminals and terrorists as a result of civil war that started in 2011. Turkey continues to be exposed to the uncontrolled consequences of the ongoing conflict in Syria. Syrian nationals seem to make up a large proportion of the foreign individuals involved in certain types of smuggling and trafficking. The Islamic State in Iraq and Syria (ISIS) generates revenue from its territorial control of culturally rich regions. One of the sources of revenue is the plundering of antiquities (see Chapter 9). In addition to various kind of smuggling and trafficking, Turkey was a preferred route for antiquities smuggling by 2016,[127] confirmed by the number antiquities trafficking cases recorded in provinces (Gaziantep, Hatay, and Adana) bordering Syria.

The Syrian economy has been connected to various facets of illicit trade for decades. Even before the civil war, Syrians took part in smuggling cases on the Turkish/Syrian border. Ongoing civil war has only led to the expansion of Syria's illicit economy. Antiquities trafficking can be divided into distinct periods of activity. By the time ISIS was a mere shadow of its former self, it was mainly the purview of terrorist organizations. Following its defeat on most fronts, criminal organizations and local smugglers were back in the game. Antiquities traffickers use southern (Lebanon) and northern (Turkey) routes in the trafficking of antiquities. Currently, Syrian antiquities are transferred more globally, geographically ranging from Thailand and China to the U.K., France, and Germany. Turkey, Lebanon, and United Arab Emirates (Dubai) are the most popular transit points.[128]

One of the principal elements of Turkey's cultural heritage is its numismatic materials. Many discoveries were made in legal excavations and controlled agricultural works as well as activities by casual or professional treasure hunters in the 1990s. There is no way of knowing the exact number of coins that arrived on foreign markets in those years, but the value of plundered coins must have been prodigious.[129] The smuggling of coins has kept its pace since the 1990s. Each year Turkish police seize tens of thousands of coins from the hands of smugglers. Turkish police increasingly seized coins. Local and international smugglers operated in this area. For example, in a case recorded in 2017, one British tourist was arrested while attempted to smuggle 13 coins out of Turkey.[130]

There are many players in antiquities smuggling.[131] In Turkey, antiquities traffickers consist of *amateurs*, *facilitators*, and *criminal groups*. The amateurs are predominantly illegal excavators who are interested in antiquities and conduct their business through personal networks or websites that facilitate the marketing of antiquities. Amateurs are the most pervasive group of traffickers in Turkey. In 2014, most of the traffickers arrested were illegal excavators. The increasing number of Turkish websites in this area is encouraging people to become more interested in antiquities.[132] It should be noted that the widespread interest in antiquities has led to the emergence of fraud cases as well. In 2011, the police discovered a laboratory that was being used to manufacture counterfeit antiquities.[133]

The facilitators are collectors and dealers who either operate individually or are linked to traffickers. Their role is to provide international connections for the marketing of antiquities. Using land- or sea-based transportation, companies transfer these antiquities to international dealers. The fact that most of the seizures have been made in the cities of Istanbul, Izmir, Antalya, and Mugla indicates that these collectors and dealers operate in metropolitan or harbor cities. It is common for legal dealers in the trafficking of antiquities to exploit their legitimate status.[134]

Criminal groups consisting of local smugglers and well-networked transnational gangs make up the third type of trafficker. The police reported 44 organized crime groups operating in this area in 2009.[135] This number decreased to 22 in 2010,[136] 24 in 2013,[137] and 13 in 2015. Criminal groups are composed of illegal excavators, collectors, and marketers, and their operations include selecting archaeological preservation areas, employing local inhabitants for excavation, maintaining their activities by means of agents in other regions, and transferring antiquities abroad. Law enforcement operations have confirmed that Turkish antiquities traffickers have operated in networks. One of the antiquities trafficking cases recorded in Turkey in 2010 included criminal networks between Turkey and Europe.[138] Law enforcement continued to detect transnational antiquities trafficking groups in 2012, arresting two groups,[139] and one transnational group in 2015.[140]

When adapting to several types of trafficking, criminal groups in Turkey are not limited to the trafficking and smuggling of drugs or humans. In the 1990s, the police seized nuclear materials and antiquities from the same group, indicating even broader flexibility among traffickers.[141] In 2004, two traffickers attempted to sell an Aphrodite statue[142] to a German purchaser. When they were arrested in Istanbul, police found them in possession of drugs and counterfeit ID cards.[143]

Antiquities traffickers continue to target the same Western European and United States destinations for trafficked antiquities as they did in the 1990s and the early 2000s. In 2012, "The Winged Seahorse Brooch" stolen from the Uşak City Museum was seized in Germany, and the "Orpheus Mosaic" smuggled from the city of Şanlıurfa was recovered in the U.S.[144] Turkish antiquities trafficking cases indicate that traffickers use diverse land and sea routes to transport antiquities, including:[145]

- the Balkans land route through Bulgaria, Romania, and Austria to Germany, France, and Switzerland;
- the Mediterranean Sea route from Turkish harbor cities to Italy and then to Germany, Scotland, the U.K., and the U.S.; and
- the Black Sea route from Turkish harbor cities to Romanian, Russian, or Ukrainian harbors and then to Germany, Scotland, the UK, and the U.S.

The existence of alternative routes demonstrates that traffickers have well-networked linkages in the transport of Turkish and Middle Eastern antiquities.

Nuclear Smuggling

Nuclear smuggling gained serious attention after the 9/11 attacks in the United States due in no small part to al Qaeda's alleged quest for nuclear weapons.[146] For terrorist groups like al Qaeda, nuclear weapons are the ultimate force multipliers, that is, offering a small group to enhance its killing power in the furtherance of its campaigns of asymmetrical warfare.[147] As of 2018, no terrorist group has demonstrated the acumen required to engage in this form of warfare, lacking the know-how and the infrastructure likely to produce such a weapon of mass destruction. Although there is trepidation among homeland security services and the like that nuclear materials could be stolen by either criminal or terrorist organizations, at this point evidence is mostly anecdotal.[148] That said, criminal and terrorist groups are much more likely to produce some type of biological or chemical device.[149]

Although the smuggling of nuclear materials is far less common than other types of smuggling, this activity creates greater fear and debate. Concern was heightened in the 1990s after the collapse of the Soviet Union. The world watched attentively as individuals and groups attempted to smuggle nuclear materials from the Soviet Union to Western European nations. A lack of safeguards to protect the sensitive materials made it possible for smugglers to act.[150] Seizures made by German police in the 1990s confirmed the route and the source countries.[151] U.S. policies aimed at controlling nuclear materials in post-Soviet states succeeded, and these materials were more effectively safeguarded in the late 1990s.

On the other hand, the interest of rogue states in obtaining nuclear materials has increased concerns about these materials falling into the wrong hands. Iran, North Korea, and Iraq were at the top of the agenda in the 1990s for precisely that reason. The mere allegation that Iraq possessed nuclear materials was enough to trigger U.S. intervention in Iraq in 2003. North Korea and Iran also have generated intense concern in terms of their desire to possess nuclear weapons. In addition to nuclear materials, however, the use of chemical weapons in the ongoing Syrian civil has focused attention on the smuggling of chemical materials used to make chemical weapons.

Turkey's geographic location made it a convenient route and transit location for the smuggling of nuclear materials from the former Soviet Union into Western European countries. In addition, insufficient controls at customs checkpoints and the lack of regulations and laws made Turkey a bridge country in the 1990s.[152] Turkey first encountered nuclear smuggling cases in 1993 when Istanbul police seized 2,530 grams of radioactive material from seven Turkish criminals. Laboratory results showed that the material included around 3% enriched uranium-235. In a 1994 case, police seized 14 kg of radioactive uranium from six criminals, three of whom were Iranian.[153] According to police statistics from 1997, nine cases involving the smuggling of radioactive materials occurred in 1993 and 1997.[154] It seems that seven of these cases occurred in 1996 and 1997.

The number of cases involving the smuggling of radioactive and nuclear materials increased steadily in 1998 and 1999. Police investigated some cases in 1999 and seized chemical materials in five of them: mercury (two cases), cesium (one case), sulfonic acid (one case), and titanium (one case). In three cases, police found "selenium, osmium or red mercury." No materials were seized in the remaining three cases.[155] Investigation of the routes used in the 1999 cases showed that Iran was the source in two cases, Georgia was the source in three cases, and the Nakhchivan Autonomous Region was the source in five cases. These materials were seized as the smugglers traveled through Istanbul and Izmir in the western part of the country, confirming Turkey's role as a transit country. In one case, the materials were seized in the province of Şanlıurfa, which lies on the border with Syria, after the smugglers crossed the Georgian border into Turkey.[156]

Most of the smuggling routes remained the same in 2000. Russia was the source in two cases where the material was transferred to the provinces of Samsun and Antalya using an air route. Georgia was used in one case where the material was sent to the province of Şanlıurfa and then on to the city of Adana over a land route. Iran was used in two cases where the materials were sent by a land route to the provinces of Iğdır and Ağrı along Turkey's far eastern border. The Nakhchivan Autonomous Region was a source in one case where the materials were flown to Istanbul.[157] Two cases occurred in the province of Hatay on the Syria border. The police seized "selenium, osmium or red mercury" in six cases, chemical materials in two cases, mercury in two cases, and plutonium in one case.[158] The evidence from the cases that proved Turkey's role as a transit country prompted U.S. authorities to donate 42 nuclear detectors to Turkey in 2004.[159] Furthermore, the U.S. authorities conducted training programs in Turkey in 2007.[160]

According to the James Martin Center for Nonproliferation Studies, data from 1993 and 1999 reflect Turkey's role as a transit country for smugglers of nuclear materials. The center found that 18 nuclear smuggling cases occurred in Turkey between these years. Small amounts of uranium and plutonium were seized in these cases. The source countries were former Soviet Union countries, Romania, and Iran. Individual opportunist criminals operating independently were involved in these cases.[161]

Police statistics from 1993 to 2006 show that the police found some amount of uranium and radioactive materials in 13 smuggling cases during that period. In these cases, the police arrested 67 criminals with a combined total of 17.1 kg of uranium, 2.91 grams of americium, a small amount of cesium, and 1.9 kg of scandium.[162] Analyses of these cases point out that the criminals were not given information about the nature of the materials they

agreed to smuggle or, as happened most often, received inaccurate information about the materials. The criminals became involved in the smuggling
cases for financial gain; therefore, they attempted to sell the materials at
exorbitant prices. The criminals also used Russian prospectuses to convince
buyers that the materials were legitimate. In most cases, the criminals committed fraud. Police seizures included red mercury, mercury oxide, mercury
iodide, and some chemicals known as "snake venom" that are used as indicator compounds to detect toxic gases in the air.[163]

According to police records, the last nuclear smuggling case in Turkey that
included uranium (1.1 gram) was in 2006, and Turkey has not experienced
any nuclear smuggling cases since then. However, Turkish media reports
on nuclear smuggling cases refute the claim by the police. For example, the
police seized 13 nuggets of pure aluminum, a material used in nuclear energy
production. In another case, two Georgian nationals were detained with some
amount of cesium and mercury in 2006. Lastly, in a case recorded in March
2018, the police seized 1.4 kg of californium with four traffickers, all used in
nuclear warheads and nuclear energy as well as in the oil and mining industries. Its market value is around 72 million USD. The police believe that the
source of this material is Russia, and that traffickers might attempt to transfer
it abroad.[164]

Of the criminals involved in nuclear-material smuggling cases in Turkey,
most have been Iranians.[165] Over the past five years several Iranian-linked
nuclear smuggling cases have occurred in Turkey. In 2013, for example,
Turkish and German police conducted a joint police investigation of a nuclear
smuggling group comprised of seven Iranian criminals. According to police
findings, the Iranian smugglers had established a front company in Istanbul
and bought nuclear materials and some tools used in nuclear technology from
India and Germany. They then tried to transfer these materials to Arak province in Iran. Investigators discovered that these criminals were suspects in the
shipment of around 900 loads of nuclear material linked to Iran.[166]

Other nuclear smuggling cases from the 1990s indicated that terrorist
groups were interested in obtaining nuclear materials. The PKK, however,
seemed to be more interested in using chemical materials rather than nuclear
materials, having carried out a chemical attack in the Turkish village of
Ormancik in January 1994 in which 16 people were killed. In another case,
the police found sarin and mustard gas in the hands of PKK militants. Other
terrorist groups targeted nuclear research centers in Turkey. In the province
of Konya in 2007, for example, the police found that al-Qaeda militants took
photographs of a nuclear research center in Istanbul. In another investigation,
the police discovered that the Iranian-directed terrorist organization Salam
Tawhid Quds Force also took the photographs of this center (see Chapter 8).[167]

NOTES

1. Rajeev K. Goel, "Cigarette Smuggling: Price vs. Nonprice Incentives." *Applied Economics Letters*, Vol. 15, No. 8, (July 2008): 587-592.
2. Sharon Melzer, "Counterfeit and Contraband Cigarette Smuggling: Opportunities, Actors, and Guardianship." Unpublished dissertation, American University, 2010, v.
3. Joe Myers, "Which Countries Have the Highest Tax on Cigarettes?" *World Economic Forum,* accessed on July 6, 2017 from https://www.weforum.org/agenda/2016/05/which-countries-have-the-highest-tax-on-cigarettes.
4. Mahmut Cengiz, *Turkiye'de Organize Suc Gercegi ve Terorun Finansmani* (Ankara: Seckin Yayinevi, 2015), 158.
5. P.C. van Duyne, "Organizing Cigarette Smuggling and Policy Making, Ending Up in Smoke." *Crime, Law, and Social Change.* Vol. 39, No. 3, (April 2003): 285-317.
6. Ayda A. Yürekli, "Worldwide Organized Cigarette Smuggling: An Empirical Analysis." *Applied Economics.* Vol. 42, No. 5, (February 2010): 545-561.
7. Luk Joossens, "From Cigarette Smuggling to Illicit Tobacco Trade." *Tobacco Control*, Vol. 21, No. 2, (March 2012): 230-234.
8. "Sigaraya Ödenen Vergi Oranı Ne Kadar?." *Guncel Fiyatlar 2017*, accessed on March 20, 2018 from http://www.guncelfiyatlari.com/sigaraya-odenen-vergi-orani/.
9. "Sigaraya Ödenen Vergi Oranı Ne Kadar?," *Guncel Fiyatlar 2017.*
10. *2015 Turkish Report of ASOD,* xvii.
11. "Workshop Cigarette Smuggling" *Directorate General for Internal Policies,* European Parliament, Brussels, 30.
12. *1995 Turkish Report of ASOD, 31-33.*
13. *1997 Turkish Report of ASOD, 25-26.*
14. *1999 Turkish Report of ASOD, 45.*
15. *2004 Turkish Report of ASOD, 8-9.*
16. *2005 Turkish Report of ASOD, 100-104.*
17. *2007 Turkish Report of ASOD, 71-72.*
18. *2009 Turkish Report of ASOD, 79.*
19. *2010 Turkish Report of ASOD, 89-93.*
20. Tom Arnold, "Smoke and mirrors in Turkey with illicit cigarette trade." *The National Business,* accessed on March 17, 2018 from https://www.thenational.ae/business/smoke-and-mirrors-in-turkey-with-illicit-cigarette-trade-1.247302.
21. *2011 Turkish Report of ASOD, 17.*
22. *2011 Turkish Report of ASOD, 21.*
23. *2011 Turkish Report of ASOD, 22.*
24. *2012 Turkish Report of ASOD, 36.*
25. *2013 Turkish Report of ASOD, 65.*
26. *2010 Turkish Report of ASOD, 89-93.*
27. *2013 Turkish Report of ASOD, 67.*
28. *2015 Turkish Report of ASOD, 28.*

29. Tom Arnold, "Smoke and mirrors in Turkey with illicit cigarette trade."

30. *2015 Turkish Report of ASOD, 27-28.*

31. *2015 Turkish Report of ASOD, 27-28.*

32. "A hazy crisis: illicit cigarette smuggling in the OSCE region." *Hearing before the Commission on Security and Cooperation in Europe, One Hundred Fifteenth Congress,* first session, July 19, 2017, 4.

33. Tom Arnold, "Smoke and mirrors in Turkey with illicit cigarette trade."

34. Mahmut Cengiz's field experience, Iğdır, September 2011-March 2014.

35. "A hazy crisis: illicit cigarette smuggling in the OSCE region," 4 and Louise Shelley, *Dirty Entanglements* (London: Cambridge University Press, 2014), 260.

36. Mahmut Cengiz's field experience, Iğdır, September 2011-March 2014.

37. Mahmut Cengiz's field experience, Iğdır, October 2013.

38. Behsat Ekici, "Illicit Transborder Trade between Iraq and Turkey in the Post Saddam Era." *Journal of International Relations,* Vol. 9, Number I8, II, (2011): 63-80, 70.

39. Husnu Babat, "Türkiye'de Başlıca Kaçakçılık Türleri Ve Kaçakçılığın Ekonomiye Zararları," *SASAM,* accessed on June 14, 2017 from http://sahipkiran.org/2017/02/12/turkiyede-kacakcilik-turleri/.

40. "Petrol Price per Litre $ around the World," *Economics,* (October 5, 2012), accessed on June 15, 2017 from http://www.economicshelp.org/blog/5862/oil/petrol-price-per-gallon-around-the-world/.

41. Suleyman Elik, *Iran-Turkey Relations 1979-2001* (New York: Routledge, 2012), 173.

42. Ali Alfoneh, *Iran Unveiled* (Washington DC: American Enterprise Institute, 2013), 190.

43. Monavar Khalaj, "Iran sees boom in cross-border fuel and goods smuggling," *Financial Times,* accessed on March 18, 2018 from https://www.ft.com/content/235e02e4-b7dd-11e2-9f1a-00144feabdc0.

44. Mahmut Cengiz's field experience, September 19, 2012, Iğdır.

45. Bilal Wahab "How Iraqi oil smuggling greases violence." *Middle East Quarterly,* Fall, Vol.13(4), (2006): 54-59.

46. Phil William, *Criminals, militias, and insurgents organized crime in Iraq* (BiblioGov, 2009), 63.

47. Bilal Wahab "How Iraqi oil smuggling greases violence."

48. William, *Criminals, militias, and insurgents organized crime in Iraq,* 84.

49. Firat Bozcali, "Managing Oil in Kurdistan-Iraq, 1991-2003." *International Association of Iraqi Studies,* London, July 16, 2008.

50. William, *Criminals, militias, and insurgents organized crime in Iraq,* 85.

51. Ekici, "Illicit Transborder Trade between Iraq and Turkey in the Post Saddam Era," 69.

52. *2004 Turkish Report of ASOD, 1.*

53. *2013 Turkish Report of ASOD, 61.*

54. *2014 Turkish Report of ASOD, 3.*

55. Hürriyet Haber, "Kaçak akaryakıtın yıllık faturası 20 milyar liraya ulaştı," *Ekonomi*, accessed on August 7, 2017 from http://www.hurriyet.com.tr/kacak-akaryakitin-yillik-faturasi-20-milyar-liraya-ulasti-40446621,.

56. Husnu Babat, "Türkiye'de Başlıca Kaçakçılık Türleri Ve Kaçakçılığın Ekonomiye Zararları."

57. *2015 Turkish Report of ASOD, 25.*

58. *2011 Turkish Report of ASOD, 15.*

59. *2013 Turkish Report of ASOD, 63.*

60. The police conducted 756 oil smuggling investigations in 2008, 1,392 in 2010, and 2,014 in 2011(*2011 Turkish Report of ASOD*, 19).

61. *2011 Turkish Report of ASOD, 15.*

62. There is a good reason to believe that the oil seizures dropped in the wake of the corruption scandals implicating President Recep Tayyip Erdogan and his inner circle. Once he fired most police investigators after the 2016 coup attempt, it only opened new opportunities for smugglers (see Chapters 6 and 7).

63. While the number of oil smuggling investigations decreased 84% in 2015 compared with 2014, the number of oil smugglers arrested decreased 79%. In 2015, arrests had plummeted to 1,491 (*2015 Turkish Report of ASOD*, 24).

64. "Böylesini görmediniz! İşte 400 Katırla Yapılan Kaçakçılık," *Hurriyet*, (April 27, 2013), accessed on June 14, 2017 from http://www.hurriyet.com.tr/video/boylesini-gormediniz-iste-400-katirla-yapilan-kacakcilik-76731.

65. "Smugglers Build Three-Kilometer Pipeline between Turkey, Iran," *Hurriyet*, accessed on June 14, 2017 from http://www.hurriyetdailynews.com/smugglers-build-three-kilometer-pipeline-between-turkey-iran.aspx?pageID=238&nID=36517&NewsCatID=348.

66. Mahmut Cengiz's field experience, January 18, 2014, Iğdır.

67. Mahmut Cengiz's field experience, September 2013, Iğdır.

68. Crystal M. Flinn, "Black Gold in the Black Market: Tackling the Issue of International Oil Smuggling through Technology, Public Policy, and Internal Corporate Controls," 28.

69. Mahmut Cengiz's field experience, December 16, 2013, Iğdır.

70. Mahmut Cengiz's field experience, December 16, 2013, Iğdır.

71. Mahmut Cengiz's field experience, May 8, 2013, Iğdır.

72. "POAŞ iddianamesi kabul edildi: Aydın Doğan ve Ersin Özince'ye 23 yıl hapis istemi," *Cumhuriyet*, accessed on June 13, 2017 from http://www.cumhuriyet.com.tr/haber/turkiye/502735/POAS_iddianamesi_kabul_edildi__Aydin_Dogan_ve_Ersin_Ozince_ye_23_yil_hapis_istemi.html.

73. "Recep Tayyip Erdoğan, Aydın Doğan ile barıştı," *Haber 3*, accessed on June 13, 2017 from https://www.haber3.com/guncel/recep-tayyip-erdogan-aydin-dogan-ile-baristi-haberi-4403361.

74. Barbara Moran, "Cracking Down and Counterfeit Drugs." *Nova Next*, (August 20, 2016), accessed on July 9, 2017 from http://www.pbs.org/wgbh/nova/next/body/uncovering-counterfeit-medicines/.

75. "20 Shocking Counterfeit Drugs Statistics." *Health Research Funding*, accessed on March 18, 2018 from http://healthresearchfunding.org/20-shocking-counterfeit-drugs-statistics/

76. "20 Shocking Counterfeit Drugs Statistics." *Health Research Funding.*

77. "20 Shocking Counterfeit Drugs Statistics." *Health Research Funding.*

78. "20 Shocking Counterfeit Drugs Statistics." *Health Research Funding.*

79. Donald deKieffer and Kevin Horgan, "The Current Policy and Law of Counterfeit Medicines," in *Counterfeit Medicines,* eds. Albert Wertheimer and Perry Wang, (Glendale, AZ: ILM Publications, 2012): 19-32, 19.

80. Obinna Obi-Eyisi and Albert Wertheimer, "The Background and History of Counterfeit Medicines", in *Counterfeit Medicines,* eds. Albert Wertheimer and Perry Wang, (Glendale, AZ: ILM Publications, 2012): 1-16

81. *2009 Turkish Report of ASOD*, 60.

82. *2013 Turkish Report of ASOD*, 41.

83. Mahmut Cengiz's field experience, February 13, 2014, Iğdır.

84. *2011 Turkish Report of Anti-Smuggling and Organized Crime*, p. 3.

85. "Ilac Kacakciligi Operasyonu," *Haberler*, accessed on July 10, 2017 from https://www.haberler.com/ilac-kacakciligi-operasyonu-8447376-haberi/.

86. "Van'da Buyuk Ilac Kacakciligi Operasyonu," *Dogan Haber Ajansi*, (June 18, 2016), accessed on July 10, 2017 from http://arsiv.dha.com.tr/vanda-buyuk-ilac-kacakciligi-operasyonu_1258267.html.

87. *Turkish Report of ASOD 2016, 34-35.*

88. Siamak Namazi, "Sanctions and Medical Supply Shortages in Iran," *Wilson Center Middle East Program*, accessed July 11, 2017 from https://www.wilsoncenter.org/sites/default/files/sanctions_medical_supply_shortages_in_iran.pdf.

89. Obinna Obi-Eyisi and Albert Wertheimer, "The Background and History of Counterfeit Medicines," 2-3.

90. Eamon Mcniff, "ABC News Investigation into Counterfeit Prescription Drug Operations in the US." *ABC News*, accessed on July 11, 2017 from http://abcnews.go.com/Health/abc-news-investigation-counterfeit-prescription-drug-operations-us/story?id=31077758.

91. Joe Eaton, "Counterfeit Drugs Are Flooding the Nation's Pharmacies and Hospitals," *AARP Bulletin*, accessed on July 11, 2017 from http://www.aarp.org/health/drugs-supplements/info-2016/counterfeit-prescription-drugs-rx.html.

92. "Second Turkish Man Sentenced for Smuggling Counterfeit Cancer Drugs," *US Food and Drug Administration News Release*, (January 23, 2015), https://www.fda.gov/NewsEvents/Newsroom/PressAnnouncements/ucm431343.htm, accessed on July 11, 2017.

93. Zachary Brennan, "USTR: 97% of Counterfeit Drugs in US Shipped from Four Countries," *RAPS*, accessed on July 11, 2017 from http://www.raps.org/regulatoryDetail.aspx?id=24853.

94. "Sahte ilaç operasyonu," *A Haber,* accessed on July 8, 2017 from http://www.ahaber.com.tr/webtv/yasam/sahte-ilac-operasyonu.

95. "Sahte Ilac Imalathanesine Baskin," *Hurriyet*, (September 26, 2016), http://www.hurriyet.com.tr/sahte-ilac-imalathanesine-baskin-40232089, accessed on July 8, 2017.

96. "İstanbul'da sahte ilaç operasyonu," *Posta*, (June 26, 2017), http://www
.posta.com.tr/istanbul-da-sahte-ilac-operasyonu-haberi-1309651, accessed on July 8,
2017.

97. Safak Yel "İzmir'de villaya sahte ilaç imalatı operasyonu." *Anadolu Ajansi,*
accessed on March 19, 2018 from https://aa.com.tr/tr/turkiye/izmirde-villaya-sahte
-ilac-imalati-operasyonu/923284.

98. Ramazan Egri, "Sancaktepe'de Sahte Ilac Operasyonu" *CNNTURK,* accessed
on March 18, 2018 from https://www.cnnturk.com/turkiye/sancaktepede-sahte-ilac
-operasyonu.

99. "Counterfeit Drugs in Turkey," *Havoscope Global Black Market Information*, (no date), http://www.havocscope.com/counterfeit-drugs-in-turkey/, accessed on
July 12, 2017.

100. "Sanal ilaç almayın" *Hurriyet*, (October 14, 2016), http://www.hurriyet.com.
tr/sanal-ilac-almayin-40249186, accessed on July 8, 2017.

101. "Sahte ilaç satan 5 bin 300 internet sitesine kapama," *Hurriyet*, accessed on
July 7, 2017 from http://www.hurriyet.com.tr/sahte-ilac-satan-5-bin-300-internet-si
tesine-kapama-40276161.

102. *2010 Turkish Report of ASOD*, 98.

103. Tim K. Macke and Bryan A. Liang, "Counterfeit Drug Penetration into
Global Legitimate Medicine Supply Chains: A Global Assessment," *Am. J. Trop.
Med. Hyg.* 92(Suppl 6), (2015): 59–67

104. *2011 Turkish Report of ASOD*, 24.

105. *2012 Turkish Report of ASOD,* 42.

106. "Fake Drugs Swamp the Middle East," *The Middle East Magazine*, accessed
on July 10, 2017 from http://www.themiddleeastmagazine.com/wp-mideastmag-live
/2013/04/fake-drugs-swamp-the-middle-east/.

107. *2015 Turkish Report of ASOD*, 35-36.

108. "Suriye'den giriş yapan TIR'da 1.5 milyon liralık ilaç ele geçti," *Karar*,
accessed on July 10, 2017 from http://www.karar.com/guncel-haberler/suriyeden-gir
is-yapan-tirda-15-milyon-liralik-ilac-ele-gecti-356382.

109. Fred M. Shelley and Reagan Metz, *Geography of Trafficking: From Drug
Smuggling to Modern-Slavery* (Santa Barbara, CA: ABC Clio, 2017), 79.

110. Matthew Bogdanos, *Thieves of Baghdad* (New York: Bloomsbury, 2005),
289.

111. Between 1993 and 1995, 55% of cases were theft of antiquities, whereas
remaining cases were randomly encountered and illegal excavations (*1995 Turkish Report of Anti-Smuggling and Organized Crime Department (ASOD)*, 42). The
number of antiquities cases was 216, and law enforcement arrested 565 suspects in
these operations. Law enforcement seized 440 antiquities between 1995 and 1997.
The number of trafficking cases increased from 216 in 1997 to 338 in 2000 (*1997
and 2000 Turkish Report of ASOD*). When examining routes of trafficking, traffickers
used Istanbul and Izmir to collect stolen objects first and transfer them abroad through
land or air (*1995 Turkish Report of ASOD*).

112. Six antiquities were repatriated from the U.S. to Turkey between 1994 and
1997 (*1997 Turkish Report of ASOD,* 37).

113. *1997 Turkish Report of ASOD,* 37-38.

114. *1997 Turkish Report of ASOD,* 40.

115. Mahmut Cengiz's field experience, August 2015, Istanbul.

116. Mahmut Cengiz's field experience, August 2015, Istanbul.

117. Mahmut Cengiz's field experience, August 2015, Istanbul.

118. Mahmut Cengiz's field experience, August 2015, Istanbul.

119. Bogdanos, *Thieves of Baghdad,* 249.

120. In 1997, law enforcement recorded 20 cases in the borderlands surrounding the Turkish and Iraqi border (*1997 Turkish Report of ASOD,* 40).

121. For instance, in Hakkari, a province bordering Iraq and Iran, 14 antiquities traffickers were arrested in three cases in 1997.

122. Milbry Polk and Angela M. H. Schuster, *The Looting of the Iraqi Museum, Baghdad: The Lost Legacy of Ancient Mesopotamia* (New York: Biblio, 2005), 17.

123. *2004 Turkish Report of ASOD,* 13.

124. *2007 Turkish Report of ASOD,* 78.

125. Karzan Sulaivany "Iraqi forces foil $13M plot to smuggle ancient artefacts from Kirkuk to Turkey." *Kurdistan24,* accessed on March 28 from http://www.kurd istan24.net/en/news/3b4c5390-1fe2-4d2b-9410-22631e179c46.

126. Shelley and Metz, *From Drug Smuggling to Modern-Slavery,* 79.

127. Neil Brodie and Isber Sabrine, "The Illegal Excavation and Trade of Syrian Cultural Objects: A View from the Ground." *Journal of Field Archaeology,* Vol 43, No. 1, (2018): 74-84.

128. Neil Brodie, Interview by Mahmut Cengiz, Personal Interview, February 13, 2018.

129. Chris S. Lightfoot, *Recent Turkish Coin Hoards and Numismatic Studies* (Ankara: British Institute of Archaeology, 1991), 1.

130. "Sussex man held in Turkey for smuggling ancient coins." *BBC,* accessed on March 30, 2018 from www.bbc.com/news/uk-england-sussex-41026849.

131. Bogdanos, *Thieves of Baghdad,* 248.

132. *2014 Turkish Report of ASOD,* 62.

133. *2011 Turkish Report of ASOD,* 26.

134. *2014 Turkish Report of ASOD,* 61.

135. *2009 Turkish Report of ASOD,* 87.

136. *2010 Turkish Report of ASOD,* 100.

137. *2013 Turkish Report of ASOD,* 73.

138. *2010 Turkish Report of ASOD,* 100.

139. *2012 Turkish Report of ASOD,* 44.

140. *2015 Turkish Report of ASOD,* 39.

141. Loise Shelley, *Dirty Entanglements: Corruption, Crime, and Terrorism* (New York: Cambridge University Press, 2014), 261.

142. It was stolen from Izmir Archeological Museum. The price of the statue, which originated from BC 30 in the Roman period, was 1 million USD (*2004 Turkish Report of ASOD,* 12).

143. *2004 Turkish Report of ASOD,* 12.

144. *2013 Turkish Report of ASOD,* 50.

145. *2013 Turkish Report of ASOD*, 50.

146. David Hafemeister, *Nuclear Proliferation and Terrorism in the Post-9/11 World* (New York: Springer, 2016), 275.

147. Siegfried S. Hecker, "Nuclear Terrorism." In *High-impact Terrorism*, ed. National Research Council (Washington DC: National Academy Press, 2002): 149-155.

148. Weapons of Mass Destruction Commission, *Weapons of Terror Freeing the World of Nuclear, Biological and Chemical Arms* (Stockholh: Grafiska, 2006), 40.

149. Louise Shelley, *Dirty Entanglements* (London: Cambridge University, 2014), 291.

150. Rensselaer W. Lee, *Smuggling Armagedon: The Nuclear Black Market* (New York: St. Martin's Griffin, 2000), 1-3.

151. Brian M. Jenkins, *Will Terrorists Go Nuclear?* (New York: Prometheus Books), 152.

152. *1997 Turkish Report of ASOD*, 30.

153. *1995 Turkish Report of ASOD, 30-31.*

154. *1997 Turkish Report of ASOD, 33.*

155. *1997 Turkish Report of ASOD, 92.*

156. *1999 Turkish Report of ASOD, 83.*

157. *2000 Turkish Report of ASOD, 136.*

158. *2000 Turkish Report of ASOD, 138.*

159. *2004 Turkish Report of ASOD, 28.*

160. *2007 Turkish Report of ASOD, 61.*

161. Mahmut Cengiz, *Turkish Organized Crime from Local to Global*, (VDM Publishing, 2011), p. 23.

162. *2006 Turkish Report of ASOD, 80.*

163. *2007 Turkish Report of ASOD, 60.*

164. "Turkish police seize radioactive Californium element in Ankara," *Daily Sabah,* accessed on March 19, 2018 from https://www.dailysabah.com/investigations/2018/03/19/turkish-police-seize-radioactive-californium-element-in-ankara.

165. Arnold and Barletta, 1999.

166. "Nuclear Materials Smugglers Arrested," *UPI*, accessed on July 13, 2017 from http://www.upi.com/Top_News/World-News/2013/03/11/Nuclear-materials-smugglers-arrested/UPI-80861362997303/.

167. Emre Ercis, *Kara Kutu Selam Tevhid Kudus Ordusu* (Istanbul: IstIkbal Matbaacilik, 2015), 66-67.

Chapter 5

Human Smuggling and Trafficking

INTRODUCTION

Human smuggling and human trafficking generate tremendous profits for criminal organizations. Prices for smuggling often depend on a prospective migrant's wealth and nationality, as well as the incorporated risks of the journey, the degree of professionalism of the service providers, and the attractiveness of the country of destination.[1] Geopolitics have only added to the increase in population movement, mostly from impoverished and conflict-ridden locales to more industrialized countries. Spurred on by the growing juxtaposition between the haves and have-nots in the developing and developed world, thanks to globalization, this environment has also offered a favorable environment for the growth of criminal groups.[2]

One way to look at human smuggling and trafficking is as two sides of the same coin.[3] One distinctive similarity is the emphasis of the words *coercion and consent* in the definition of both types of trafficking. With human smuggling, illegal immigrants voluntarily agree to go with their handlers. Human trafficking, on the other hand, involves persons being coerced into service by their handlers—the traffickers—becoming victims in the process. It is not uncommon for human trafficking cases to begin as simple smuggling operations. However, for law enforcement, the difference between coercion and consent is not always clear.[4]

Turkey is a source, transit, and target country for both human smuggling and human trafficking. A considerable number of illegal immigrants have been smuggled along a route through Turkey, presenting opportunities for Turkish smuggling groups to operate transnationally. Similarly, Turkey has seen an increase in sex trafficking and labor trafficking. Both crimes represent a multibillion-dollar industry in the country. This chapter analyzes the existing situation of human smuggling and human trafficking. Using official reports, international reports, field experiences, and interviews,[5] this chapter often focuses on how Syrians have been exploited by smugglers and traffickers.

Human Smuggling

There is a growing concern over unregulated international immigration. Whereas there were 156 million migrants in 1990, by 2010 it rose to at least 214 million, driven by issues closely related to globalization and social transformation, inequality, state and human security, technology, law and governance, and labor demand.[6] Out of the 130 million international migrants, an estimated 20 to 30 million are categorized as illegal immigrants; at any time, around 4 million are actively pursuing immigration. The tightening of borders has forced illegal immigrants to rely on smuggling groups. Organized crime groups are involved in human smuggling, including the prominent Chinese snakeheads and the coyotes of Mexico.[7]

Human smuggling is a criminal activity in which smugglers illegally transport consenting immigrants across international borders without the required travel documents. The desire for a better life or desperation in the face of persecution by tyrannical regimes drive people into the hands of criminal groups in order to move clandestinely across borders. The source countries are often located in South America, Africa, the Middle East, and Asia.[8] Turkey is not only a source country, but also a transit and destination country, a bridge if you will, that facilitates transnational smuggling operations.[9] Moreover, conflicts in Iraq and Syria have turned Turkey into the epicenter for the smuggling of illegal immigrants into European Union countries.[10]

Turkish criminal statutes targeting human smuggling date back to the 1970s. However, Turkish law enforcement officials only published their first report on human smuggling in 1999. According to the report, human smugglers used many locations in Turkey's northeastern, eastern, and southern border provinces as entrance points; and many locations in its western and southwestern provinces as exit points by both sea and land. In 1999, 115 human smuggling investigations were undertaken.[11] Subsequent reports the following year reveal that the source regions were Middle Eastern, Asian, and African countries. That same year, illegal immigrants from East African countries began using the Turkish route, taking advantage of the well-networked connections of Turkish human smugglers.[12] The number of human smuggling cases rose to 154 in 2000.[13] By the early 2000s, human smugglers regarded their illegal activities as akin to a profession.[14] From this year on, the number of human smuggling cases increased slightly and nearly doubled to around 300 investigations in 2014.[15]

In the early 2000s, it became clear that given Turkey's geographical location along transnational human smuggling routes, the country needed to focus on creating laws to deter the smuggling activity. It did not help that loopholes in the judicial system often freed convicted smugglers after insignificant punishment. Further challenging for Turkish authorities was the fact that the police did not have access to centers capable of providing maintenance services such as lodging, food, and health care after illegal immigrants are apprehended.[16] By 2018, little had changed in this regard.

Turkey has grappled with many issues that provide a favorable environment for human smuggling. Of these, the country's geographical location is preeminent; not surprisingly illegal immigrants prefer the prominence of well-networked Turkish human smugglers. Turkish crime groups are extremely resourceful, enabling them to move easily between various other types of illicit smuggling activities into human smuggling. For example, a considerable number of drug traffickers have expanded into the arena to meet the increasing demand from Syrians seeking to escape the ongoing conflict in Syria.[17] Criminal groups in European countries have also diversified into human smuggling.[18] It is not uncommon for these operations to traffic concurrently in drugs, cigarettes, and antiquities across Turkey's borders.[19]

It should be noted that the nonchalant attitude of former Turkish administrations (as well as the Justice and Development Party- AKP) plays a key role in facilitating human smuggling. Providing accommodations or health care for smuggled people is a burden for the Turkish government, which lacks the funds to offer such services. To evade these onerous responsibilities, the government instructs law enforcement officials to put little effort into apprehending illegal immigrants. In a case recorded in 2013, for example, word was passed on to the authorities that Afghan and Pakistani immigrants were en route to Istanbul from the province of Iğdır, in the far eastern part of the country. Despite these tips, authorities intentionally ignored the intelligence. By most accounts, the police responded as they did due to the dearth of maintenance services in Turkey. Budget issues also have had an impact on the deportation of illegal immigrants. Law enforcement officials prefer to transfer the immigrants back to the neighboring countries from which they came.[20]

Human smugglers use several intricate strategies to transport illegal immigrants to their destination countries. One option is to traverse the rocky and mountainous parts of Turkey's porous eastern and southeastern borders either on foot or by bus with fake documents in hand. Other immigrants are transported in the secret storage compartments of trucks or buses. In another strategy, deported immigrants—mainly from Azerbaijan, Armenia, Georgia, and Uzbekistan—use counterfeit travel documents to reenter Turkey through border gates in Iğdır and Artvin provinces. Some immigrants come to Turkey as tourists with visa exemptions but remain in the country and travel to

European Union countries illegally. Other immigrants cross the eastern or southeastern borders of Turkey and board buses that bring them to Istanbul. From Istanbul they are smuggled into Europe through either the Edirne province or Kırklareli province along the Maritza River or through some Aegean provinces (Muğla, Izmir, and Aydın) to the Greek islands.[21]

Smugglers use at least two types of boats to ferry the immigrants to the islands and pass the cost on to the immigrants. For example, transportation on a rubber boat costs between 1,000 and 1,200 euros per immigrant, a jet boat costs 1,500-2,000 euros, and a luxury yacht costs double that at from 1,500 to 4,000 euros.[22] Cargo ships docked in northeastern ports, have also been utilized to smuggle immigrants from Turkey to European Union countries such as Bulgaria and Romania. Those headed to Greece and Italy, embark from the country's southern ports. Other illegal immigrants use counterfeit Turkish travel documents to enter Serbia, Croatia, Macedonia, and Bosnia—countries that do not require visas for Turkish citizens—and then travel illegally to Western European countries.[23]

One popular ruse for smugglers is to direct recent immigrants to their consulates once in Turkey. Stating that they have lost their passports, they receive temporary travel documents, allowing smugglers to doctor their original passports, creating a counterfeit visa that enables the immigrants to move on to European countries.[24] The cost of this smuggling regimen is around 12,000 euros.[25]

Interviews with law enforcement shed light on the various sources of funding. While some immigrants fund their illegal travel by selling their properties, others use money obtained from drug trafficking or organ trafficking. In one case, for example, the police apprehended a group of Afghan people with 5 kg of heroin who were on a bus en route to Istanbul. They were able to travel with the heroin all the way from Afghanistan to Turkey, freely passing across the Iranian and Turkish borders. There is also anecdotal evidence that human smugglers have interacted with organ traffickers. The price for a kidney is typically 10,000 USD and can be sold for at least 150,000 USD.[26] This is more than enough lucre to pay one's smuggling fees.[27]

Turkish human smugglers have been characterized by professional flair and physical violence.[28] Having become transnational in scope since at least the 1990s, in the following decade their activities have only broadened. In one 2004 case, police detected a human smuggling network operating between Turkey and China. Further investigation revealed that Chinese illegal immigrants were flown from China to Jordan and then smuggled overland to Turkey. In this instance, police arrested 30 human smugglers with 117 counterfeit passports. In another investigation that same year, Turkish and British law enforcement collaborated to disband a human smuggling group comprising Turkish, Iranian, and Iraqi smugglers who were connected to smuggling operatives in the United Kingdom.[29] Smugglers commonly operate in these countries. They are by most accounts, well-informed about asylum procedures and accessible points of entry in a host of countries.[30]

Many Turkish human smuggling operations have a Greek connection. The convergence of smuggling activities in both countries offers an enticing opportunity for human smugglers targeting European Union countries.[31] Since the 1990s, Greece has seen an influx of immigrants. By the early 2000s, 6.4 percent of the Greek population was made up of immigrants.[32] A human smuggling investigation conducted in 2004 revealed the existence of transnational networks linking operations in China, Pakistan, Turkey, and Greece. Illegal immigrants from these countries are brought to Turkey and smuggled to European countries using sea routes. Jet boats have been used to transfer immigrants to the Greek islands. The police arrested 30 Turkish and Greek human smugglers in possession of a jet boat, counterfeit passports, long-barrel weapons, and several small arms. In total, the police recorded 324 human smuggling cases in 2004.[33]

Turkish human smugglers have networks in source, transit, and target countries. For example, a police investigation conducted in 2005 revealed that Turkish, Pakistani, and Bangladeshi human smugglers had collaborated in the smuggling of Asian illegal immigrants via Turkey. Turkish human smugglers also have used alternative routes as well. In one case, human smugglers attempted to transfer 39 Syrian illegal immigrants from the port of Mersin in southern Turkey to Northern Cyprus, the Turkish part of the eastern Mediterranean island of Cyprus.[34]

The nationalities of illegal immigrants apprehended in Turkey offer insight into the transnational capacity of Turkish human smuggling groups. For example, Eritreans,[35] Mauritanians, Somalians, and Myanmarians were among the illegal immigrants apprehended in Turkey in 2008.[36] In addition to these nationalities, illegal immigrants from Georgia, Palestine, Pakistan, Afghanistan, Azerbaijan, Russia, Syria, and Iraq have been seized in Turkey.

Palestinians were the leading group of illegal immigrants between 2005 and 2009;[37] however, Syrians, as one might expect, has become the leading group after the start of the Syrian civil war in 2011. They have two options to leave Syria, either using legal protocols such as family reunification, university fellowships and scholarships, and training programs or illicit strategies, such as relying on smugglers utilizing the most prominent Balkans route that passes through or near Turkey, Greece, Macedonia, Serbia, Croatia, and Slovenia.[38] In 2015, 56 percent of the 856,273 illegal immigrants who traveled from Turkey to the Greek islands were Syrians.[39]

Turkish and Syrian human smugglers cooperate in the smuggling of Syrians. However, given their familiarity with the language and the Syrian people, Syrian smugglers have begun to dominate the smuggling partnership in the region.[40] Afghan, Tunisian, and Iraqi smugglers have also been identified as actors in the network. Turks typically supply the equipment used for smuggling Syrians. Some Turkish and Syrian companies have even gone as far as purchasing pockets of land in close proximity to the sea to facilitate smuggling operations. According to the unwritten agreements between the smugglers and their customers, the smugglers are expected to provide Syrian refugees with transportation, food, lodging when necessary, life jackets, and swimming rings.[41] The prices for transportation from Syria vary widely, ranging from 300 USD for locals to more than 20,000 USD if counterfeit documents, bribes, and luxury services are required.[42] Smugglers operating along Turkey's western shores can earn around 16,000 USD per trip.[43] Some Syrians have amassed huge amounts of money from these activities. For example, one Syrian smuggler admitted in a 2015 interview that he had already earned $800,000 for his part in the activity.[44]

Large cargo ships owned by wealthy Syrian businessmen are capable of smuggling between 400 and 500 Syrians per trip from Istanbul and Mersin provinces. When intensive patrols of the Greek islands are in effect, the cargo ships travel to Romania. Occasionally, Syrian immigrants have been transferred to the larger cargo ships after they have been transported by small boats to either of the two Turkish provinces. The large cargo ships also transfer the Syrian immigrants to smaller boats when the cargo ship is near the coasts of the target countries. Albanians take an active role in providing this kind of transportation.[45]

Human smugglers share their craft with others. During a human smuggling investigation, for example, the police found that the leader of the criminal organization being targeted was a former Syrian shoe repairman. When he arrived in Turkey, he tried to cross the border into Greece three times but failed each time. During these attempts, however, the shoe repairman met human smugglers and learned their smuggling techniques. He then established a criminal organization comprised of Turkish and Syrian smugglers and became part of several transnational smuggling networks. He smuggled not only Syrians but also persons from Guinea, Somalia, Cameroon, Kenya, Rwanda, Senegal, Afghanistan, and Palestine. The diverse nationalities of the smuggled immigrants are an indication of how broad the shoe repairman's transnational smuggling had become.[46]

Syrian smugglers are based in the city of Aksaray in Istanbul province. Immigrants who want to travel to European countries meet intermediaries there, where together they cobble out an agreement about the conditions of their illegal trek. In one police video, taken by a hidden camera, an intermediary and a prospective immigrant bargain over the costs for traveling to Greece over a land route. The intermediary charges everyone except for children under 2 years old. The same video includes price negotiations between a

Syrian immigrant from the city of Raqqa and a smuggler in Izmir province, where the Basmane mosque is used as a base for intermediaries to meet with immigrants. The negotiated price typically is $550 per passenger.[47]

Past and current governments in Turkey have failed to adopt effective policies for suppressing human smuggling. Between 2004, when Turkey began the negotiation process to enter the European Union, and 2011, the outbreak of the Syrian conflict in 2011, police apprehended an average of 55,000 illegal immigrants in the country each year.[48] After 2011, the massive influx of Syrian refugees seeking a safer haven in Turkey, Turkish police face an insurmountable obstacle to enforcing the government's anti-smuggling policies. As a result, despite the rise in illegal immigration, the number of illegal immigrants apprehended in Turkey decreased dramatically. In the three years after the start of the civil war, the number of illegal immigrants apprehended in Turkey totaled 10,119,[49] a decrease of 91 percent from the 139,471[50] illegal immigrants apprehended in the three years before the civil war started. The Turkish government's response to the decreased apprehensions was to adopt a policy that allowed Syrians and other immigrants to leave the country. According to critics in Europe, human smuggling in Turkey has been ignored since then.[51]

European Union countries have been challenged by a massive influx of Syrians. As of March 2016, Syrians had scattered over 20 countries.[52] The situation of the Syrian immigrants prompted critics of the European Union to speak out. One critic noted that if the European Union had been active in seeking solutions to political conflicts such as the current one in Syria and had provided enough humanitarian assistance abroad, it would not have encountered the massive immigration issue.[53] In response to such criticism and the influx of Syrian immigrants seeking asylum in its member countries—most of whom had arrived after first entering Turkey—the European Union negotiated an agreement with Turkey to halt the flow of Syrian immigrants. According to the deal signed in 2016, Turkey would take back the Syrians who had illegally passed into Greece and would increase its efforts to stop Syrian immigrants from leaving Turkey in return for selectively sending immigrants staying in Turkish refugee camps to European Union countries. Turkey would also receive several billion euros[54] to cover the cost of hosting more Syrian immigrants. The agreement, however, did not produce permanent and effective results. Well-networked Turkish and Syrian smugglers simply used different routes to transfer Syrian immigrants from the western shores of Turkey to the Greek islands. As of August 2017, for example, the number of Syrian asylum seekers in European Union countries was 952,000,[55] with most having passed through Turkey. The business of smuggling in Turkey remains exploitative and portrays a growing relationship with other types of crimes, especially human trafficking.[56]

Human Trafficking

Human trafficking impacts almost every country in the world. It is considered the fastest-growing and the second most lucrative form of transnational crime after drug trafficking. Human trafficking is the result of multiple conditions, including poverty, corruption, gender, ethnic and racial discrimination, and political instability.[57] Like the business of human smuggling, human trafficking is exploitative and related to other types of crime.[58] Human trafficking is defined as the recruitment, transportation, or transfer of people by means of coercion—such as threat, use of force, abduction, fraud, deception, or the abuse of power. The victims are forced to work in the sex or labor sectors.[59]

Human trafficking is among the crimes that affect national security, economic stability, migration, and environmental sustainability. It attracts transnational crime groups, worsens irregular migratory flows, harms labor markets, and is linked to other illicit activities.[60] It is estimated that 27 million people are victimized each year and represents a crime sector worth 32 billion USD.[61] Turkey has faced two forms of human trafficking: sex trafficking and forced labor. While sex trafficking has been a growing concern since the 1990s, forced labor has been a problem since the start of the Syrian civil war in 2011 when millions of Syrians sought ways to flee the violence in their country.

Sex Trafficking

Sex trafficking is the most prevalent kind of human trafficking in Turkey. Although thousands of foreign victims are deported after being charged with committing prostitution the human trafficking sector remains active. Victims are promised jobs in entertainment, modeling, or domestic work but instead are forced into the sex sector upon arriving in the country. Traffickers mostly use psychological coercion and debt bondage to force victims into sex trafficking, though they also use social media to lure victims and hire foreign recruiting and management assistants to find victims.[62]

Turkey has been a target country for human trafficking since the collapse of the Soviet Union. Victims have traveled to Turkey either by coercion or voluntarily.[63] Turkey's current and former governments have paid little attention to the problem of human trafficking.[64] International reports have criticized Turkey for not doing enough to eliminate human trafficking.[65]

The first Turkish police report on human trafficking was published in 2004 and showed that the police arrested 227 traffickers that year. In 2005, the number of human traffickers arrested rose to 379.[66] Police investigations in 2006 showed that human trafficking groups were operating transnationally. Of the 422 traffickers arrested in 2006, 375 of them were Turks. Others were from Moldova (12), Russia (12), Azerbaijan (7), Kyrgyzstan (5), Uzbekistan (5), Ukraine (4), Georgia (3), and Turkmenistan (1). The nationalities of the victims were, in some cases, reflective of the proportion of arrested traffickers with that same nationality. Of the 246 victims in 2006, for example, 75 were from Moldovia and 45 from Russia—the two countries that topped the list for the number of traffickers (12 each) arrested. The remaining victims came from Ukraine (35), Kyrgyzstan (27), Azerbaijan (22), Uzbekistan (18), Iran (2), Kazakhstan (2), Bulgaria (2), Armenia (1), and Belarus (1).[67] Some of the traffickers were female and previously victims of human trafficking.[68]

In 2007, traffickers from two additional countries, Pakistan and Romania, were arrested, and victims from Sri Lanka and Tunisia were deported. A striking difference between the cases in 2007 and those from the previous year were the number of traffickers compared to the number of victims. In 2007, the number of traffickers was 308, while the number of victims was 148.[69] The number of victims in 2007 was less than half the number of traffickers. In 2006, the number of victims and the number of traffickers were about equal. The large gap in 2007 stems from the reluctance of victims to cooperate with the law enforcement officials. The victims were frightened by the traffickers, knowing that if they cooperated as a victim, they would be deported and not returned again to Turkey.[70]

The number of traffickers arrested decreased steadily after 2010, with about 89 arrests in 2013, 91 in 2014, and 87 in 2015.[71] This decline was the result of changes in the characteristics of human trafficking. The victims who had connections in Turkey did not need a trafficker to help them find work in the sex sector when they returned to Turkey. Instead, they used their own contacts to find work. Findings from human trafficking investigations in Turkey concur with conclusions from analogous investigations around the world. The investigations indicate that victims come from countries such as Russia, Turkmenistan, Kazakhstan, Kyrgyzstan, Morocco, and Azerbaijan and depending on their qualifications they can earn up to $1,000 per night. Victims frequently cooperate and collaborate with one other. It is not uncommon for some to be brought into Turkey illegally, put into debt bondage, and threatened by their traffickers.

Human traffickers also tend to trap civil servants, businessmen, and bureaucrats by videotaping their sexual relations with the trafficking victims, so the documentation can be used as blackmail if the recipients should threaten the traffickers. Another tool that traffickers use to control civil servants and bureaucrats is bribery. The bribes enable human traffickers to easily bring victims back into the country shortly after they have been deported. The traffickers' strategies include using counterfeit passports, bribing customs officers, or crossing borders illegally,[72] all of which have been seen in other countries around the world.[73] Furthermore, victims are less cooperative about the identities and modus operandi of the traffickers when victims are captured by the police.[74]

Case Study: The Investigations in Iğdır City

Iğdır is a city of about 571 square miles in the eastern part of Turkey. It has a high potential for human trafficking despite its relatively small population of around 85,000 people. Many of the police investigations conducted in Iğdır between 2011 and 2013 involved human trafficking. More than half of the country's 14 human trafficking investigations that were treated as organized crime[75] in 2012 occurred in Iğdır province. Similarly, five of the nine human trafficking investigations across the country in 2013 took place in Iğdır province.[76] These statistics do not mean that Iğdır is more prone to human trafficking than other parts of the country or that Iğdır province represents more than half of the country's human trafficking incidents. Rather, the investigations were the result of Iğdır province being selected as the pilot region for developing a national and regional model to combat human trafficking.[77]

Iğdır province has a mixed population divided almost equally between Turks of Azeri origin and Kurds. Azeri traffickers have opened hotels in the city and brought victims from Azerbaijan to work at the nightclubs of these hotels.[78] International reports confirm that Turkey is one of the target countries for the exploitation of Azeri women in the sex sector.[79] In this small city, more than 20 hotels have been linked to sex trafficking. Some victims have become leaders in the sex sector, helping to coordinate efforts to bring victims from Azerbaijan. Azeri hotel owners—the traffickers—have contacts with other Turkish traffickers who have transferred Kyrgyz victims to Iğdır. When some of these victims have worked in the sex sector in other cities, they have met victims from different countries and invited them to work in Iğdır. As a result, Iğdır has become a trafficking hotbed for predominantly Azeri and Kyrgyz victims in addition to victims from Morocco, Armenia, Russia, and Uzbekistan.[80]

Exoticism of women based on race and ethnicity is a valuable asset in the human trafficking sector.[81] Knowing that customers do not underestimate the women's ethnic and racial identity in choosing their victims,[82] the hotel owners have an entrepreneurial mindset, using the business in ways that will yield the highest profits. For example, they deliberately have lured Armenian victims to attract more customers because it is culturally meaningful for Azeris to have sex with Armenians. As a result of ongoing animosity between Azeris and Armenians, Azeris acknowledge that having sex with an Armenian woman is viewed as a way of taking revenge on Armenians. Additionally, the hotel owners treat victims brutally, forcing pregnant victims to have sex with customers and to take medicines to delay their menstrual periods. They even have exploited underage victims at the nightclubs.[83]

The Iğdır hotel owners have close relationships with bureaucrats and law enforcement officials, who provide protection for the owners' illicit activities. The hoteliers either bribe law enforcement officials or send them victims to have sex with in order to entrap them in their activities, thus ensuring against any possible investigation into their activities. Relying on these relationships, the hotel proprietors intimidate victims to keep them from reporting their abusers to the police. The hotel owners' tactic is to tell the victims they have connections with the police and that the police would instantly let the hotel owners know if any of the victims had contacted the police.[84]

As an added layer of protection, the hotel owners developed other techniques to allow them to operate unhindered, such as dodging the law. According to Turkish law, being an intermediary or providing a place for prostitution to occur is a crime. The hotel owners therefore built high walls around the hotels and attached iron wires and pieces of glass on the walls (see Figure 5.1). The walls, of course, were not intended to protect the hotels from thieves but to prevent the police from discovering that the hotels were being used for prostitution. The hoteliers also check the identity cards of customers before allowing them to enter the hotel and station lookouts along routes to the hotels to watch for approaching police cars. The lookouts utilize encrypted radios to communicate with the watchmen in the hotels.[85]

Figure 5.1 **Pieces of glass on the walls surrounding hotels.** *Source*: Police Raid Made on May 8, 2013.

When the organized crime police attempted to conduct an investigation in December 2011, they learned that the hotel owners had been tipped off to the raid in advance by police officers who were colluding with the hotel owners in the prostitution operation. After the aborted investigation, the police developed new techniques to detect human trafficking cases, this time deploying undercover agents to infiltrate the hotels in the guise of wealthy businessmen. Some of the hotel owners were suspicious about the businessmen's true identity and feared they might actually be police officers, but, because the tactic was being used for the first time, many did not notice the identities of undercover agents. To allay their suspicions, some proprietors hired psychologists to uncover the truth. The well-trained undercover agents, however, succeeded at keeping their true identities secret and collected a considerable amount of solid evidence on how victims were forced into the sex sector.[86]

The police deployed separate pairs of undercover agents to other hotels for the same purpose. After collecting all of the evidence, the police raided the hotels and arrested the suspects.[87]

Agents involved in the Iğdır undercover operation discovered many details about the complicated human trafficking crime sector and links between human trafficking and other types of crime. Agents discovered that the human trafficking was committed by an organized crime group comprised of the hotel owners and their accomplices. Additionally, they found secret cameras in several hotel rooms, with video recordings intended to be used to blackmail wealthy businessmen and state officials when necessary.[88]

This human trafficking operation could not have flourished without corruption. In some cases, hotel owners bribed law enforcement officials to get information in advance about pending police raids. For example, hotel owners and cooperating police officers might use cryptic language to communicate with each other, such as "What does the weather look like today?", "Did you see the keys?", and "I have a stomachache today." When the police officers used these codes in their communication with the hotel owners, it meant that the police would make a raid. The owners therefore let victims leave the hotels or hid them in secret places within the hotel as seen in Figure 5.2.

Human trafficking was also linked to extortion practices as hotel owners coerced money from victims. The investigation uncovered networks between human traffickers and smugglers. When trafficked victims were deported, smugglers immediately brought them back into the country. Each deported victim paid the smugglers around $1,500 to reenter the country. Victims who were smuggled back into the country through the uncontrolled parts of the border had to walk for up to 10 hours on steep and rocky terrain. There have been reports of victims being stopped and raped by PKK militants. Another detail uncovered in the Iğdır operation was the practice of counterfeiting. Some victims, especially those from Kyrgyzstan, used fake travel documents as well as genuine passports with a different name.[89]

Figure 5.2 One of the secret places used by traffickers in a hotel. *Source*: Police Raid Made on May 8, 2013.

The undercover operation also revealed that some female workers at the hotels also were traffickers. After working in the sex sector in Iğdır, they attempted to bring new victims from Azerbaijan and provided the victims with accommodations and connections to the hotel owners. Putting the victims in debt bondage, the female traffickers extorted large sums of money from the newcomers,[90] much the same way that victims are extorted by perpetrators in the transportation, recruitment, and sale of trafficked victims.[91] According to findings from the undercover operation, each victim was earning 100 Turkish liras, approximately 30 USD dollars, from each customer. The customer also paid for the hotel room, which cost 50 Turkish liras for one hour. Considering that the monthly average salary for an Azeri victim was around 200 USD in her home country, the victims had the opportunity to make more than that amount in one night. The prospect of losing that income explains why victims did not want to be caught by the police. In some cases, when the victims were captured, they wept and pleaded not to be deported, saying that they had to come back into the country and that their deportation would only put them in debt bondage because they needed to get help from the hotel owners to pay the debt. Some hotel owners earned up to $50,000 in a month.[92]

Profiles of the trafficking victims in Iğdır explains much about why they kept working in the sex sector and corroborated the results of previous research conducted in 2010. The research concluded that most victims were single or divorced women, one-third of them having children. Their income was low when compared with the income of women in Turkey.[93] The situation in Iğdır was similar. Most of the victims were divorced. Their families did not know that they were involved in the Turkish sex sector, believing instead that the women were working in Turkey as housekeepers. The average age of the Iğdır victims was in the range of 20 to 30 years old. Older victims left the hotels and opened houses in Iğdır to earn money from prostitution in the city.[94]

Some victims captured in Iğdır province in 2013 were deported many times but returned thanks to established connections between traffickers with smugglers operating in Turkey's border regions, again confirming the results of research conducted in 2010. According to the research, one-fifth of the victims in the sample reported that they would seek opportunities to reenter Turkey to work again in the sex sector.[95] It should be emphasized, however, that victims who return voluntarily to work in the sex sector are still considered to be victims. Interviews with victims in 2012 and 2013 indicated that victims are caught in a tricky situation: They voluntarily return to Turkey after deportation but continue to work in the sex sector when they arrive. According to the interviewees, they regret working in the sex sector but feel pressured to provide financial assistance to their families and children in their home countries. Many, if not most of the victims have asserted that they cannot have sex with the customers without drinking alcohol first.[96]

The money flowing through the sex sector in Iğdır is handled in diverse ways by traffickers and victims. The traffickers, for example, put part of their cash into the construction and car dealership sectors in Iğdır and transfer some of the remaining cash to Baku, the capital and commercial hub of Azerbaijan. Victims, however, use underground money transfer systems, such the trust-based hawala system that allows for the transfer of money without the actual movement of any funds. Several exchange offices and jewelry stores that had contacts with hawaladars in Azerbaijan were used by the victims. Also, state banks with branches in Central Asia were used by Central Asian victims. The victims deposited small amounts of money that their relatives could then withdraw with a debit card.[97]

It is common for corrupt government officials, such as border and customs officials, and law enforcement officers to help human traffickers operate unimpeded.[98] In Iğdır, human trafficking often involved the exploitation and revictimization of the women involved in the sex sector. According to findings from the Iğdır undercover operation, some victims were raped by police officers. The agents also found that most Azeri victims used a route through the Nakchivan Autonomous Region to reach Turkey. After taking an airline flight that landed late at night in the Nakchivan Autonomous Region, the Azeri victims boarded a shuttle bus for transportation to Turkey. When the bus arrived at the customs checkpoint on the Turkish border, police officers checking passports ordered some victims off the bus for trivial reasons and then raped them. Fearful of being deported, the victims did not report the crimes to the police; instead, they kept secret what they had experienced at the customs checkpoint. In their statements to the police, shuttle bus drivers confirmed removals and rapes of women by police officers. Drivers also said that they told the women they should wear head scarves like Iranian women and warned them not to wear makeup. One of the bus drivers related an incident in which the victim was hospitalized because she was forced to have anal intercourse by several police officers. Police investigators found the victim and confirmed the bus driver's story.[99]

Syrians in Human Trafficking

With hundreds of people seeking to escape civil war and tyrannical regimes in Middle Eastern countries, human traffickers have a new stream of immigrants to victimize. Syrian refugees are especially vulnerable, as they flee a country mired in a civil war (since 2011). The war has sparked an extensive and ongoing migration of refugees into surrounding countries, particularly Turkey. Turkey has been the most generous country, hosting almost half of the Syrian refugees scattered over 20 countries. Almost 10 percent of Syrians who have fled their country now live in refugee camps.

Syrians living in or out of refugee camps are exposed to sex trafficking and labor trafficking. In 2016, 36 out of 183 trafficking victims identified in Turkey were Syrians, representing the largest segment of this group of trafficking victims.[100] Syrian women were routinely subjected to early and forced marriages, polygamy, sexual harassment, human trafficking, prostitution, and rape at the hands of criminal groups.[101] According to one Syrian victim, Syrian women have been sold in Turkish refugee camps, often using methods used by terrorist groups operating in Syria, who sold women at slavery markets.[102] In return for being given a promise of marriage, families in the refugee camps are paid, and their underage daughters are forced to work in the sex sector when they leave the camps. Most of these victims, however, are sold at nightclubs in metropolitan cities.[103] In other cases, pimps collect Syrian women under the pretext of having found work for them in the agriculture sector; however, the women instead are forced into prostitution.[104] Thousands of Syrians have been victimized by human traffickers.[105]

Traffickers who take advantage of the destitution of Syrian refugees target underage girls, particularly those between the ages of 15 and 20. Girls as young as 13 also have been targeted, but such instances are rare. Traffickers deceive desperate Syrian families with the promise of a better life for their daughters after they get married. It should be noted that Syrians without legal travel documents are much more vulnerable to being forced to work in the sex sector. The parents of Syrians are paid between $700 and $1,700, an enormous sum for a Syrian parent, to hand over the bride. Some Syrians use this money to pay a smuggler who can take them to a European Union country.[106] The practice of polygamy is a pervasive part of the culture in eastern and southeastern regions of Turkey, even though it is prohibited by Turkish law. Syrian girls are married under religious law as a second or third wife of older customers. Even aging men in other Gulf States purchase underage Syrian girls from refugee camps, including camps in Turkey.[107]

Syrians also are vulnerable to organ trafficking, which involves people selling one of their kidneys to traffickers. According to an interview in Lebanon, one organ trafficker said he sold the kidneys of 30 Syrians in the last three years.[108] Syrians in Turkey also sell their kidneys at prices ranging from 6,000 euros to 11,000 euros through some social media accounts. Allegedly, some hospitals in the eastern region of the country have been used illegally for kidney transplantation. Clients are typically Saudi Arabians and Europeans.[109]

Another type of trafficking that ensnares Syrians, particularly migrants, is forced labor in Turkey.[110] Fifty-five percent of Syrians in Turkey are under the age of 18, and only about one-fourth of them attend school. In the province of Izmir, only 6,000 out of a total of 21,000 Syrian children attend school. Most of the unschooled children work in the underground economy,[111] usually in the service and agriculture sectors.[112] Some children, though, work in textile factories that export clothes to European Union countries. The children are employed in low-level jobs that require few skills, receive meager salaries, and are treated badly.[113] All of the shoe manufacturing factories in Gaziantep, a city in the western part of Turkey, employ at least one or two child workers who are paid only half of what an adult worker would be paid, and they are exposed to harmful chemicals.[114] The number of children beggars in Turkey is roughly 100,000, and a considerable number of them are Syrians.[115]

NOTES

1. Mitchel P. Roth, *Global Organized Crime* (New York: Routledge, 2017), 215.

2. Louise Shelley, *Human Trafficking*, (New York: Cambridge University Press, 2010), 2.

3. Roth, *Global Organized Crime,* 215.

4. Jessica Elliott, *The Role of Consent in Human Trafficking*, (New York: Routledge, 2015).

5. This chapter used seven interviews made with law enforcement officials. Interviews with Le1, Le2, Le3 were made in Hatay, Le4 and Le5 in Istanbul, Le7 and Le8 in Ankara. As explained in the introduction chapter, these codes were given to the respondents. Also, this chapter used field experiences of Mahmut Cengiz, the

co-author, who worked as the chief of organized crime department in the province of Iğdır between September 2011 and March 2014.

6. Stephen Castles, "The Forces Driving Global Migration." in *Human Trafficking,* eds. Natividad G. Chong and Jenny B. Clark (New York: Routledge, 2016): 6-24.

7. Roth, *Global Organized Crime, 216.*

8. Tolu Ogboru and Salome Kigbu, "Human Smuggling, Human Trafficking, Transnational Organised Crime." *Beijing Law Review,* Vol. 6, No. 4 (December 2015): 224-231.

9. Mahmut Cengiz, *Turkiye'de Organize Suc Gercegi.* (Ankara: Seckin Yayinevi, 2015)

10. Al Rousan and Nabil Al-Tikriti, "Syrian and Iraqi Conflicts Move Turkey to the Heart of Europe's Refugee Crisis," *Turkish Review,* Vol. 5, No. 3 (May 1, 2015): 190-193.

11. *1999 Turkish Report of Anti-Smuggling and Organized Crime Department (ASOD),* 51-52.

12. *2000 Turkish Report of ASOD, 88.*

13. *2000 Turkish Report of ASOD, 90.*

14. Ahmet Içduygu and Ş. Toktaş, "How Do Smuggling and Trafficking Operate via Irregular Border Crossings in the Middle East? Evidence from Fieldwork in Turkey." *International Migration,* (2002): 25-54.

15. *2015 Turkish Report of ASOD, 44.*

16. *2000 Turkish Report of ASOD, 89.*

17. Le1, Le2, and Le3. Interviews by Mahmut Cengiz, Personal Interviews, April 24, 2015, Hatay.

18. Michael Birnbaum, "Human Smuggling a New Growth Industry," *Edmonton Journal,* (September 5, 2015), A17.

19. Le1, Le2, and Le3. Interviews by Mahmut Cengiz, Personal Interviews, April 24, 2015, Hatay.

20. Le4 and Le5, Interviews by Mahmut Cengiz, Personal Interviews, July 26, 2015, Istanbul.

21. *2014 Turkish Report of Anti-Smuggling and Organized Crime, 70.*

22. "Gocmen Kacakciligi Dosyasi," *Cagdas Haber,* accessed on August 8, 2017, from http://cagdashaber.net/Ozel-Haber/gocmen-kacakciligi-dosyasi.html.

23. *2013 Turkish Report of ASOD, 75-76.*

24. *2014 Turkish Report of ASOD, 70.*

25. "Gocmen Kacakciligi Dosyasi," *Cagdas Haber,* accessed on August 8, 2017, from http://cagdashaber.net/Ozel-Haber/gocmen-kacakciligi-dosyasi.html.

26. Roth, *Global Organized Crime, 218.*

27. Le4 and Le5, Interviews by Mahmut Cengiz, Personal Interviews, July 26, 2015, Istanbul.

28. Tülin Günşen İçli, Hanifi Sever, and Muhammed Sever, "A Survey Study on the Profile of Human Smugglers in Turkey." *Advances in Applied Sociology,* 05, 01, (1), (2015): 1-12.

29. *2004 Turkish Report of ASOD, 26-27.*

30. Sebnem Koser Akcapar, "Re-Thinking Migrants' Networks and Social Capital: A Case Study of Iranians in Turkey," *International Migration*, Vol. 48, No. 2 (April 2010), pp. 161-196.

31. Theodaire Baird, *Human Smuggling in the Eastern Mediterranean*, (New York: Routledge, 2017).

32. Georgios A. Antonopoulos, "The Smuggling of Migrants in Greece: An Examination of Its Social Organization," *European Journal of Criminology*, Vol. 3, No. 4 (October 2006), pp. 439-461.

33. *2004 Turkish Report of ASOD, 26-27.*

34. *2005 Turkish Report of ASOD, 113.*

35. *2012 Turkish Report of ASOD, 49.*

36. *2008 Turkish Report of ASOD, 68.*

37. *2009 Turkish Report of ASOD, 93.*

38. Luigi Achilli, "The "Good" Smuggler: The Ethics and Morals of Human Smuggling among Syrians." *The Annals of the American Academy of Political and Social Science.* 676 (1), (03/2018): 77 - 96.

39. "İşte madde madde AB - Türkiye göçmen anlaşması," *Haber*, (October 5, 2017), accessed on May, 2017, from http://www.internethaber.com/iste-madde-madde-ab-turkiye-gocmen-anlasmasi-foto-galerisi-1577305.htm?page=3.

40. "Gocmen Kacakciligi Dosyasi," *Cagdas Haber*, accessed on August 8, 2017, from http://cagdashaber.net/Ozel-Haber/gocmen-kacakciligi-dosyasi.html.

41. Yasser Alawi, "A Syrian Smuggler Working on Turkey's Shores Speaks Out," *Huffington Post*, (March 30, 2016), accessed on August 10, 2017, from http://www.huffingtonpost.com/entry/syria-deeply-interview-people-smuggler-turkey-greece_us_56facd51e4b0143a9b497365.

42. Theodaire Baird, *Human Smuggling in the Eastern Mediterranean*, (New York: Routledge, 2017).

43. "Migrant Crisis: The Syrians Exploited by People-Smugglers in Turkey," *BBC*, (September 8, 2015), accessed on August 10, 2017, from http://www.bbc.com/news/av/world-europe-34183454/migrant-crisis-the-syrians-exploited-by-people-smugglers-in-turkey.

44. Patrick Kingsley, "Syrians in Turkey: The Human Smuggler and the Young Refugee," *New York Times*, (March 24, 2017), accessed on August 10, 2017, from https://www.nytimes.com/2017/03/24/world/europe/turkey-human-trafficking-refugee-crisis.html.

45. "Gocmen Kacakciligi Dosyasi," *Cagdas Haber*, accessed on August 8, 2017, from http://cagdashaber.net/Ozel-Haber/gocmen-kacakciligi-dosyasi.html.

46. "Suriyeli Ayakkabıcının Kurduğu İnsan Kaçakçılığı Şebekesi Çökertildi," *Haberler*, (May 26, 2017), accessed on August 10, 2017, from http://haberler.com/suriyeli-ayakkabicinin-kurdugu-insan-kacakciligi-9661516-haberi.

47. Alex Forsyth, "Suriyeli mültecilerin sırtından para kazanan organ taciri," *BBC*, (April 26, 2017), accessed on August 10, 2017, from http://www.bbc.com/turkce/haberler-dunya-39704728; "Türkiye'deki mülteciler ve kaçakçılık şebekeleri," *euronews*, (May 2, 2016), Accessed on August 10, 2017, from https://www.youtube.com/watch?v=3C0VBww0qh4.

48. *2005 Turkish Report of ASOD, 113.*

49. *2015 Turkish Report of ASOD, 44.*

50. *2010 Turkish Report of ASOD 106.*

51. Anna Triandafyllidou, "Governing Migrant Smuggling: A Criminality Approach Is Not Sufficient," *open Democracy*, (April 6, 2016), accessed on December 25, 2017, from https://www.opendemocracy.net/beyondslavery/hsr/anna-trianda fyllidou/governing-migrant-smuggling-criminality-approach-is-not-sufficien.

52. Danilo Mandic, "Trafficking and Syrian Refugee Smuggling: Evidence from the Balkan Route," *Social Inclusion*, Vol. 5, No. 2 (June 1, 2017): 28-38.

53. Bakare Najimdeen, "Middle East Refugees' Crisis: Europeans' Three Dimensional Approaches." Policy Perspectives, Vol. 13, No. 2 (2016): 63-91.

54. It is highly likely that some of this money has gotten into the wrong hands. Turkish money spent for Syrians in refugee camps is not audited, creating opportunities for corrupt politicians and bureaucrats.

55. "Syrian Refuge Regional Response," *UNHCR*, accessed on August 4, 2017, from http://data.unhcr.org/syrianrefugees/regional.php.

56. Elif O. Carmikli and Merve U. Kader, "Migrant Smuggling in Turkey: The Other Side of the Refugee Crisis," *USAK Report*, No. 45 Ekim (2016), 34.

57. Natividad G. Chong and Jenny B. Clark , "Introduction: Trafficking in Persons," in *Human Trafficking,* eds. Natividad G. Chong and Jenny B. Clark (New York: Routledge, 2016): 1-5.

58. Elif O. Carmikli and Merve U. Kader, "Migrant Smuggling in Turkey: The Other Side of the Refugee Crisis," *USAK Report*, No. 45 Ekim 2016, 34.

59. "What Is Human Trafficking?," *Human Rights Commission*, accessed on August 11, 2017, from http://sf-hrc.org/what-human-trafficking.

60. "2017 Trafficking in Persons Report," U.S. State Department, (June 2017), accessed on August 14, 2017, from https://www.state.gov/documents/organization/271339.pdf, 18.

61. Veerendra Mishra, *Combating Human Trafficking: Gaps in Policy and Law*, (California: Sage Publications, 2015), 1.

62. "2017 Trafficking in Persons Report," U.S. State Department, (June 2017), accessed on August 14, 2017, from https://www.state.gov/documents/organization/271339.pdf, p. 402.

63. Oguzhan O. Demir and James Finckenhaur, "Victims of Sex Trafficking in Turkey: Characteristics, Motivations, and Dynamics," *Women & Criminal Justice*, Vol. 20 (2010): 57-88.

64. Le4 and Le5, Interviews by Mahmut Cengiz, Personal Interviews, July 26, 2015, Istanbul.

65. "2017 Trafficking in Persons Report," U.S. State Department, (June 2017), accessed on August 14, 2017, from https://www.state.gov/documents/organization/271339.pdf, 400.

66. *2005 Turkish Report of ASOD, 116.*

67. *2006 Turkish Report of ASOD, 111.*

68. *2008 Turkish Report of ASOD, 64.*

69. *2007 Turkish Report of ASOD, 83-84.*

70. Le4 and Le5, Interviews by Mahmut Cengiz, Personal Interviews, July 26, 2015, Istanbul.

71. *2015 Turkish Report of ASOD, 45.*

72. Mahmut Cengiz's field experience, 2011 September-2014 March. Iğdır.

73. "2017 Trafficking in Persons Report," U.S. State Department, (June 2017), accessed on August 14, 2017, from https://www.state.gov/documents/organization/271339.pdf, p. 9.

74. Le4 and Le5, Interviews by Mahmut Cengiz, Personal Interviews, July 26, 2015, Istanbul.

75. This format includes wiretapping, surveillance, and deployment of undercover agents because human trafficking groups are considered to be criminal organizations.

76. *2013 Turkish Report of ASOD, 77*; Le6 and Le7, Interviews by Mahmut Cengiz, Personal Interviews, August 15, 2015, Ankara.

77. Mahmut Cengiz's field experience, 2011 September-2014 March. Iğdır.

78. Mahmut Cengiz's field experience, 2011 September-2014 March. Iğdır.

79. "2017 Trafficking in Persons Report," U.S. State Department, (June 2017), accessed on August 14, 2017, from https://www.state.gov/documents/organization/271339.pdf, p. 76.

80. Mahmut Cengiz's field experience, 2011 September-2014 March. Iğdır.

81. Natividad G. Chong, "Human Trafficking and Sex Industry: Does Ethnicity and Race Matter?", in *Human Trafficking,* eds. Natividad G. Chong and Jenny B. Clark (New York: Routledge, 2016):109-127, 122.

82. Joane Nagel, *Race, Ethnicity, and Sexuality: Intimate Intersections, Forbidden Frontiers* (New York, Oxford University Press, 2003), 55.

83. Mahmut Cengiz's field experience, 2011 September-2014 March. Iğdır.

84. Mahmut Cengiz's field experience, 2011 September-2014 March. Iğdır.

85. Mahmut Cengiz's field experience, 2011 September-2014 March. Iğdır.

86. Mahmut Cengiz's field experience, 2011 September-2014 March. Iğdır.

87. Mahmut Cengiz's field experience, 2011 September-2014 March. Iğdır.

88. Mahmut Cengiz's field experience, 2011 September-2014 March. Iğdır.

89. Mahmut Cengiz's field experience, 2011 September-2014 March. Iğdır.

90. Mahmut Cengiz's field experience, 2011 September-2014 March. Iğdır.

91. "2017 Trafficking in Persons Report," U.S. State Department, (June 2017), accessed on August 14, 2017, from https://www.state.gov/documents/organization/271339.pdf, 17.

92. Mahmut Cengiz's field experience, 2011 September-2014 March. Iğdır.

93. Oguzhan O. Demir and James Finckenhaur, "Victims of Sex Trafficking in Turkey: Characteristics, Motivations, and Dynamics," *Women & Criminal Justice*, Vol. 20 (2010), pp. 82-83.

94. Mahmut Cengiz's field experience, 2011 September-2014 March. Iğdır.

95. Oguzhan O. Demir and James Finckenhaur, "Victims of Sex Trafficking in Turkey: Characteristics, Motivations, and Dynamics," Vol. 20 (2010), p. 84.

96. Mahmut Cengiz's field experience, 2011 September-2014 March. Iğdır.

97. Mahmut Cengiz's field experience, 2011 September-2014 March. Iğdır.

98. Louise Shelley, "Human Security and Human Trafficking," in *Human Trafficking and Human Security*, ed. Anna Johnson, (New York: Routledge, 2009): 10-26.

99. Focus group with eight former Istanbul law enforcement officials conducting 2012 and 2013 investigations, May 2015.

100. "2017 Trafficking in Persons Report," U.S. State Department, (June 2017), accessed on August 14, 2017, from https://www.state.gov/documents/organization/271339.pdf, 402.

101. Uzay Bulut, "Turkey: The Business of Refugee Smuggling, Sex Trafficking," *Gatestone Institute International Policy Council*, (April 3, 2016), accessed on August 13, 2017, from https://www.gatestoneinstitute.org/7756/turkey-refugees-sex-trafficking.

102. Interview with Istanbul law enforcement officials, August 2015.

103. Le4 and Le5, Interviews by Mahmut Cengiz, Personal Interviews, July 26, 2015, Istanbul.

104. Le4 and Le5, Interviews by Mahmut Cengiz, Personal Interviews, July 26, 2015, Istanbul.

105. Le4 and Le5, Interviews by Mahmut Cengiz, Personal Interviews, July 26, 2015, Istanbul.

106. Uzay Bulut, "Turkey: The Business of Refugee Smuggling, Sex Trafficking," *Gatestone Institute International Policy Council*, (April 3, 2016), accessed on August 13, 2017, from https://www.gatestoneinstitute.org/7756/turkey-refugees-sex-trafficking.

107. Uzay Bulut, "Turkey: The Business of Refugee Smuggling, Sex Trafficking," *Gatestone Institute International Policy Council*, (April 3, 2016), accessed on August 13, 2017, from https://www.gatestoneinstitute.org/7756/turkey-refugees-sex-trafficking.

108. "Suriyeli Multecilerin Sirtindan Para Kazanan Organ Taciri," *BBC*, (April 26, 2017), accessed on August 13, 2017, from http://www.bbc.com/turkce/haberler-dunya-39704728.

109. "ARD: Türkiye'deki Suriyeliler böbreklerini satıyor," *ARD*, (February 21, 2017), accessed on August 13, 2017, from http://www.dw.com/tr/ard-t%C3%BCrki yedeki-suriyeliler-b%C3%B6breklerini-sat%C4%B1yor/a-37646452.

110. "2017 Trafficking in Persons Report," U.S. State Department, (June 2017), accessed on August 14, 2017, from https://www.state.gov/documents/organization/271339.pdf, p. 17.

111. "Suriyeli çocuk işçiler eğitim alamıyor, ucuza çalıştırılıyor," *Evrensel*, (April 23, 2016), accessed on August 13, 2017, from https://www.evrensel.net/haber/2782 48/suriyeli-cocuk-isciler-egitim-alamiyor-ucuza-calistiriliyor.

112. Department of Anti-Smuggling and Organized Crime (KOM), Turkish National Police, 2015, p. 43.

113. "Çocuk mülteciler Türkiye'de tekstil atölyelerinde çalıştırılıyor," *BBC*, (October 24, 2016), accessed on August 13, 2017, from http://www.bbc.com/turkce/haberler-turkiye-37748847.

114. "Suriyeli çocuk işçiler eğitim alamıyor, ucuza çalıştırılıyor," *Evrensel*, (April 23, 2016), accessed on August 13, 2017, from https://www.evrensel.net/haber/2782 48/suriyeli-cocuk-isciler-egitim-alamiyor-ucuza-calistiriliyor.

115. Deniz Gök, "Binlerce Cocuk Dilencilerin Cetelerinin Aginda," *Onedio*, (January 29, 2016), accessed on August 13, 2017, from https://onedio.com/haber/ binlerce-cocuk-cetelerin-aginda-668408.

Chapter 6

Political Corruption and the Illicit Economy

Impacts of the December 2013 Graft Scandals

INTRODUCTION

Corruption provides an incubator for terror and crime, allowing both to flourish in a self-reinforcing, tangled web of deceit and underworld connections.[1] The higher the level of corruption in a country the more hospitable it becomes for organized crime and terrorist groups. Among types of corruption, political corruption plagues many parts of the world. Massive government corruption cases have helped fuel the growth of the illicit economy.

Corruption, in varying degrees, negatively impacts both developed and developing countries.[2] According to one 2014 survey in the United States, 50 percent of respondents said that political corruption was common at the federal level of government.[3] In recent years, Turkey has been linked to numerous corruption scandals at the highest levels of government. Two of them that occurred on December 17 and 25 in 2013 are considered turning points in terms of their impact on the illicit economy.

These investigations implicating President Recep Tayyip Erdogan, his family members, inner circle, ministers, and bureaucrats, by most accounts have contributed to the current government's destruction of not just the rule of law and the nation's judiciary system, but also Turkey's 100-year-old democratic gains. This chapter focuses on the impacts of political corruption, with the December 17 and 25 scandals serving as the backdrop. It additionally uses the results of a focus group study[4] conducted with 5 Turkish experts and researchers in 2015 as well as media interviews with an investigator and the prosecutor. It was necessary to use these media interviews because the December 25 investigation was especially exposed to the strict pressure of the government due to its direct implications with Erdogan. The only available source is the media interviews of the prosecutor Muammer Akkaş and the police chief Yasin Topçu who spoke to the media after the December 25 scandal. They were the most active investigators of the December 25 Investigation.

Political Corruption

The term and concept of corruption, as used in this chapter, refers to behavior that deviates from the normal duties of a public servant. This deviant behavior is usually associated with private gains, such as monetary compensation at public expense.[5] For example, corruption can be understood as an illegal payment to a public agent to acquire benefits the person otherwise would not be entitled to. Corruption can be as simple as the transfer of money or goods to a low-level agent who agrees to overlook the payment of a traffic ticket or as serious and far-reaching as a head of state who accepts millions of dollars to favor an international firm in return for reducing a customs fee.[6]

Despite its common elements, the definition of corruption can vary among cultures, nations, and regions. Deviant behavior in the political context often includes bribery (use of rewards to influence a person's judgment), nepotism (favoring ascription rather than merit), and misappropriation (illegal taking or use of public resources).[7] Less precise is what constitutes "normal duties." For example, accepting gifts may not be considered a corrupt act in some countries and may instead be perceived as a normal, or non-deviant, act. Another example is a contractor taking a government purchasing officer and the officer's family on an all-expenses-paid vacation.[8] Other examples include granting a position to a relative rather than to a qualified person, removing all officeholders who supported the opposition party in an election, establishing a part-time consulting firm to parlay inside knowledge and contacts in business dealings, and awarding government contracts to political supporters and favored friends.[9]

Bribery and related actions often come to mind in any discussion of corruption.[10] The scope of political corruption, however, is much broader. Activities related to political corruption include: bribery and graft (extortion and kickbacks), kleptocracy (stealing and privatizing public funds), misappropriation (forgery, embezzlement, misuse of public funds), nonperformance of duties (cronyism), influence peddling (favor-brokering and conflict of interest), acceptance of improper gifts (speed money), protecting maladministration (cover-ups and perjury), abuse of power (intimidation and torture), manipulation of regulations (bias and favoritism), electoral malpractice (vote buying and election rigging), clientelism and patronage (politicians giving material favors in exchange for citizen support), and illegal campaign contributions (giving unregulated gifts to influence policies and regulations).[11]

There are various categories of corruption—grand corruption, petty corruption, and political corruption. Grand corruption is characterized by the involvement of high-level public officials who make decisions based on large-volume public contracts. Petty corruption involves public servants who participate in small-scale wrongdoing.[12] In Turkey, high-level politicians and bureaucrats systematically provide government contracts in return for bribes. Similarly, a considerable number of public servants have been involved in bribery and embezzlement cases.[13] For example, the percentage of customs officials charged with corruption and prosecuted was 71 percent in 2013.[14]

Political corruption can involve private individuals who finance the campaigns of political parties in exchange for political favors. Privately financed campaigns are vulnerable to corruption because the money can influence the actions and decisions of the public officials who receive it.[15] According to public opinion, political corruption extends beyond the generally accepted forms of corruption such as bribery and influence peddling, to include practices that may be legal but are discomfiting, such as favoritism in the awarding of government contracts and the passage of regulations and legislation favorable to specific interest groups.[16]

Intrinsic to all acts of political corruption is the complicity of a public official. Moreover, the official must have violated the public's trust in a way that harms the public interest, knowingly engaged in conduct that exploits the office for private gain and ignores accepted rules of conduct for holding public office within the political culture and provided a third party with access to a good or a service. These criteria are part of a political culture composed of clear, shared norms and rules governing the conduct both of public officials and members of the public.[17]

Political corruption often is related to the quest for unlimited power. As Lord Acton has aptly put it, "power tends to corrupt, and absolute power corrupts absolutely." For example, politicians who believe they have unlimited power, are prone to lose their ability to distinguish right from wrong in terms of actions and conduct. Acton's statement reflects the link between power and morals. Corruption is a form of coercion.[18] Powerful leaders have the authority to influence the judgment of others who exercise governmental functions.[19]

Research conducted in Turkey in 2009 indicated that most of the respondents limited the definition of corruption to bribery.[20] Corruption in Turkey, however, is most prevalent in the political arena among politicians and political parties.[21] Corrupt practices seen most often are "fraud against public agency," "embezzlement," "bid rigging," "extortion," "fraud in performance of contract," and "unjust acquisition of property/ concealment of assets."[22] Clientelism also is common in Turkey. Typically, the patron exercises power and influence in favor of a client, receiving in return personal gifts, electoral support, and political donations.[23]

Political Corruption in Turkey

Turkey's legacy of political corruption can be traced back to the Ottoman Empire, which was characterized by a highly educated but corrupt bureaucracy. Even though Turkey is a member of the G20 (Group of Twenty) countries representing industrialized and emerging economies, corruption has hindered its development.[24] The public perception in Turkey is that political corruption is widespread in the country.[25] According to a 2009 survey, 89 percent of respondents felt that corruption was a serious issue; 37 percent of the respondents admitted having given bribes to public officials at one time or another.[26]

Global results by subsector in 2013 showed that corruption is entrenched in political parties and those political parties are perceived as the most corrupt institutions in the world, followed by police and parliaments/legislatures.[27] These findings mirror the situation in Turkey. Political parties in Turkey have been often implicated in corruption cases. Such involvement is not surprising, given that corruption has been inherent in Turkish politics for so long. Turkish political parties have a long history of awarding government contracts to their supporters. Exemplars include those given followers of the Republican People's Party during the administrations of Mustafa Kemal Ataturk and Ismet Inonu in the 1930s and 1940s and to supporters of the Justice Party led by Suleyman Demirel in the 1960s.[28]

Corruption has also influenced several military coups beginning in the 1960s.[29] The years leading up to the 1980 military coup were marked by a flourishing shadow economy dominated by smugglers and traffickers. After 1980, corruption became more complicated. High-level bureaucrats and politicians engaged in fictitious export, money laundering, and real estate operations that involved speculation and public-contract paychecks.[30] During these years, center-right political parties were exposed to intensive corruption.[31] In the 1990s, many political parties that epitomized political corruption, clientelism, and nepotism were discredited by the Turkish people who shifted their support to parties representing political Islam, such as the Welfare Party (WP-Refah Partisi), which ostensibly distanced itself from corruption and was rewarded with the support of the Turkish people.[32]

Current President Recep Tayyip Erdogan and his predecessor President Abdullah Gül were founders of the AKP and were originally closely aligned with Necmettin Erbakan who founded the WP in 1987.[33] Erbakan's involvement in the political process began in the 1970s with the founding of Islamic political parties. Those parties, however, were shut down because they violated the secular constitution. Erbakan was not deterred; the WP won municipal elections in 1993 and became a partner in the country's coalition government in 1997. The WP was banned in 1997, and Erbakan replaced it with the Virtue Party (VP-Fazilet Partisi) in 1998. Three years later, the VP was banned. It was replaced by two political parties when reformers (Recep Tayyip Erdogan, Abdullah Gül, and Bülent Arınç) in the VP established the AKP and the traditional wing of the VP established the Felicity Party (FP-Saadet Partisi).

The WP and the VP parties have been critics of Turkey's endemic corruption since the 1980s. By most accounts they tied the corruption to the machinations of several political parties.[34] For example, the Motherland Party (Anavatan Partisi-ANAP), which ruled the country from 1983 to 1991, lost considerable support in the 1989 municipal elections when it was tied to corrupt activities.[35] In the 1990s, as more and more citizens responded to graft scandals, the abuse of public funds, and rampant corruption, Erbakan's Islamist political parties grew in popularity.[36]

A litany of scandals plagued Turkish politics in the 1990s, including one in Istanbul in 1993, when the director of the Water and Sewage Administration was convicted of bid-rigging and was imprisoned for seven years.[37] The following year brought the scandal dubbed "Civangate." In this case, the director of a state bank was charged with taking 5 million USD in bribes and incarcerated.[38] The Susurluk scandal in 1996 came to light after a traffic accident involving a luxury vehicle. The car's occupant happened to be a criminal with an arrest warrant hanging over his head. What made matters worse was other occupants at the car, a high-level police chief and member of the True Path Party (Dogru Yol Partisi-DYP), partnered with the country's coalition government. The accident led to revelations of corruption within the government (see Chapter 1). As a result, several of the political parties that were partners in the governing coalition were forced out of power.[39] In these cases, the judicial results might not have been perfect, but compared to the results of the December 2013 scandals, officials in the judiciary system were at least permitted to investigate the scandals, and perpetrators were convicted for their activities.[40] The scandals in the 1990s prompted the outraged populace to gravitate toward the WP and the VP parties.

The 1990s was an era when coalition governments were in power since no political party received 25 percent of the popular votes cast.[41] In the 1999 elections, corruption rocked nearly all political parties that were part of the coalition government.[42] The corrupt image of other political parties paved the way for Erbakan's WP to win the election in 1995 and for Bulent Ecevit's Democratic Left Party to win the election in 1999.[43] Research conducted in the early 2000s by nongovernmental organizations verified the people's trust of political parties had substantially declined. In one survey, 75 percent of respondents attributed their distrust to the parties to perceptions of rampant corruption.[44]

Some sources suggest Turkey has never witnessed the level of systemic corruption that fuels the AKP.[45] The party has seized every opportunity to enhance its power base by transferring money to so-called Islamist groups as a result of marketization of education and health care, and the privatization of businesses and industries.[46] The AKP has created and perpetuated a favorable environment for corruption with actions such as providing government contracts solely for the benefit of its affiliates. When the police unintentionally discovered the corruption perpetrated by the AKP in December 2013, the country's political, economic, and governmental systems paid the price.[47]

The AKP falls into the legacy of corrupt political parties that has persisted since the Turkish Republic was founded in 1923. Initially, the AKP targeted the fight against the 3Ys in Turkish—*yoksulluk* (poverty), *yasaklar* (restrictions), and *yolsuzluk* (corruption)—a strategic priority since 2002 when it began to rule the country.[48] In its campaign against corruption, the AKP fulfilled the promises of President Erdogan, ordering that the corruption files of former ministers be sent to Turkey's Supreme Court. The party then passed legislation that required all elected officials to reveal their wealth. However, Erdogan's attitude changed, prompting the AKP to abandon its determined stance against corruption.[49]

The consequences for the country were significant. First, a report by the Organization for Security and Cooperation in Europe (OSCE) criticized the dearth of transparency in campaign financing as well as practices that damaged the impartiality of the 2015 elections. What's more, Turkey plunged to 66th place in 2015 from 53rd place two years earlier in the Corruption Perception Index. The AKP also weakened anticorruption legislation, including the Public Procurement Law,[50] which allowed the party to take bribes and approve bids from its affiliates. Audits were weak, and little was done to sanction those who engaged in bribery. For example, law enforcement investigated only one percent of more than 300,000 government contracts made in 2012. The law does not authorize law enforcement to trace bribes even though tip-offs have been received on many of them.[51] Further shattering its image, the AKP eliminated the rule that required yearly reports from the Court of Accounts to be submitted to parliament, eroding the legislature's ability to review public spending. Offering a glimpse into the near future, when former Prime Minister Binali Yıldırım was appointed[52] he refrained from mentioning a word about fighting corruption during his first speech to parliament in May 2016.

Although the previous Prime Minister, Ahmet Davutoğlu, had established an anticorruption unit and unveiled a corruption package, President Erdogan thwarted pending investigations.[53] Ultimately, the AKP has moved light years away from its promises of its early years. As a result, the AKP, more than previous administrations, has failed to take on the challenges of governmental corruption. The current system has been described as a "kleptocracy" as the heads of state continue to use their power to exploit the Turkish people and the country's natural resources in exchange for personal wealth and political power.[54]

Following in the footsteps of former political parties that had vowed to fight corruption but were unsuccessful,[55] the AKP not only failed to enact effective legislation, but also abolished an independent anti-corruption unit. In doing this, the AKP protected itself from any potential corruption investigations. For example, the AKP government received a draft corruption law in 2003 when the party assumed national power but rejected it.

Anticorruption investigations in Turkey, while rare, have mostly focused on political parties, targeting opposition parties or businessmen. For example, the Anti-Smuggling and Organized Crime Department (ASOD) of the Turkish National Police (TNP) ostensibly was in charge of conducting anti-corruption investigations involving the exploitation of state power to repress political opposition.[56] The real intent, however, was to intimidate political opponents.[57] Rare police investigations of AKP municipalities were undertaken to make it look like the government was fighting against corruption.[58]

Endemic corruption has marked the tenure of the AKP. Although President Erdogan touted principles of honesty, ethics, and virtue in the 1994 municipal elections,[59] he created a so-called pool system in the 1990s that was built on false rhetoric about honesty. In one speech, Erdogan said, "...Do you know why some people are poor? Because they are not good at stealing. Do you know why some people are wealthy? Because they are good at stealing."[60] In another speech, he said, "...robbery inherits to the child from his father, not from child to his father. When rulers in a country are thieves, it mirrors to subordinates and public...."[61]

When Erdogan was invited to an art exhibition in 1994, he said, "I only owned this ring on my finger as an asset." Erdogan was not born into wealth and did not have a life of luxury until later in his life. The son of a very poor family, he owned only a small, inexpensive apartment in Istanbul in the 1980s. He was proud of owning very humble assets. After Erdogan was elected mayor of Istanbul in 1994, however, the value of his assets skyrocketed. By 2002, he was worth $1 billion.[62]

December 17 Investigation: Zarrab's Economic Jihad (ZEJ)

When the international community imposed an embargo on Iran, Iranian officials went to great lengths to violate the embargo. One strategy was to hire facilitators to transfer money to Iran. Of these, the most prominent was

Reza Zarrab, who had been released from a Turkish prison thanks to connections in the corridors of power but was arrested in the United States. Babak Zanjani was another conspicuous facilitator. Both facilitators justified their efforts in terms of economic jihad on behalf of the Iranian government. Iran's supreme leader, Ayatollah Ali Khamenei, proclaimed 2011 as the year of economic jihad and a turning point for economic reforms.[63] A letter written by Zarrab's father emphasized that the Zarrab family was ready to contribute to the Iranian economy in line with the government's proclamation.[64] These facilitators were responsible for creating a system that could circulate Iranian money while skirting the embargo imposed by the United Nations (UN), the U.S., and the European Union. However, the pragmatic Iranians were not above deviating from their economic jihadism ideology in order to line their own pockets with a significant amount of money. Both Zarrab and Zanjani operated in Turkey clandestinely and have been tied to numerous acts of corruption.[65]

The Islamic Revolutionary Guard Corps (IRGC) in Iran is credited with masterminding efforts to exploit the facilitators. Established during the 1979 Iranian Revolution, Ruhollah Khomeini, former supreme leader of Iran, established the IRGC to protect the regime. Subsequently, the Revolutionary Guards moved into Iranian politics and the country's economy. In 1989, Akbar Hashemi Rafsanjani, former president of Iran, empowered the IRGC to control and manage a significant portion of the Iranian economy. The IRGC not only developed models to launder Iranian money during the embargo, but it also became an active part of Iranian nuclear armament policy.[66] Based on Iran's ongoing interest in shipping aircraft-related raw materials for use in an advanced weapons program,[67] the facilitator Zanjani's trustee, Mehdi Shams, bought Onur Air,[68] a low-cost Turkish airline based in Istanbul, to transport the motors of old aircraft to Iran in order to use motor parts to produce advanced nuclear weapons.[69]

The initiation of the police investigation of Zarrab was based on various pieces of information, including a fax notice dated July 18, 2012. The fax suggested that Zarrab and Abdullah Happani and their accomplices were laundering money at Turkey's Durak Exchange Office and helping drug traffickers to transfer the illicit proceeds. After examining the July 18 document, police uncovered a notice from 2010 describing the involvement of Zarrab and his father in transferring illegal money through the Durak Exchange Office. This information was confirmed by a 2008 report from Turkey's Financial Crimes Investigation Board (Mali Suclari Arastirma Kurulu-MASAK). According to the report, Reza Zarrab earned enormous sums of money to fund his extravagant lifestyle. He engaged in a number of suspicious money transactions, which required police investigation. A MASAK report on the seizure of heroin at the Kapikule border gate in 2007 titled, "The Evaluation Report of Happani Group," revealed that money transfers by drug traffickers were made through the Durak Exchange Office. This report was sent to the TNP's ASOD on June 3, 2011.[70]

In another instance, four couriers connected to Reza Zarrab were arrested at Moscow's Vnukova Airport with 14.5 million USD and 4 million euros in cash in 2010. One of the couriers was Reza Zarrab's driver.[71] An analysis by the ASOD found that some companies owned or co-owned by Reza Zarrab were involved in the illegal export of gold bars to Iran. Other monies, whose source was obscure and earned abroad, were transferred from Dubai of the United Arab Emirates (UAE) to Russia through Turkey. This analysis was forwarded to the Financial Crimes Unit of the Istanbul Police Directorate because Reza Zarrab's illegal activities and his companies were in Istanbul. The Financial Crimes Unit then prepared a report and contacted the local prosecutor on September 13, 2012. The prosecutor initiated an investigation charging Zarrab with conspiracy to set up a money laundering organization for money obtained from smuggling and criminal activities. The Financial Crimes Unit used wiretapping and surveillance during the investigation, which lasted until December 17, 2013. The prosecutor merged the charges of bribery when the investigation broadened. As a result of 15-month investigation, the police found that Reza Zarrab's group committed the following crimes:[72]

- Transferred huge amount of cash to Russian banks through front companies in return for commissions from couriers who carried the money from Turkey to Russia (old system).
- Engaged in gold trading and transferred money through front companies to bypass legal international systems for transferring money and gold in order to skirt the international embargo (new system).
- Used another transfer system to carry money belonging to the Iranian government. Reza Zarrab's accomplices submitted fraudulent documents to Turkey's Halkbank regarding the fictitious export of food and medicine in return for commissions on these transactions. For one of these fictitious exports, the group prepared fraudulent documents that listed 150 tons of food on a ship with capacity of only five tons.
- Transferred 1.5 tons of gold bars from Ghana to Turkey. The goal was to collect gold bars in Turkey and then transfer them to Iran.
- Gave bribes to high-level Turkish politicians and bureaucrats while committing all of the illegal transactions described above.

- Mediated prostitution at hotels in Istanbul for Dubaian officials[73] who were exploited to commit fictitious export deals between Dubai and Istanbul.

The Russian Connection

For a commission of 0.2 percent to 0.3 percent, Reza Zarrab used three couriers to open 10 bank accounts in Russia into which the illicit money would be deposited. After withdrawing money several times a week from Turkish banks, the couriers carried the cash to Russian banks. Russian police seized the money during one of these transfers. In response to this incident, Zarrab changed tactics and began circulating Iranian money in return for commissions. Turkey's MASAK and Tax Department prepared reports describing his violation of banking rules and regulations. In addition, the crafty Zarrab paid bribes to prevent the media from disclosing his Russian connections.

The Iranian Connection

Although Reza Zarrab's new corruption scheme was linked to Iran, Turkish police focused instead on fraud, bribery, and counterfeiting committed in Turkey for the purpose of skirting the embargo imposed on Iran, rather than on violations of international rules on embargoes. The Turkish prosecutor therefore focused on how Turkish officials committed crimes linked to Reza Zarrab.

The UN and EU imposed economic sanctions on Iran, with the U.S. imposing its own embargo after the 1979 Iranian revolution. Subsequently, it expanded the scope of economic sanctions to firms linked to Iran. The reason for stiffening the embargo was Iran's continuing illicit nuclear activities. The goal of the sanctions was to censure Iran and prevent further improvements to the country's nuclear capabilities and to put pressure on Tehran to address the international community's concerns about Iran's nuclear program.

Expanded U.S. sanctions on the sale of Iranian petroleum impacted Reza Zarrab's corrupt activities in Turkey. Starting in 1995, the United States passed several acts and issued orders affecting the sale of Iranian petroleum. A December 2011 act, for example, barred countries from engaging in transactions with the Iranian Central Bank and Iranian firms. The United States amended the act in 2013 to protect close allies such as Turkey. According to amendments enacted on February 6, 2013, countries that wanted to import petroleum or natural gas from Iran must make the payment to a bank located in the importing country, and the payment could not be transferred to Iran. Iran could buy only food, medicine, and industrial materials with money earned from the sale of its petroleum and natural gas.

Likewise, the EU passed legislation targeting Iran, including an act signed in 2010 that froze the assets of the Iranian Central Bank in member states. In March 2012, the EU prohibited transactions with Iranian firms and expanded sanctions on importing Iranian petroleum. The EU also barred all transportation companies linked to Iran from purchasing insurance.[74]

Turkish banks also felt the effects of these sanctions. When asked for an interpretation of the sanctions, the Turkish Banks Association responded that its banks were prohibited from engaging in correspondence, making swift or normal transfers, and engaging in foreign trade operations with Iranian banks and firms. The Association further held that branches of Turkish banks in countries that are imposing embargoes on Iran must obey the rules of those embargoes.[75]

International embargoes on Iran created more opportunities for Reza Zarrab, who received assignments from the Ahmadinejad government. The Turkish investigation of Zarrab focused on how Reza Zarrab gave bribes to the Turkish ministers and bureaucrats, smuggled gold between Ghana and Turkey, and circulated Iranian money in violation of international rules. The investigation also examined how Reza Zarrab prepared and submitted counterfeit documents to the Halkbank.[76]

Why Iran Deployed Facilitators

To be prepared financially for the possibility of a war, Iran used facilitators such as Reza Zarrab and flexible strategies to skirt the embargoes and stockpile gold. One strategy was to use existing linkages between the Halkbank and Iranian banks in order to transfer Iranian money in gold from Turkey to Iran. For example, after the Iranian Central Bank buys Toman[77] from Bank A in Iran, the money in the central bank's euro and Turkish lira account at the Halkbank is transferred to the account of Bank A at the Halkbank. Then the money is transferred to the account of Reza Zarrab. Therefore, gold is bought in Turkey and sent to firms in UAE (Dubai). As a result, Iran circulates its currency in the domestic market and carries gold to Iran. Reza Zarrab's group used this money-circulating system primarily in 2012 and 2013.

After Iran was publicly revealed as complicit in this money-circulating scheme, Zarrab's group switched its money-transferring route and included China. The new system transferred Iranian money in China to Iran via Turkey and UAE (Dubai). Reza Zarrab's group established front companies in China and transferred money in the form of Toman and Yuan currencies to the accounts of the front companies as fictitious payments for nonexistent goods. The companies transferred the Toman and Yuan money to a Chinese bank in the form of Euros and Turkish liras and then retransferred that money to the bank accounts of firms linked to Reza Zarrab in Turkey. Because real firms in Turkey used the Halkbank, front companies used other Turkish banks. Reza Zarrab's groups used the money held by their Turkish firms to buy gold bars and exported them to Dubai via couriers sent to Iran. Zarrab's group gave bribes to high-level Chinese bank officials for their help in operating the money-transfer system among China, Turkey, UAE, and Iran.

When the United States passed resolutions in 2013 that barred Turkey from making payments to Iran in gold while allowing Turkey to import Iranian petroleum and natural gas, Reza Zarrab's group developed a third system to circumvent the embargo. Because the embargo exempted food and medicine, Reza Zarrab's group resorted to bogus trade among Turkey, UAE, and Iran. Members of the group prepared counterfeit export documents for food and medicine and submitted the papers to the Halkbank. After transferring money from Iran to Turkey and UAE, the group converted it into cash in Dubai and shipped the cash to Iran. In addition to crimes such as money laundering and illegal money transferring, Reza Zarrab's group committed fraud.

In return for his criminal efforts in the three money-transfer systems, Reza Zarrab received a 0.030 percent commission for every cent of money transferred to Iran. Reza Zarrab then paid a 0.008 percent commission to the Halkbank, a bribe of 0.005 percent to the minister of economy, Zafer Çağlayan, and a bribe of 0.004 percent to the director of the Halkbank, Suleyman Aslan. That 0.004 percent share in the scheme explains why Turkish police found enormous amounts of cash in the bank director's house.

The police established that Reza Zarrab was the leader of three subgroups whose members were linked to each other. The groups committed the crimes of fraud, smuggling, and giving and taking bribes. The first subgroup was comprised of couriers and accomplices of Reza Zarrab. The second subgroup was comprised of the minister of economy and his son, his brother, and two secretaries and the director of the Halkbank. The third subgroup, whose leader was the minister of interior, Muammer Güler, was linked to Reza Zarrab. This group also included the son of the minister of interior and the minister's secretaries.[78]

Different motives prompted these subgroups to become involved in corruption. The motives for Reza Zarrab and members of the first subgroup were to receive commissions in return for transferring money to Iran, aid fraudulent food trading, earn Turkish citizenship, reduce the legal commission rates of banks, aid in the transfer of smuggled gold bars from Ghana to Turkey and leave without being arrested, create a monopoly in relations with the Halkbank, reassign public officials who became aware of the corrupt activities, squelch media reports that might be related to Reza Zarrab's activities, receive assistance from the minister of interior for coping with difficulties encountered by front companies used in money transfers in China, and develop strategies to prevent law enforcement investigations of the subgroup's activities. The motives for the second and third groups were to accept many bribes along with jewelry, luxury items, expensive watches, and a monthly salary in the form of a consultancy.[79]

Findings of Police Investigation

The police found solid evidence of corruption by wiretapping the phone conversations of the minister of economy and Reza Zarrab, discovering that the minister accepted bribes in the amount of 32 million euros, 6.7 million USD, 3.5 million Turkish liras, and 300,000 Swiss francs. Both men had private phone numbers and used code words to mask their conversations. In one of the wiretapped conversations, Reza Zarrab called the minister's son and said, "Is 24 available?" In another wiretapping, Reza Zarrab called the undersecretary of the minister of economy and said, "Please tell the minister that 18 is open," which meant that both sides used different phone numbers just to transfer bribes. Reza Zarrab and the minister of economy also were careful about where they exchanged bribes, sometimes exchanging the money in shopping center restrooms.[80] The minister of economy also linked Reza Zarrab to other ministers, including the minister of the European Union.[81]

The minister of the economy provided connections between Reza Zarrab and the director of the Halkbank, who played a critical role in transferring money from China to Turkey and committing fictitious trade between Turkey and Dubai in return for a large monetary bribe. The police were able to prove that Zarrab gave 15 bribes to the director of the Halkbank for a total of 3 million euros, 3.9 million USD, and 1 million Turkish liras.[82]

Zarrab's strong links to the AKP government provided him with opportunities to influence other ministers. One of them was the minister of interior, who took bribes in return for illegally granting Turkish citizenship to individuals connected to Reza Zarrab, for punishing the police chief who threatened Reza Zarrab, for providing privileged transportation for Zarrab while he was in Istanbul, for intervening with media stations that were going to publish news about Reza Zarrab, and, more importantly, for sending a reference letter for Reza Zarrab's front companies to ease the challenging formalities of Chinese banks.

The minister of interior also attempted to find out whether the Istanbul Police Directorate had conducted any investigations of Reza Zarrab. The minister's son, in one of his contacts with Reza Zarrab, suspected that he was being followed by a police squad. To mask the son's corrupt relationship with Reza Zarrab, the son had been appointed as a consultant to Reza Zarrab; therefore, the bribes were shown as payment for his consultancy job. According to the police investigation, the total amount of bribery money paid to the minister of interior was close to 10 million USD.[83]

Another active corruption participant was the minister of the European Union, Egemen Bağış. He was given 1.5 million USD in return for giving Turkish citizenship and an Italian visa to Reza Zarrab's brother and for his efforts to censure the publication of news that might reveal Reza Zarrab's corrupt activities. Reza Zarrab also exploited the minister's close relationships in Europe and the United States to cover up corrupt transactions of the Aktif Bank in Turkey, which was used for the first two money transfer systems involving UAE-Turkey-Russia and Turkey-UAE-Iran.[84]

How Shoeboxes Became the Symbol of
the December 17 Investigation

Turkey was shocked when media outlets reported that among the 89 suspects who had been arrested were the sons of four ministers, Reza Zarrab and the director of the Halkbank. However, after the government intervened to stop their trials, the judge dropped the case on October 17, 2014.[85] The police found cash in the houses of some of the suspects, including 4.5 million USD in shoeboxes in the house of Halkbank director Suleyman Aslan[86] and around 700,000 Turkish liras in the house of the son of the minister of interior. Although it was alleged that the money was put in the houses of the suspects during police raids, the suspects reclaimed the money, with interest, when the judge closed the case.[87] In another odd twist, Aslan told the prosecutor that he was going to build a religious high school in Çorum province. The explanation, however, was dubious because it would have made more sense for Aslan to keep the money for the school building in a bank rather than at his home.[88]

International Confirmation of Zarrab Investigation

The government succeeded in shutting down the police investigation of Reza Zarrab in Turkey, that is until Zarrab and his two accomplices were arrested in Miami, Florida, on March 19, 2016. This development arose after the United States District Court for the Southern District of New York filed an indictment against the suspects in the December 17 Turkish investigation for engaging in transactions worth hundreds of millions of dollars on behalf of the government of Iran and other Iranian entities, violating U.S. sanctions prohibiting such transactions. The indicted individuals were alleged to have laundered the proceeds of those illegal transactions and to have defrauded several financial institutions by concealing the true nature of the transactions.[89] The U.S. prosecutor included the report of the December 17 Turkish investigation as evidence for the indictment, confirming the findings of Turkish investigators. The prosecutor also indicted Reza Zarrab for his links to Erdogan's family. Reza Zarrab, for example, made donations to the Social

Development Center Association (Toplumsal Gelisim Merkezi Dernegi - TOGEMDER) founded by Erdogan's wife, Emine Erdogan.[90]

Erdogan has tried several strategies to meddle in the Zarrab case in the United States. He first made a concerted effort to secure Zarrab's release from U.S. custody. His effort was a clear message to Zarrab: do not plead guilty or testify in court. Erdogan also visited former President Barack Obama and President Donald Trump to ask how Zarrab could be extradited.

In the meantime, the Erdogan regime arrested some Americans to use as bargaining chips for Zarrab's release. For example, Resurrection Church Pastor Andrew Craig Brunson was arrested by Izmir police for allegedly having ties to Fethullah Gülen. Next, Istanbul police arrested U.S. drug liaison officer Metin Topuz, who had been in charge of working on drug-law enforcement in both countries for 32 years. The theory in Turkey was that Topuz was a Gülenist who worked with U.S. and Turkish police to launch the Zarrab investigation and then overthrow Erdogan's government. The evidence used to arrest Brunson and Topuz, however, was spurious at best.

After it was clear that Zarrab would testify in the U.S. district court in New York, Erdogan took a different tactic, using the pro-government mass media under his control to blame the United States for ongoing efforts to overthrow Erdogan's government and for instigating the so-called military uprising in July 2016.

Zarrab retained a dream-team of lawyers after he was arrested in the United States. His Turkish experience as the target of an investigation motivated him to seek his release in the United States; however, Zarrab failed in his efforts. The U.S. investigators also arrested Mehmet Hakan Atilla, a Turkish banker and Aslan's deputy director, on March 27, 2017. Atilla was charged with conspiracy to violate the International Emergency Economic Powers Act and conspiracy to commit bank fraud. Because Zarrab had agreed to testify as a government witness, Atilla was the only suspect to face a trial by jury.

Zarrab pleaded guilty and made a cooperation deal with U.S. Justice Department attorneys in October 2017. He testified for six days at a federal trial in December 2017. In his testimony, Zarrab admitted to all of the charges against him and said that he devised the scheme to evade U.S. embargoes on Iran while in Turkey. Zarrab also testified that he gave bribes of around 50 million euros to Çağlayan and a large sum of money to Güler, Aslan, and Bağış; that he gave bribes to have the charges against himself in Turkey dropped; and that he used Turkey's Aktif Bank and Halkbank for his corrupt oil-for-gold and oil-for-food transactions. When he failed to establish a money-laundering system in India and China, Zarrab testified, he transferred Iranian money from those countries to Turkey and then sent the money to Iran. Zarrab also noted in his testimony that he continued to launder money in Turkey after the December 17 and 25 Turkish investigations and pointed out

Berat Albayrak, Erdogan's son-in-law and current minister of economy, who asked for Erdogan's approval for evading sanctions in June 2014.

U.S. attorneys accused Atilla, the Turkish banker, of being an embargo fixer who oversaw the creation of new methods for Zarrab to launder money when Zarrab had difficulty transferring Iranian money from Turkey to Iran. Atilla's lawyers, who were paid by the Turkish government, stated before the jury that Zarrab was a money launderer who distributed bribes on different continents to Turkish politicians and bureaucrats, confirming the findings of the December 17, 2013 Turkish police investigation. The jury found Atilla guilty on five out of six counts, including bank fraud and conspiracy on January 3, 2018.

Reactions of the AKP Government

The December scandals unearthed overarching bribery, cronyism, and illegal rent-seeking mainly in the construction and energy sectors where pro-AKP businessmen were beneficiaries.[91] It was stunning for everyone in Turkey. The Erdogan government was shocked by the arrests of the sons of ministers. The operation also caused Erdogan to panic and allegedly hide large amounts of money. According to a documentary produced by Turkish journalist and columnist Can Dundar, Erdogan called his son in the early hours of police raids of the houses of the suspects and told him to move all of the cash out of his house in Istanbul.

One of the statements Erdogan made to his son—"leave zero money" (*paraları sıfırla*) at the house—was used to symbolize the corruption investigation. Erdogan called his son several times to determine whether his son had succeeded in moving the huge amount of money from the house. In an afternoon call, Erdogan's son said, "We moved most money, and a small amount left which was 30 million Euros."[92] Later comments aimed at estimating the amount of money discovered at the house of Erdogan's used the phrase "a small of amount of money"—meaning that if 30 million euros was a small amount, then the total amount of money must have been huge. The efforts of Erdogan's son to leave no money in the house were verified in the following days when the son bought four villas in Istanbul for a total price of 12 million USD. The registration of the four houses bought on December 26, 2013, verified the efforts of Erdogan's son to leave no money in his house.[93] It is uncertain why Erdogan's son struggled to move money and where the money was earned.

After the investigation, the Erdogan government declared that all police officers and prosecutors were now regarded as followers of Fethullah Gülen, an Islamic cleric living in self-imposed exile in Pennsylvania. According to explanations from Erdogan and his ministers, the investigation was instigated by Gülen to subvert the government.

Erdogan and Gülen were allies in the early years of the AKP government until 2010. During this period, Erdogan exploited allegedly Gülenist law enforcement officials and prosecutors to remove the shadows of the elites over Turkish democracy, resorting to periodic military coups. Turkey witnessed these coups in 1960, 1971, 1980, and 1997. These elites utilized death squads, when they needed to, and became involved in dark cases in the government similar to the roles of death squads in South American countries.[94] As a matter of fact, the police, based on solid evidence, conducted two investigations against elite groups, dubbed Ergenekon and Balyoz. In the Ergenekon investigation, the police revealed that a small group of people who kept ruling power in their hands became involved in many violent actions. In the Balyoz investigation, the police found many materials, showing the attempts of a group of soldiers controlled by elites, to begin a military coup in the country in the early 2000s. According to speculations, Erdogan gave instructions to use fake evidence to imprison people who were allegedly members of Ergenekon. After eliminating the elites and breaking their power, Erdogan began to target Gülenists in the government in 2010, acknowledging that they cannot be controlled when it comes to covering up his crime and terrorism linkages. In response to the December corruption scandals, Erdogan started a crackdown on Gülenists and purged over 170,372 officials[95] from the government. Some observers believe that Erdogan concocted the July 15, 2016 military uprising because he needed a strong and internationally accepted pretext for further purges. It should be noted that the government has failed to satisfactorily explain the specifics of the military uprising since July 2016.[96]

Several days after the December 17 investigation was made public, Erdogan praised Reza Zarrab for being a philanthropic businessman. Meanwhile, the government reassigned police officers from the Financial Crimes Unit to other units and a new chief of the Istanbul Police Directorate was appointed and flown to the city in an Erdogan-owned aircraft. The government's swift actions left many people wondering why the government was in such a hurry to reassign police officers and whether the move was an attempt to cover up other corrupt acts that might be investigated. Even more questions would arise after the announcement of another police investigation on December 25.

December 25 Investigation: Erdogan's Pool System

In 1994, Erdogan established the so-called "pool system," which stipulated that the AKP would receive a 10 percent commission from all government bids. The ideological justification for the pool system was the need to raise funds for political Islam.[97] The system is based on creating a corrupt network, involving the listing of businessmen who could support political Islam, open as many bids as possible, award the bids to the businessmen, and then extort a 10 percent commission.[98] In return for the commission, the businessmen were not audited. Going back to the oft-repeated adage, that "systems corrupt people more than people corrupt systems,"[99] Erdogan's Pool System (EPS) has influenced many politicians and bureaucrats.[100]

The pool system took on international dimensions while Erdogan served as prime minister between 2003 and 2014. Connections to Iran and the Gulf states were uncovered through investigations and announced on December 17 for the ZEJ case and December 25 for the EPS case. The money-pool system crossed the boundaries of kleptocracy into the realm of political corruption.[101] Kleptocrats siphon money intended for the public good and share it with others in exchange for the support of those individuals.[102]

Though it has been difficult to measure the costs of the corruption at the root of the pool system, studies suggest that a negative correlation exists between economic growth and corruption. Government functionaries in corrupt countries prioritize the pursuit of economic power and their own interests, which undermines economic development. Research shows that a one-unit increase in corruption lowers public spending 0.2 percentage point of GDP (Gross Domestic Product); therefore, poor people who are dependent on the provision of public services are harmed the most.[103]

In Turkey, the cost of corruption is masked by government-funded infrastructure projects in the form of highways, hospitals, schools, and university buildings that dazzle people and give the misleading impression of economic development. Turks at the lowest rungs of the economic ladder readily buy into the government façade, which credits Erdogan for any social aid provided to legions of poor and marginalized Turks. By most accounts they have been persuaded that the aid will continue as long as President Erdogan rules the country. Turkey, however, has paid a huge cost for the ongoing corruption. Several billion Turkish liras line the pockets of politicians and bureaucrats. By some calculations, one fourth of the Turkish budget goes toward corruption. On the other hand, it is accurate to say that Turkey now has more highways than ever before. The sad truth is that this infrastructure is the result of contracts divvied out to businessmen who are obedient to the AKP, a practice that siphons money from the Turkish budget.[104] For example, 83 percent of the highways built during Erdogan's tenure have required substantial repairs. In 2008, Turkey spent 685 million Turkish liras on highway repairs; in 2014, that amount increased to 1.6 billion Turkish liras.[105] The reason for the spike is mostly related to corrupt government contracts that are awarded to affluent businessmen without any auditing and oversight.[106] Corruption has become deeply rooted in modern day Turkish politics.[107]

Systematic corruption is a political phenomenon, and high-level politicians exploit their power to transfer illicit benefits.[108] The December 25 scandal illustrated how high-level politicians systematically corrupt the bidding process in public tenders under the auspices of President Erdogan.[109] This type of corruption exists in many countries. A 2012 survey of 3,000 business executives found that 27 percent of respondents believed that corruption in public procurements caused them to lose government contracts to their competitors who offered bribes. Most affected was Brazil, where 87 percent of respondents had the same response. In another survey, respondents said that they were asked for bribes when dealing in public tenders.[110]

The public procurement process presents opportunities for corrupt officials and investors competing for public tenders to engage in illegal activity. Officials in high places favor capital-intensive public projects while ignoring ongoing operations and maintenance of infrastructure. It is not uncommon for corrupt leaders to intentionally present investors with white-elephant projects that have little value in terms of economic development but offer a conduit for them to take bribes from the firms bidding on the projects. Legitimate investors often abstain from making investments in public-tender projects because of the risk that the completed project will be expropriated or confiscated unless a bribe was paid.[111]

The December 25 investigation into President Erdogan's pool system revealed that the AKP government procures bids mostly for profitable projects in order to extort commissions from the bidders. Investors in these lucrative projects were a group of businessmen who had been granted exclusive access to public tenders as well as low-interest loans from both state and Islamist banks. The businessmen, although extremely wealthy from public procurement schemes, still had the audacity to complain about being extorted by the Erdogan government. Police wiretappings of the businessmen involved[112] confirmed their grievances and complaints about a government request to donate money for the government's purchase of a media company.

This investigation also disclosed another international link to President Erdogan's pooling system (in addition to the Iranian connection). This link was considered the most serious aspect of the investigation because it involved President Erdogan's son and Yasin El Qadi, an al Qaeda financier, also involved with other high-level politicians and bureaucrats in the AKP government.[113] The investigation of Erdogan's pooling system began in 2012 on the basis of randomly obtained evidence regarding bid rigging and police wiretappings conducted during a separate 2011 investigation. The prosecutor, Muammer Akkaş, authorized the police to search for government connections to the bid rigging and instructed the police to execute wiretappings.[114] This surveillance uncovered links between the government and Bosphorus 360, a company that rigged the bid on the sale of the Etiler Police School building. When Akkaş widened the investigation, he determined that Bosphorus 360 had, in addition to two legally registered owners, partners such as high-level bureaucrats, politicians, and the son of President Erdogan. These partners were following the activities of Bosphorus 360 and rigging bids using their state powers.[115]

Bid-rigging Schemes

During the December 25 investigation, police found evidence of bid-rigging in five separate cases. First, the police investigated the sale of an expensive property, the Etiler Police School building, which belonged to Istanbul, a metropolitan municipality. The investigation showed that Bosphorus 360 attempted to buy the property at a lower price. Normally, the sale of a state property requires valuation by experts who determine the market price. If the valuation of a property comes in below the market price, then it is possible that corruption was involved. In the Etiler Police School building case, the police found that the expensive property was valued at 430 million Turkish liras for Bosphorus 360 rather than at the property's market price of 1.5 billion Turkish liras. The mayor of Istanbul made a declaration with respect to this police investigation, offering a land register as evidence that the property in question had not actually been sold. The mayor's declaration, however, was misleading because the police had discovered irregularities in the first step of the sales process—the valuation of the property. If the police had not uncovered the wrongdoing, then the property would have been sold to Bosphorus 360. The police substantiated how valuation bid was rigged.[116]

In another case, a criminal group of entrepreneurs rigged a bid to run a coal mine. One of them attempted to run a mine in the Beykoz district of Istanbul; however, he encountered a number of bureaucratic roadblocks stemming from government regulations. As a result, he failed to get a license until he formed a relationship with the partners of Bosphorus 360. This relationship helped the entrepreneur to get a license for the Beykoz mine despite previous official reports that the bid had been rejected.[117]

A third investigation revealed a criminal act related to the purchase of a media company owned by Calik Holding. Some businessmen were forced to be part of a fundraising effort to buy a media company in return for being granted public tenders. Contrary to media news reports in favor of the corrupt AKP government, it was not simply a collaboration to raise funds; rather, the businessmen were part of a conspiracy established to acquire enough money to purchase the media company. They earned money from public tenders that lacked competitiveness and transparency. For one of the fundraising activities, the businessmen donated $630 million to buy the Sabah-ATV media group.[118]

The police investigation showed that President Erdogan had wanted to buy the Sabah-ATV media group and had ordered the creation of a new company, Zirve A.S., with the sole purpose of purchasing the Sabah-ATV media group. The Sabah-ATV media group, however, had been purchased for $1.1 billion in 2007 by Calik Holding. Zirve A.S., nonetheless, had only 380 million Turkish liras (around $100 million). Therefore, the pool was created to raise funds under the control of the son and son-in-law of President Erdogan in coordination with Binali Yıldırım, who was appointed as prime minister in 2016. Businessmen who had become wealthy from government contracts intentionally granted to them were involved in the pool.[119] For example, the report from the police investigation listed government contracts provided illegally to the members of the pool system.[120] These businessmen not only were enriched by contracts, but they had their taxes reduced or eliminated altogether by the government. In 2010, for example, the $130 million tax bill for Cengiz Construction, an active member of the government pool system, was eliminated.[121] The police recorded all money transfers by these businessmen until the pool owned $630 million, which was enough to purchase the Sabah-ATV media group.[122]

President Erdogan's motive in forcing the businessmen to raise this amount of money was to consolidate his power through the media. He was well aware that the media was an effective tool for influencing the public perceptions of the government and for disseminating propaganda favorable to the government.[123] After the December 17 and December 25 investigations, President Erdogan began to take control of a considerable number of media groups, some of which were owned by businessmen who were suspects in the December 25 investigation.[124]

In another investigation, friends of President Erdogan planned to construct the Urla Villas in Izmir, an area where construction had been formerly prohibited because it had been identified as a site that needed to be protected. When unlicensed construction began in this area, the court ordered that the property be destroyed. Izmir Mayor Cahit Kirac attempted to implement the court's decision, but he was reassigned as the mayor of Diyarbakir before he could do anything. To invalidate the report that marked the site as protected, some businessmen bribed the board of experts to prepare a counterfeit report that would enable them to construct the villas. Based on this counterfeit report, some villas were constructed in Urla. The experts on the board attempted to have the bribery money sent to them through secret money transfers. The attitude of board experts proved that they had prepared the report illegally.[125] When a journalist asked President Erdogan if he owned villas in Urla, he responded harshly, saying that the villas were built 35 years ago.[126] However, a map of the area on Google Earth cast doubt on Erdogan's explanation since it showed that the villas were newly built.[127]

The fifth case involved the Turkey Youth and Education Foundation (Turkiye Genclik ve Egitime Hizmet Vakfi - TURGEV) and its board. The foundation forced businessmen to make donations in return for receiving more government contracts and construction permits.[128] The foundation exploited the government's influence on contractors and entrepreneurs because several members of Erdogan's family—including Erdogan's son, daughter, and brother-in-law—served on the foundation's board. The police found 19 suspicious donations to the foundation during its investigation.[129] The foundation's link to the government and Erdogan's family also were uncovered during the investigation of the Reza Zarrab case. From a wiretapped conversation, the police learned that Reza Zarrab called one of the Foundation's directors, who mentioned the minister of economy and the son of President Erdogan and then said that a donation had been made to the foundation.[130]

After the December 25 investigation, pro-government media outlets criticized the police. The prosecutor Akkaş, who had permitted the police wiretaps responded to the critics, emphasizing the lawful evidence that had been collected. According to Akkaş, the investigation was recorded in the National Judiciary Informatics System[131] (Ulusal Yargi Agi Bilisim Sistemi - UYAP) as required by law, proving that all evidence was gathered legally, and all wiretappings were conducted with proper authorization. Investigators, however, did not wiretap President Erdogan, his son, his son-in-law, or any politicians who were immune from investigation. Akkaş had also intended to wiretap President Erdogan's son because of his active role in corruption schemes. However, Akkaş gave up because he was concerned about the leakage of investigation. Akkaş's experience with other cases led him to be more careful about confidentiality in subsequent investigations.[132]

Akkaş continued to pursue corruption activity, especially after the extent of corruption uncovered during an investigation that lasted almost 20 months. Akkaş said he oversaw every step of the investigation and, as evidence was gathered, the investigation broadened, revealing that the suspects were gaining millions and even billions of dollars from government bids by using their power of influence. Akkaş noted that he was upset about not being able to finalize the investigation and apologized to the Turkish people for failing to do so. He said:

> I owe an apology not to finish this investigation. When I was appointed to the Tekirdag province as a prosecutor, I conducted investigations about thieves who stole trivial materials cost of several ten Liras, and these thieves were sentenced to two or three years of imprisonment. In a case, I prosecuted a thief who stole

10 Turkish Liras. I enforced the rule as required. However, in the December 25th investigation, the amount of money stolen from the government was over billion US dollars. I feel a twinge of guilt about not enforcing law equally on every criminal irrespective of his political power. No one has interfered in my investigations including the December 25th one since I started to work as a prosecutor. No one has been informed about this investigation as required by law. I shared some information about the investigation on the 24th of December, one day before the failed operation. Even though I was knowing some suspects such as Bilal Erdogan and other high-level bureaucrats, I only focused on my investigation. I am obligated to investigate crime as a prosecutor.[133]

Akkaş then summarized what he experienced the day before the investigation was disclosed on December 25:

On the 24th, some police officers came my office to inform me about a plan to interfere with my investigation. I was told that newly-assigned police officers learnt about the December 25th investigation, and they were going to hamper it. Then I tried to take measures and made preparations. As required by a newly-issued regulation after the December 17th operation, I called the chief attorney and informed him about bids rigged in instances such as Urla Villas, Etiler Police School buildings, illegal railroad and land road contracts, and a bid on the mine property. I told chief attorney that this investigation is the most comprehensive and substantiated one I have ever made. During the brief of chief attorney, my first impression was that the chief did not look interested in the suspects and evidence in the investigation and asked me two questions whether this investigation used the appropriate law article and why Urla Villas in Izmir was investigated in Istanbul. I responded that the group can be identified as a qualified criminal group since the suspects resorted to use of threat and force, and one of the suspects was Yasin El Qadi who funded terrorism.[134] There is no jurisdiction when it comes to investigate any qualified criminal group. Therefore, investigating Urla Villas within the same context in this investigation is legal. The chief attorney tried to put pressure on me and said "I am having you followed. How dare you say me that you want to do raids in this investigation?" Finally, I have decided to conduct this operation whatsoever it costs me.[135]

Akkaş witnessed how, for the first time in Turkish legal history, law enforcement officials refused to obey a court decision. He said:

Rather than identifying December 17th and 25th operation as coup attempts to overthrow government, the intervention of government should be defined as a coup on Turkish law system. Even though I sent court decision to the police, they did not apply it. As wiretapped from newly-assigned Minister of Interior who said "intrude the house of prosecutor and break it if there is any need," the police violated law.

What Happened on December 25?

Prosecutor Akkaş ordered the police to conduct an investigation and to arrest any suspects; however, newly replaced police officers violated the law and did not obey the court order. Akkaş then wrote a letter to journalists, saying that the justice was illegally obstructed. He disseminated the letter because of his concern about the evidence gathered during the investigation. In his letter, Akkaş emphasized how he responded to the risks involved in undermining the investigation. After explaining the content of the investigation to the chief attorney of Istanbul, Akkaş received orders from the court and conveyed them to the police.[136] The investigation became an instrument for the persecution of Akkaş. President Erdogan in one of his speeches, for example, insulted and threatened Akkaş.[137] As expected after Erdogan's speech, Akkaş was relieved of his duties, reassigned, suspended, forced out of his job, and prosecuted. The court issued a warrant for his arrest. When he was reassigned to Tekirdag, he was harassed and followed by the members of the intelligence service. His wife and parents were harassed as well.[138] Even his home was illegally searched by the police without an attorney or witness present. After the search, the police changed the lock on the home, and Akkaş' family was not allowed to reenter.[139]

Political Influence on ZEJ and EPS Cases

Both December cases have devastated Turkey's constitutional, institutional, and bureaucratic systems as well as the ability of law enforcement and the judiciary to enforce and apply the rule of law. The examination of corrupt groups using social network analysis[140] in both cases gives clues about the extent to which political influence is involved.

The group density[141] in the Zarrab Economic-Jihad (ZEJ) case from December 17 is 0.21 whereas it was 0.24 in the Erdogan Pool-System (EPS) case from December 25, meaning that the actors in the EPS case are highly connected. Figure 6.1 and Figure 6.2 graphically represent these connections. The more intense lines in Figure 6.2 confirm the greater connectedness between the actors in the EPS case compared with the ZEJ case where the lines are less intense.

Groups also have cliques, or subsets of actors closely tied to each within the same group.[142] These cliques are crucial because they essentially dictate the nature, purpose, and activities of the larger group.[143] The number of cliques within a group indicates the level of acquaintanceship among the group's members. In a group with a relatively large number of cliques, the group members most likely know each other well. The number of 10-person cliques in the ZEJ case was 3, while the number of 10-person cliques in

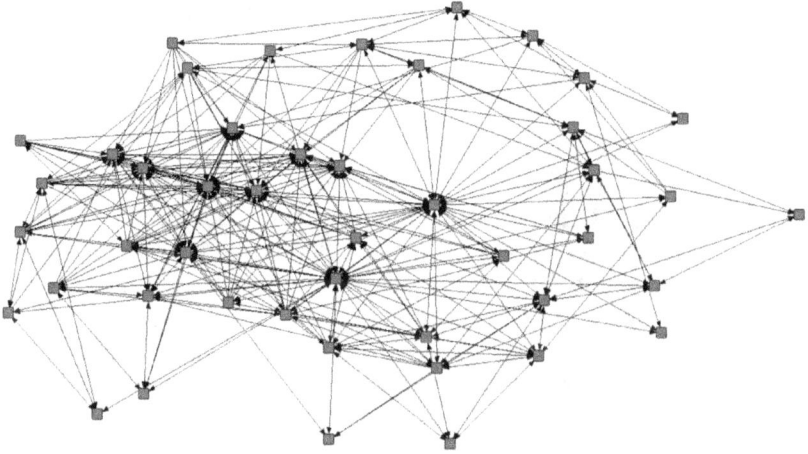

Figure 6.1   Graphic representation of the ZEJ case from December 17

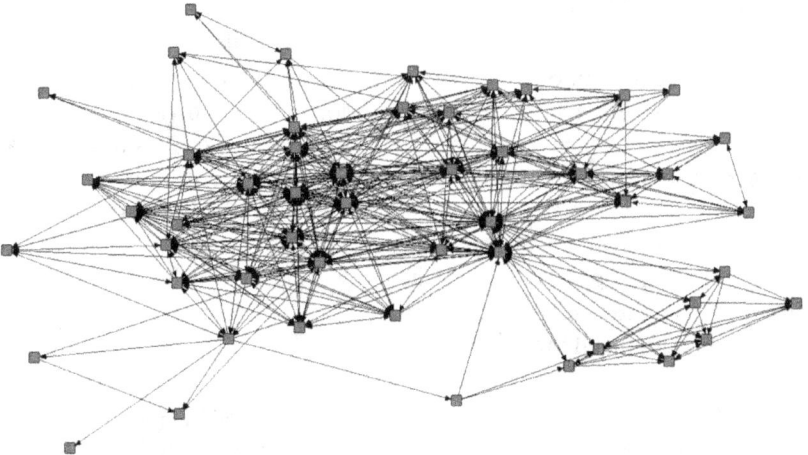

Figure 6.2   Graphic representation of the EPS case from December 25

the EPS case was 30, which means that the suspects in the EPS case were more acquainted with each other and therefore could breed 30 subgroups, or cliques, consisting of 10 members who know each other.

The analysis of group density and the number of cliques shows that political influence was much greater in the EPS case than in the ZEJ case because Prime Minister Yıldırım and President Erdogan were members of the group. The presence of these two individuals enabled the group members to believe that they could break the law with impunity, unlike the members of the group in the ZEJ case. The members of the group in the EPS case, therefore, were less concerned about the need for confidential communications than were the members of the group in the ZEJ case.

Transition to Authoritarianism and Public Attitude in Corruption Scandals

Authoritarianism only presents more opportunities and protection for corrupt leaders.[144] The corruption scandals surrounding the AKP in Turkey have threatened the viability of a democratic regime that had been touted as a model for other Middle Eastern countries. In its attempt to retain power, the AKP transitioned to an authoritarian presidential system where high-level political corruption is prevalent, the rulers can engage in any type of activity with impunity, and public criticism is prohibited. The media become more dependent on the government for information, competitive political parties were banned, and all citizens were expected to be submissive to the government's will, leaving the rule of law and the judiciary dependent on the whims of the government.[145]

The AKP has seized any opportunity to move the country toward an authoritarian regime in order to reach its ultimate goal: total immunity from investigations of its actions. President Erdogan went so far as to call the attempted military coup on July 15, 2016, "a gift from God," using the phrase as a pretext to silence opponents of the government and to indoctrinate the public about the value and appropriateness of a dictatorial presidential system. Almost 200 media and newspaper outlets were shut down, and several deputies from an opposition political party were arrested. President Erdogan's priority is to shelter himself from public criticism and to be immune from investigation and prosecution.

Despite being a democratic country, the public's apathetic reaction to the ZEJ and EPS corruption revelations contrasted sharply to the public's reaction in the wake of the 1997 Susurluk scandal, when millions of Turks responded with outrage and demonstrations against the government. Their ire was sparked by revelations of corruption that leaked from a traffic accident in the small town of Susurluk in Balikesir Province. The occupants of the car, which was loaded with assassination weapons, included a mafia leader wanted on an arrest warrant, a police chief, and a member of the Turkish parliament. In response to the public backlash, the government prosecuted the individuals involved and voted the member of parliament out of office.[146]

The different public reactions stem from the way government corruption is perceived based on the wealth of the country. Research shows that the perception of corruption is higher in poor countries than it is in wealthy countries.[147] When the economic situation in the country improved during the first years of the AKP government in the early 2000s, the people were not interested in corruption scandals. When the economic situation is bleak, interest in corruption scandals increases.

In a country with a single-party government, whose leader and high-level politicians apparently have been involved in corruption, the AKP has continued to win elections. Four explanations are proposed for why voters persistently support corrupt leaders. First, inherent corruption leads people to tolerate any kind of corruption. Second, when the pool of candidates is comprised of corrupt politicians, voters have no alternative candidates to elect. Third, when voters are not informed about the corrupt behavior of politicians, they unknowingly support them in elections. Fourth, voters knowingly support corrupt politicians because they believe that the benefits of electing such candidates outweigh the harm that can come from the politicians' corrupt actions. Research in Brazil in 2000, for example, showed that 47 percent of respondents would vote for a corrupt politician who could resolve the municipality's problems even though the person is reputed to be corrupt. Subsequent research in Brazil in 2002 and 2007 verified the year of 2000 finding that voters were willing to tolerate corrupt politicians. In a more recent study, 40 percent of the respondents said they would be willing to vote for a corrupt politician who could meet the needs of the people rather than an honest politician who could not do so.[148] Such is the case in Turkey, where the people chose personal well-being at the expense of jeopardizing the country's democratic system of government.

Economics and the hope for a better standard of living explain the Turkish people's willingness to support corrupt politicians. When the AKP began to rule the country, the economy improved. People with a low level of education were focused only on attaining a better standard of living and believed that with the AKP in power, they would be able to do so. These individuals essentially looked the other way and remained apathetic about the government's corrupt actions.[149] As time went on, they lost their ability to see that the AKP was turning into an authoritarian regime.[150] During the AKP's tenure, human rights violations, torture, and restrictions on freedom of the press emerged and have continued. In 2012, for example, Turkey was ranked second after Russia in the number of appeals made to the European Court of Human Rights.[151] In 2016, Turkey surpassed China in arbitrarily jailing journalists.[152]

President Erdogan's divisive politics polarized Turkish people, further complicating the situation.[153] The president apparently knew that the more people who support a dominant group, the less aware they are of organizational corruption,[154] and used this knowledge to his advantage. President Erdogan exploited that support to consolidate his support among the voters, push them to cast their ballot for the AKP,[155] and solidify his position as a dominant and autocratic leader.

The Attitude of the Government towards the Corruption Scandals

Ruling-party corruption scandals have occurred in many countries, and each country has responded differently. In some countries, confidence in the judiciary has increased because of its efforts to disclose corrupt acts. Such was the case in Italy in 1973 when an oil scandal beset that country, in Spain in 1993 when illegal financing of political parties was uncovered, and in France in 1987 when it was discovered that the Socialist Party had received funding in return for political favors. In each case, the judiciary was strengthened as a result of its performance in investigating government corruption.[156] In other countries, the public response to government corruption was to call for the ruling party to resign or to vote it out in the next election.

Rather than punishing the politicians and bureaucrats who were implicated in the corruption scandals, the AKP government covered up the wrongdoing and developed measures to prohibit anticorruption investigations in the future—despite a considerable amount of robust evidence and confessions made by some of the suspects. For example, the minister of environment and urbanization, Erdogan Bayraktar, whose son was arrested during the December 17 investigation, told the NTV news channel after a few days from the investigation, "I am rejecting the pressure put on me to resign. Whatever I have done is under the approval of Prime Minister Erdogan. I am resigning from my party and my member position at the parliament; in the same way, Erdogan must resign, too."[157]

Erdogan responded with more retaliatory actions against investigators.[158] He then set out to cast an even wider net. Because he knew that watchdogs and independent media outlets were allowed to scrutinize and publicize political corruption in democratic regimes,[159] Erdogan seized the control of the media and increasingly repressed social media.[160] But he did not stop there and took new steps to cover up the scandals. For example, hundreds of civil servants were reassigned, the judiciary was rendered dysfunctional, public officials were intimidated by being thrown in jail or tortured, and the country's system of government was reconstructed to protect Erdogan from all investigations (see Chapter 7).

NOTES

1. Louise Shelley, *Dirty Entanglements* (New York: Cambridge University Press, 2014), 65.

2. Zoe Pearson, "An International Human Rights Approach to Corruption." in *Corruption and Anti-Corruption*, eds. Peter Larmour and Nick Wolanin, (Asia Pacific Press, 2001): 30-61.

3. Jeffrey Milyo, "Corporate Influence and Political Corruption: Lessons from Stock Market Reactions to Political Events." *The Independent Review*, Vol. 19, No. 1 (Summer 2014): 19-36.

4. The focus group took place in X city of Turkey in 2015. Because of the concerns shared in the previous chapters, this chapter does not give any details on the demographics of the participants. They were given guarantees that their identities would be kept confidential. The information given by them is verifiable from the media.

5. Carl J. Friedrich, "Corruption Concepts in Historical Perspective." in *Political Corruption: Concepts & Contexts*, eds. A. Heidenheimer and M. Johnston, (New Brunswick: Transaction Publishers, 2002): 15-24.

6. S. Rose-Ackerman, "When Is Corruption Harmful?" in *Political Corruption: Concepts & Contexts*, eds. A. Heidenheimer and M. Johnston, (New Brunswick: Transaction Publishers, 2002): 353-371.

7. Joseph Nye, "Corruption and Political Government: A Cost Benefit Analysis." *American Political Science Review*, Volume 61, Issue 2 June (1967): 417-427.

8. John A. Gardiner, "Defining Corruption." in *Political Corruption: Concepts & Contexts*, eds. A. Heidenheimer and M. Johnston, (New Brunswick: Transaction Publishers, 2002): 25-40.

9. Gardiner, "Defining Corruption", 27.

10. Laura S. Underkuffler, *Captured by Evil: The Idea of Corruption in Law* (Yale University Press, 2013), 7.

11. Roberta Ann Johnson and Shalenda Sharma, "About Corruption." in *The Struggle against Corruption*, ed. Roberta Ann Johnson, (New York: Palgrave, 2004): 1-21.

12. Pearson, "An International Human Rights Approach to Corruption," 33.

13. Focus Group Study with five experts and researchers, By Mahmut Cengiz, August 2015, X City.

14. Focus Group Study with five experts and researchers, By Mahmut Cengiz, August 2015, X City.

15. Samuel Issacharoff, "On Political Corruption." *Harvard Law Review*, Vol. 124, No. 1 (November 2010): 118-142.

16. Jeffrey Milyo, "Corporate Influence and Political Corruption: Lessons from Stock Market Reactions to Political Events," 19-36.

17. M. Philp, "Conceptualizing Political Corruption." in *Political Corruption: Concepts & Contexts*, eds. A. Heidenheimer and M. Johnston, (New Brunswick: Transaction Publishers, 2002): 41-57.

18. John Dalberg-Acton, *Essays on Freedom and Power* (The Free Press, 1948), 364.

19. C.J. Friedrich, "Corruption Concepts in Historical Perspective." in *Political Corruption: Concepts & Contexts*, eds. A. Heidenheimer and M. Johnston, (New Brunswick: Transaction Publishers, 2002): 15-24.

20. Mahmut Cengiz, "Kamu Burokrasisinde Yolsuzlugun Yapilasmasi," Unpublished Dissertation, Ankara University, 2009, 136.

21. Focus Group Study with five experts and researchers, By Mahmut Cengiz, August 2015, X City.

22. *2015 Turkish Report of ASOD*, 4.

23. Penny Green and Tony Ward, *State Crime: Governments, Violence and Corruption* (Pluto Press, 2014), 21.

24. Shelley, *Dirty Entanglements*, 64.

25. Simon Wigley, "Parliamentary Immunity in Democratizing Countries: The Case of Turkey." *Human Rights Quarterly*, Vol. 31, No. 3 (August, 2009): 567-591.

26. Mahmut Cengiz, "Kamu Burokrasisinde Yolsuzlugun Yapilasmasi," Unpublished Dissertation, Ankara University, 2009: 134, 135.

27. Susan Rose-Ackerman and Bonnie J. Palifka, *Corruption and Government*, (New York: Cambridge University Press, 2016): 22-23.

28. Zeyno Baran, "Corruption: The Turkish Challenge." *Journal of International Affairs*, Vol. 54, No. 1, Turkey: A Struggle between Nation and State (Fall 2000): 127-146.

29. Baran, "Corruption: The Turkish Challenge," 132.

30. Baran, "Corruption: The Turkish Challenge," 133.

31. David Phillips, *An Uncertain Ally: Turkey under Erdogan's Dictatorship*, (New York: Transaction Publishers, 2017), 45.

32. Kayhan Delibas, *The Rise of Political Islam in Turkey* (New York: I.B. Tauris, 2015), 289.

33. Delibas, *The Rise of Political Islam in Turkey*, 266.

34. Delibas, *The Rise of Political Islam in Turkey*, 18.

35. Delibas, *The Rise of Political Islam in Turkey*, 67.

36. Delibas, *The Rise of Political Islam in Turkey*, 161, 163, and 165.

37. Ugur Dundar, "ISKI Skandali Okyanusta Damla Kalir," *Oda TV*, accessed on January 2017, from http://odatv.com/iski-skandali-okyanusta-damla-kalir-2501151200.html.

38. Erhan Ozturk, "ABD kazan Civan kepçe," *Sabah Gazetesi*, accessed on January 28, 2017, from http://www.sabah.com.tr/gundem/2011/03/07/abd_kazan_civan_kepce.

39. Baran, "Corruption: The Turkish Challenge," 137-139.

40. Focus Group Study with five experts and researchers, By Mahmut Cengiz, August 2015, X City.

41. Delibas, *The Rise of Political Islam in Turkey*, 161, 163, and 165.

42. Delibas, *The Rise of Political Islam in Turkey*, 132.

43. Baran, "Corruption: The Turkish Challenge", 127-146.

44. Diba Nigar Goksel, "A Civil Society Initiative in the Fight against Corruption in Turkey." *SEER: Journal for Labor and Social Affairs in Eastern Europe*, Vol. 4, No. 2 (July 2001): 33-36.

45. Focus Group Study with five experts and researchers, By Mahmut Cengiz, August 2015, X City.

46. Pinar Bedirhanoğlu, "The Neoliberal Discourse on Corruption as a Means of Consent Building: Reflections from Post-Crisis Turkey," *Third World Quarterly*, Vol. 28, No. 7 (2007): 1239-1254.

47. Focus Group Study with five experts and researchers, By Mahmut Cengiz, August 2015, X City.

48. "Has Turkey Given up Fighting Corruption?," *Al Monitor*, accessed on January 9, 2016, from http://www.al-monitor.com/pulse/originals/2016/06/turkey-akp-abandons-fighting-corruption.html.

49. "Has Turkey Given up Fighting Corruption?," *Al Monitor*.

50. Pinar Bedirhanoğlu, "The Neoliberal Discourse on Corruption as a Means of Consent Building: Reflections from Post-Crisis Turkey." 1247.

51. Focus Group Study with five experts and researchers, By Mahmut Cengiz, August 2015, X City.

52. Binali Yıldırım is known as the loyalist minister in Erdogan's inner circle. The reason for this status had not been understood for some time. Yıldırım is one of the most corrupt ministers in Erdogan's cabinet. Erdogan and Yıldırım collaborated in bribery cases. According to a European Investigative Collaboration's examination of the Malta Files, Yıldırım clandestinely owned 11 cargo ships that cost 140 million USD. ("Malta Belgelerinden Şimdiye Kadar Neler Çıktı," *Washington Hatti*, (May 29, 2017) https://washingtonhatti.com/2017/05/29/malta-belgelerinden-simdiye-kadar-neler-cikti/, accessed June 13, 2017. Furthermore, a 2014 police investigation in Izmir proved that Yıldırım, like Erdogan, provided opportunities for corrupt activity for his family members. Yıldırım's brother-in-law was video recorded receiving a bribe in a corruption case related to the port operations manager, who was connected to Yıldırım. ("Binali Yıldırımi'in Bacanagina Kotu Haber," *Hurriyet*, (January, 22, 2014), accessed June 13, 2017 http://www.hurriyet.com.tr/binali-Yıldırımin-bacanagina-kotu-haber-25626990).

53. "Has Turkey Given up Fighting Corruption?," *Al Monitor*.

54. Focus Group Study with five experts and researchers, By Mahmut Cengiz, August 2015, X City.

55. Baran, "Corruption: The Turkish Challenge", 129.

56. Barry Hindess, "Good Government and Corruption," in *Corruption and Anti-Corruption*, eds. Peter Larmour and Nick Wolanin, (ANU Press, 2013): 1-10.

57. Mahmut Cengiz, *Turkiye'de Organize Suc Gercegi ve Terorun Finansmani* (Ankara: Seckin Yayincilik, 2015), 223.

58. Focus Group Study with five experts and researchers, By Mahmut Cengiz, August 2015, X City.

59. David Phillips, *An Uncertain Ally: Turkey under Erdogan's Dictatorship*, 45.

60. "Recep Tayyip Erdoğan: Fakir neden fakirdir? Zengin neden zengindir?," *YouTube*, accessed on January 21, 2017, from https://www.youtube.com/watch?v=pzymE4VuiBk.

61. "Recep Tayyip Erdoğan: Hırsızlık babadan oğula geçer", *Youtube*, accessed on January 21, 2017, from https://www.youtube.com/watch?v=Z5Wt-5AzFrE.

62. Ahmet Donmez, *Yuzde On Adil Duzenden Havuz Duzenine*, (Istanbul: Klas Kitapcilik, 2014), 82-83.

63. "Iran's Bold Economic Reform: Economic Jihad," *The Economist*, accessed on January 2, 2017, from http://www.economist.com/node/18867440.

64. "Turkish National Arrested for Conspiring to Evade U.S. Sanctions against Iran, Money Laundering and Bank Fraud" https://www.justice.gov/opa/pr/turkish-national-arrested-conspiring-evade-us-sanctions-against-iran-money-laundering-and.

65. Focus Group Study with five experts and researchers, By Mahmut Cengiz, August 2015, X City.

66. Emmanuelle Ottolenghi, *The Pasdaran inside Iran's Islamic Revolutionary Guard Corps,* (Washington, DC: FDD Press, 2011).

67. Emanuele Ottolenghi, "Should Boeing and Airbus Sell Planes to Iran Air?," *Foundation for Defense of Democracies,* accessed on January 23, 2017, from http://www.defenddemocracy.org/media-hit/emanuele-ottolenghi-should-boeing-and-airbus-sell-planes-to-iran-air/.

68. Ipek Yazdan, "Zencani Icin Onur Air Davasi," *Hurriyet,* accessed on January 30, 2017, from http://www.hurriyet.com.tr/irandan-zencani-icin-onur-air-davasi-4 0004264.

69. Focus Group Study with five experts and researchers, By Mahmut Cengiz, August 2015, X City.

70. Focus Group Study with five experts and researchers, By Mahmut Cengiz, August 2015, X City.

71. Ugur Soysal "Şoföründe 150 milyon dolar!", Haber Turk, (April 15, 2011), accessed on September 12, 2017, from http://www.haberturk.com/yasam/haber/620 972-soforunde-150-milyon-dolar

72. Focus group study with five police officers who became involved in December 17 and 25 investigations, Istanbul, May 2014.

73. "Tayyip Erdoğan'ın Hayırsever Rezası, Reza Zarrab Dubaili Heyete Kadın Ayarlıyor," *YouTube,* accessed on January 30, 2017, from https://www.youtube.com/watch?v=13BzmwatthY.

74. Focus Group Study with five experts and researchers, By Mahmut Cengiz, August 2015, X City.

75. Focus Group Study with five experts and researchers, By Mahmut Cengiz, August 2015, X City.

76. Focus Group Study with five experts and researchers, By Mahmut Cengiz, August 2015, X City.

77. The toman "unit of ten thousand" is a super unit of the official currency of Iran, the rial. It is divided into 10,000 dinar.

78. Focus Group Study with five experts and researchers, By Mahmut Cengiz, August 2015, X City.

79. Focus Group Study with five experts and researchers, By Mahmut Cengiz, August 2015, X City.

80. "Zafer Çağlayan Reza İle Görüşüyor 17 Mart 2014 - Otobanda Buluşma ve Tuvalette Rüşvet," *YouTube,* accessed on January 3, 2017, from https://www.you tube.com/watch?v=PoEz6eulfa4.

81. Focus Group Study with five experts and researchers, By Mahmut Cengiz, August 2015, X City.

82. Focus Group Study with five experts and researchers, By Mahmut Cengiz, August 2015, X City.

83. Focus Group Study with five experts and researchers, By Mahmut Cengiz, August 2015, X City.

84. Focus Group Study with five experts and researchers, By Mahmut Cengiz, August 2015, X City.

85. Mahmut Hamsici, "10 soruda: 17-25 Aralık operasyonları." *BBC*, accessed on November 11, 2016, from http://www.bbc.com/turkce/haberler/2014/12/141212_17_25_aralik_operasyonu_neler_oldu_10_soruda.

86. Selahattin GÜNDAY - Cem TURSUN, "Süleyman Aslan'ın evinde 4.5 milyon dolar bulundu." *Hurriyet*, accessed on November 25, 2017, from http://www.hurriyet.com.tr/suleyman-aslanin-evinde-4-5-milyon-dolar-bulundu-25388816.

87. Firat Alkac, "Paralar faiziyle iade," *Hurriyet*, accessed on January 14, 2017, from http://www.hurriyet.com.tr/paralar-faiziyle-iade-27802186.

88. Serbay Mansuroglu, "Hırsızın parasından imam hatip olmaz," *Birgun,* accessed on November 25, 2016, from http://www.birgun.net/haber-detay/hirsizin-parasindan-imam-hatip-olmaz-95739.html.

89. Tim Aranco, "After an Indictment, Turks Give U.S. Prosecutor a Hero's Welcome Online." *New York Times.* accessed on May 18, 2016, from http://www.nytimes.com/2016/03/27/world/europe/turkey-preet-bharara-reza-zarrab-indictment.html?_r=0.

90. "Zarrab, Togem-Der'e para yağdırmış," *Evrensel,* accessed on December 20, 2016, from https://www.evrensel.net/haber/280487/zarrab-togem-dere-para-yagdirmis.

91. Bilge Yesil, *Media in New Turkey: The Origins of an Authoritarian Neoliberal State* (University of Illinois Press, 2016), 116.

92. "Erdogan'in En Uzun Gunu 17 Aralik Belgeseli - Can Dundar," *YouTube*, accessed on January 3, 2017, from https://www.youtube.com/watch?v=zQI8QMjE-S0.

93. "Şehrizar Konakları'ndaki dairelerin tapusu Albayraklar'a geçti," *Sozcu*, accessed on January 3, 2017, from http://www.sozcu.com.tr/emlak/sehrizar-konaklarinda-flas-gelisme.html.

94. According to the theory of Julie Mazzei, power elites develop paramilitary groups based on their perceptions. They are against structural shifts because they perceive that they can lose the power. They are opposed to reform and employ death squads against group of people who attempt to get power from the hands of power elites (Julie Mazzei, *Death Squads or Self-Defense Forces? How Paramilitary Groups Emerge and Challenge Democracy in Latin America* (Chapel Hill: University of North Carolina Press, 2009), 1-24).

95. "Turkey's post-coup crackdown." *Turkey Purge,* accessed on October 24, 2018 from https://turkeypurge.com/.

96. Mahmut Cengiz, "Why Turkey Failed to Remove the Shadows on the Coup." *Vocale Europe,* accessed on April 4, 2018 from http://www.vocaleurope.eu/why-turkey-failed-to-remove-the-shadows-on-the-coup/.

97. Donmez *Yuzde, On Adil Duzenden Havuz Duzenine*, pp. 98-99. It is believed that the bribes are normalized because of fatwas given by Islamic law professor Hayrettin Karaman. In one of his articles, he stressed that corruption is not a robbery. "Hayrettin Karaman: Yolsuzluga Hirsizlik Denilmez," accessed on January 26, 2017, from http://odatv.com/yolsuzluga-hirsizlik-denilmez-1112141200.html.

98. Donmez, *Yuzde On Adil Duzenden Havuz Duzenine*, 100.

99. Shihata Ibrahim F.I., "The Role of the World Bank in Combating Corruption," in *Combating Corruption in Latin America*, eds. Joseph Tulchin and R. Espach, (Washington, DC: Woodrow Wilson Center Press, 2000): 205-209.

100. Focus Group Study with five experts and researchers, By Mahmut Cengiz, August 2015, X City.

101. Focus Group Study with five experts and researchers, By Mahmut Cengiz, August 2015, X City.

102. Penny Green and Tony Ward, *State Crime: Governments, Violence and Corruption,* (Pluto Press, 2014), 16.

103. Roberta Ann Johnson and Shalenda Sharma, "About Corruption," 9.

104. Focus Group Study with five experts and researchers, By Mahmut Cengiz, August 2015, X City.

105. "Duble Yollar Patladı, Onarım Parası İkiye Katlandı," *Haberler,* (September 15, 2015), accessed on January 13, 2017, from http://www.haberler.com/duble-yollar-patladi-onarim-parasi-ikiye-katlandi-7690794-haberi/.

106. Focus Group Study with five experts and researchers, By Mahmut Cengiz, August 2015, X City.

107. Tim Jacoby, "Turkey and Europe: Culture, Capital and Corruption," *Review of International Studies*, Vol. 36, No. 3 (July 2010), pp. 663-684. In research conducted in 2009, 75% of respondents agreed that gifts given to public officials in the course of business transactions are not considered bribes. This finding shows the impact of cultural factors on the definition of corruption. (Mahmut Cengiz, "Kamu Burokrasisi'nde Yolsuzlugun Yapilasmasi," Unpublished Dissertation, Ankara University, 2009, 139).

108. K. Balachandrudu, "Understanding Political Corruption," *The Indian Journal of Political Science*, Vol. 67, No. 4 (October-December, 2006): 809-816.

109. Focus Group Study with five experts and researchers, By Mahmut Cengiz, August 2015, X City.

110. Susan Rose-Ackerman and Bonnie J. Palifka, *Corruption and Government*, 93.

111. Susan Rose-Ackerman and Bonnie J. Palifka, *Corruption and Government*, pp. 101, 103.

112. "Mehmet Cengiz & bilal erdoğan küfür ediyor ses kaydı& akp," *YouTube*, accessed on January 10, 2017, from https://www.youtube.com/watch?v=kFvoSzAFyw8. When businessmen were forced to give bribes in the form of donations, they spoke with each other to complain about the amount of money they have to pay.

113. Focus Group Study with five experts and researchers, By Mahmut Cengiz, August 2015, X City.

114. "25 Aralik Iddianamesi -Yasin Topcu," *YouTube*, accessed on January 12, 2017 from https://www.youtube.com/watch?v=SPRb1deMMkU.

115. "25 Aralık Savcısı Muammer Akkaş İlk Kez Konuştu," *YouTube*, accessed on November 8, 2016, from https://www.youtube.com/watch?v=LNGLrfJ1JNk.

116. "25 Aralik Iddianamesi -Yasin Topcu," *YouTube*.

117. "25 Aralik Iddianamesi -Yasin Topcu," *YouTube*.

118. "25 Aralik Iddianamesi -Yasin Topcu," *YouTube*.

119. Ahmet Donmez, *Yuzde On Adil Duzenden Havuz Duzenine*, (Istanbul: Klas Kitapcilik, 2014), 24.

120. Donmez, *Yuzde On Adil Duzenden Havuz Duzenine*, p. 23.

121. "Cengiz İnşaat'ın vergi borcu nasıl sıfırlandı?," *Sozcu*, accessed on December 18, 2017, from http://www.sozcu.com.tr/2016/gundem/cengiz-insaatin-vergi-borcu-nasil-sifirlandi-1125649/.

122. Donmez, *Yuzde On Adil Duzenden Havuz Duzenine*, 29.

123. Donmez, *Yuzde On Adil Duzenden Havuz Duzenine*, 23.

124. Focus Group Study with five experts and researchers, By Mahmut Cengiz, August 2015, X City.

125. "25 Aralik Iddianamesi-Yasin Topcu," *YouTube*.

126. "Recep Tayyip Erdoğan'dan Zaman Muhabirine Sert Yanıt 11 Şubat 2014," *YouTube*, accessed on December 21, 2016, from https://www.youtube.com/watch?v=64cFlcWbejM.

127. "İşte Urla villaları," *Sozcu*, accessed on December 21, 2016, from http://www.sozcu.com.tr/2014/gundem/iste-urla-villalari-555231/.

128. "25 Aralik Iddianamesi-Yasin Topcu," *YouTube*.

129. David Philips, "Turken Foundation: A Wolf in the Neighborhood." accessed on December 22, 2016, from http://www.huffingtonpost.com/david-l-phillips/turken-foundation-a-wolf_b_12688412.html.

130. "Zarrab'ın Zafer Çağlayan Aracılığıyla TÜRGEV'e Gönderdiği Rüşvet," *YouTube*, accessed on January 3, 2017, from https://www.youtube.com/watch?v=Itvh_zn4P_A.

131. "The National Judiciary Informatics System (UYAP) is an e-justice system which has been developed as a part of the Turkish e-government system by the Ministry of Justice to ensure a fast, reliable, soundly operating and accurate judicial system. As a central network project, it includes all of the courts, public prosecutor's services, law enforcement offices, prisons, other judicial institutions and other government departments in Turkey." "National Judiciary Informatics System," *Public Sector Innovation*, accessed on September 12, 2012 from https://www.oecd.org/governance/observatory-public-sector-innovation/innovations/page/nationaljudiciaryinformaticssystem.htm.

132. "25 Aralık Savcısı Muammer Akkaş İlk Kez Konuştu," *YouTube*, accessed on November 8, 2016, from https://www.youtube.com/watch?v=LNGLrfJ1JNk.

133. "25 Aralık Savcısı Muammer Akkaş İlk Kez Konuştu," *YouTube*.

134. The police report of December 25th scandal revealed that El Qadi frequently claimed to make meetings regarding ongoing conflict in Syria with Chief of Intelligence and higher level politicians and bureaucrats.

135. "25 Aralık Savcısı Muammer Akkaş İlk Kez Konuştu," *YouTube*.

136. "Akkaş bildiri dağıttı Öz gece emniyete geldi." *Hurriyet*, accessed on November 7, 2017, from http://www.hurriyet.com.tr/Akkaş-bildiri-dagitti-oz-gece-emniyete-geldi-27867350.

137. "Tayyip Erdoğan: O Savcıyla daha işimiz var." *YouTube*, accessed on December, 7, 2017, from https://www.youtube.com/watch?v=lUxkgUfTk3k.

138. "25 Aralık Savcısı Muammer Akkaş İlk Kez Konuştu," *YouTube*.

139. "Polis kilidi değiştirmiş, savcının ailesi 2 gündür evine giremiyor." *YouTube*, accessed on November 7, 2016, from https://www.youtube.com/watch?v=UlJkxeKebHg.

140. UCINET 6.0 was used to analyze the structure of both groups. The data relating to edges between actors were compiled from police reports of the December 17th investigation with 46 suspects and from reports of the December 25th investigation with 51 suspects. The name of each person in the police reports is filtered and the person's ties with other people are specified. Any kind of relationship, including phone call or face-to-face connection, is accepted as a tie between those people. Zeros and ones are used in the matrix. A zero means no connections; a one means that a relationship exists between two people.

141. Group density indicates whether the ties between groups and/or individuals are loose or tight and represents the proportion of observed ties to possible ties. A higher density indicates greater connectedness among group members, while a lower density indicates less connectedness. John Scott, *Social Network Analysis* (Thousand Oaks, CA: Sage Publications, 2005).

142. Robert Hanneman, "Introduction to Social Network Methods," *University of California,* accessed on February 20, 2017, from http://faculty.ucr.edu/~hanneman/ne ttext/C11_Cliques.html#subgraph.

143. J.M. McGloin, "Policy and Intervention Considerations of a Network Analysis of Street Gangs," *Criminology and Public Policy*, Vol. 4, No. 3 (2005), pp. 607-636.

144. Eric Chang and Miriam A. Golden, "Sources of Corruption in Authoritarian Regimes," *Social Science Quarterly*, Vol. 91, No. 1 (March 2010), pp. 1-20.

145. L. Whitehead, "High Level Political Corruption in Latin America: A Transitional Phenomenon." in *Political Corruption Concepts & Contexts*, eds. A. Heidenheimer and M. Johnston, (New Brunswick: Transaction Publishers, 2002): 801-818.

146. Shaazka Beyerle, *Curtailing Corruption: People Power for Accountability & Justice* (London: Lynne Rienner Publishers, 2014), 210.

147. Xiaohui Xin and Thomas K. Rudel, "The Context for Political Corruption: A Cross-National Analysis." *Social Science Quarterly*, Vol. 85, No. 2 (June 2004): 294-309.

148. Matthew S. Winters and Rebecca Weitz-Shapiro, "Lacking Information or Condoning Corruption: When Do Voters Support Corrupt Politicians?," *Comparative Politics*, Vol. 45, No. 4 (July 2013): 418-436.

149. Focus Group Study with five experts and researchers, By Mahmut Cengiz, August 2015, X City.

150. Focus Group Study with five experts and researchers, By Mahmut Cengiz, August 2015, X City.

151. Huseyin Gül and Hakan M. Kiris, "Democratic Governance Reform in Turkey and Their Implications." in *Public Policy Administration and Policy in the Middle East,* ed. Alexander Dawoody, (New York: Springer, 2014): 25-61.

152. "New York Times Editorial Board: Turkey's Relentless Attack on the Press." *New York Times*, accessed on January 18, 2017, from https://www.nytimes.com/ 2017/01/14/opinion/sunday/turkeys-relentless-attack-on-the-press.html.

153. Tim Aranco, "In Turkey, U.S. Hand Is Seen in Nearly Every Crisis," *New York Times,* (January 4, 2017), accessed on January 5, 2017, from http://www.nyti mes.com/2017/01/04/world/europe/istanbul-attack-nightclub.html?_r=0.

154. Valerie Rosenblatt, "Hierarchies, Power Inequalities, and Organizational Corruption," *Journal of Business Ethics*, Vol. 111, No. 2 (December 2012), pp. 237-251.

155. Focus Group Study with five experts and researchers, By Mahmut Cengiz, August 2015, X City.

156. V. Pujas and M. Rhodes, "Party Finance and Political Scandal: Comparing Italy, Spain, and France," in *Political Corruption Concepts & Contexts*, eds. A. Heidenheimer and M. Johnston, (New Brunswick: Transaction Publishers, 2002): 739-760.

157. "Canlı yayında istifa! Erdoğan Bayraktar NTV konuşması," *NTV*, accessed on December 26, 2017, from https://www.youtube.com/watch?v=RqrKvxU-KzM.

158. Focus Group Study with five experts and researchers, By Mahmut Cengiz, August 2015, X City.

159. Strom C. Thacker, "Democracy, Economic Policy, and Political Corruption in Comparative Perspective: Corruption and Democracy in Latin America," in *Corruption and Democracy in Latin America*, eds. Charles H. Blake and Stephen D. Morris, (University of Pittsburgh Press, 2009): 25-45.

160. Yesil, *Media in New Turkey: The Origins of an Authoritarian Neoliberal State*, 116.

Chapter 7

How "Dirty Entanglements" Paralyze the Capacity of Law Enforcement

INTRODUCTION

The December 2013 corruption scandals (see Chapter 6) support Louise Shelley's theory of "dirty entanglement," which posits that crime, corruption, and terrorism often become "entangled," and can continue to influence each other even when they are not overlapping.[1] Based on this theory, the best model in countering criminal and terrorist groups is to develop a model that concurrently includes effective fighting tools against crime, corruption, and terrorism. The Turkish case has given lessons in terms of finding the best model in countering criminal and terrorist groups, which ignored fighting against corruption. Until the destructive impacts of the 2013 corruption scandals, the police were widely regarded as a well-educated[2] and swiftly modernizing police unit.

Any victories in countering criminal and terrorist organizations have been for naught since the crackdown began after the December 2013 scandals. By most accounts, President Erdogan's intent is not just reorganizing the government, but is introducing protections that will prevent future investigations into his activities related to crime, corruption, and terrorism. As a result, Turkey has witnessed the unprecedented purges of law enforcement officials and judiciary members, effectively hindering the legitimate operations of entire state institutions. It should be noted that, as opposed to the Erdogan government's ruthless persecutions on Turkish investigators, U.S. prosecutors and FBI agents who conducted the Zarrab investigation (incorporating Turkish evidence), were presented with the Alberto Nisman Award for Courage by Foundation for Defense of Democracies (FDD) in August 2018.[3] This chapter analyzes the consequences of the 2013 December corruption scandals on law enforcement through the comparison of data related to smuggling, trafficking, and terrorist financing using cases that took place between 2012 and 2016.

Post-Corruption Investigations Period

In the aftermath of the graft scandals, four ministers, whose sons were implicated in the corruption scandals, resigned. Efgan Ala, who had dedicated himself to ruthlessly punishing the investigators, replaced the minister of interior.
Police chiefs involved in the investigation were replaced by their colleagues
who unconditionally obeyed whatever the government commanded, even if
it meant breaking the law. For example, the police chief of Istanbul, Huseyin
Capkin, was replaced with Selami Altinok, who immediately was transported to Istanbul on Erdogan's private jet. The government then replaced
all Anti-Smuggling and Organized Crime Department (ASOD) chiefs across
the country in charge of anticorruption investigations. It was unclear at first
why the government replaced police chiefs across the country when the
investigation of the graft scandals was only carried out by the Istanbul Police
Directorate and its Financial Crimes Unit. It was soon revealed that President
Erdogan, his family members, and inner circle were targets of various crime,
corruption (see Chapter 6), and terrorism (see Chapter 9) investigations, and
this was the government's strategy for shutting down these cases.

Prosecutors involved in two December 2013 investigations were also
replaced,[4] and many wiretapped conversations among high level politicians
and bureaucrats were leaked on social media. These wiretappings indicated
that previous Interior Minister Ala was active in covering up the corruption
scandals. He made numerous phone calls to Istanbul police chief Altinok
inquiring how many police officers had been reassigned. In one wiretap
between Altinok and Ala, Altinok responded, "I reassigned two police chiefs
as you commanded to the farthest points from their homes."[5] Indeed, the
government reassigned thousands of police officers who were working for
ASOD, including members of the Anti-Terror Department and the Intelligence Units. Reassignments also hit the Financial Crimes Investigation Board
(MASAK) and other governmental organizations authorized to participate
in anticorruption investigations. The reassignments served the AKP well,
enabling it, for example, to learn about a December 25 police investigation
and stop its progress when newly assigned police officers refused to implement a court decision in the matter.

Efgan Ala was strategic in his reassignments of the police chiefs. He
deliberately replaced former police chiefs with many previously investigated
or convicted police chiefs, putting them in position to slake their appetite
for revenge against former police officers. As a result of the reassignments,
years of investigative efforts have come to a screeching halt, and all ongoing
anticorruption, organized crime, terrorist financing, and even antiterrorism
investigations were disclosed and dropped.

In addition to reassignments, the government immediately altered regulations that applied to the initiation of police investigations. An article in the

Regulation on Judicial Law Enforcement that had previously protected confidentiality, prohibiting prosecutors and law enforcement officers from sharing investigation information with their superiors, was replaced by a provision that reversed this protection, enabling officials not involved in an investigation to be privy to the content of investigations. The government further meddled in the judicial system when it reassigned two more prosecutors involved in trials arising from the December 17 investigation. One of the prosecutors had approved the arrest of several suspects; however, he changed his mind and dropped the case after 10 months[6] in return for having his previous sentence dismissed.[7] It should be noted that the main suspect of the December 17 investigation, Reza Zarrab, testified that he bribed officials to be released from Turkish jail.[8]

Intimidation of Investigators

The retaliation continued with government intimidation of investigators through persecution and torture. The goal was to discourage investigations of the AKP. After the reassignments and replacements, the AKP reportedly fabricated evidence to arrest police investigators—regardless of their involvement in the December 17 and December 25 investigations. The first arrests occurred on July 22, 2014, when 104 police officers were taken into custody. Although it was illegal to do so, the officers were arrested at midnight and handcuffed and detained for eight days rather than the maximum of four days allowed by law. They were also harshly treated while in custody.[9] The AKP government also arrested the wives and children of some of these police chiefs in 2017.[10]

Because the AKP gave priority to the arrest of police officers who worked in antiterrorism and intelligence units, suspicions arose that the government was implicated in other criminal or nefarious activities. Officers in both units were experts on illegal Iranian activities in Turkey and in the region. These officers, for example, had experience investigating not only Iranian spies who had infiltrated the government but also high-level Turkish officials who were under the influence of Iranian ideology. During one investigation, officers found that the suspects were members of the Tawhid Salam Quds Force, a group that the Turkish Supreme Court had declared a terrorist organization in 2006 (see Chapter 8). Although it was not understood initially why the government gave priority to arresting these police officers rather than the officers who had investigated the December 17 and December 25 corruption scandals, it was learned later that the targeted officers found vital linkages between the suspects and the AKP. Retaliation against police officers conducting corruption investigations affected the entire country. Thousands of judges, prosecutors, and police officers were arrested, while many more were suspended and forced out of their job on the basis of fabricated evidence. Nearly all were persecuted and tortured in the prisons.

How the December 2013 Scandals Squelched the Investigation Capacity of Investigators

The unprecedented scale of purges after the December corruption investigations not only created favorable ground for criminals and terrorists in the illicit economy, but it also caused Turkey to lose institutional memory, knowledge, and culture. When the AKP government came to power in 2002, it invested heavily in modernizing the police force, in an effort to bolster its bona fides to earn membership in the European Union. The investment paid off. Turkish police officers began to fight effectively against criminals, and the TNP was seen as a global actor in the fight against transnational criminals and terrorists. During this period, institutional memory emerged and spread throughout entire crime-fighting units. The retaliatory attitude of the government in response to two December investigations obliterated this memory of how best to fight crime, leaving the Turkish police incapable of fighting against criminal and terrorist groups. Gone also was a trove of institutional knowledge. Expert police officers who had acquired years of experience fighting criminal and terrorist groups were replaced by inexperienced and inadequately trained police officers. The government did not even allow the ousted officers to pass their knowledge on to the replacement officers. Perhaps the government deemed the knowledge transfer unnecessary, given that the newly assigned officers were frequently ordered to complete assignments outside the scope of their duties. For example, organized crime units were diverted from their focus on criminals and were required instead to investigate opponents of the government and protect the AKP regime.

As a result, the country has lost its capacity to fight against corruption, crime, and terrorism. Ultimately, a considerable number of investigations were dropped as a result of government interference or the blundering of newly appointed police officers. The comparison of police statistics shows massive decreases in the number of smuggling and trafficking cases before and after the purges. The results indicated that the ability of the police to fight crimes has been paralyzed by the purges. This goes for all types of crimes or investigations, including anti-corruption and financial crimes, smuggling and trafficking, mafia-type criminal organizations, confiscation of crime proceeds, terrorist financing, and capacity to fight international smuggling and trafficking.

Anti-corruption and Financial Crimes Investigations

While corruption has plagued various segments of Turkey for decades, its conspicuousness has become much more glaring in the period after the purges. According to the Corruption Perception Index, Turkey fell 28 places in the ranking of 180 countries between 2013 and 2017, falling to 81st place out of 180 countries in 2017.[11] This was one of the sharpest drops in the country index. Prior to the anticorruption investigation, the Turkish police saw a modest number of successes. In the aftermath of the graft scandals, the police were deprived of their capacity to investigate corruption. There are three explanations for this: First of all, law enforcement became reluctant to conduct anticorruption investigations because of the inherent personal and professional risks investigating high level politicians and high-level bureaucrats. Secondly, the government has the power to pressure law enforcement by labeling investigators as terrorists and putting them in jails when they challenge the interests of the AKP government. Finally, newly assigned police officers are Erdoganists who have a stake in unconditionally protecting the government from accusations of wrongdoing. The number of public servants arrested in anticorruption investigations decreased 91.9 percent between 2013[12] and 2016.[13] These decreases were much more visible in the number of anticorruption investigations made against municipalities (Figure 7.1).

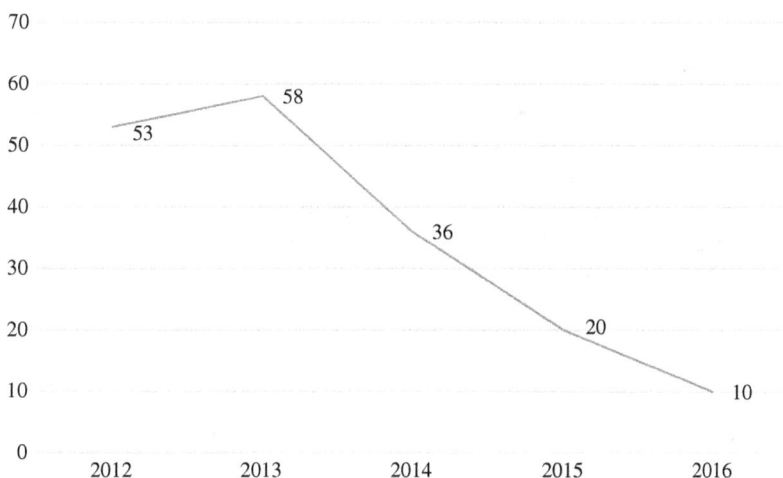

Figure 7.1   The number of corruption investigations in municipalities. *Source: 2016 Turkish Report of ASOD, 7.*

The decrease has continued in financial crimes as seen in Figure 7.2. Financial crimes investigations require more knowledge and skills than other types of crimes since these criminals are typically more sophisticated and have developed a higher level of criminal acumen. Turkish profiles of these criminals indicate they are not surprisingly the most educated underworld actors. In a perfect world, law enforcement would be better equipped and trained to elevate their expertise level, however, an examination of the data indicates the inadequacy of current police officers to meet these challenges. This phenomenon is best exemplified by the 61.2 percent decrease in financial crime investigations utilizing wiretapping, surveillance, and undercover agents between 2013 and 2016.[14]

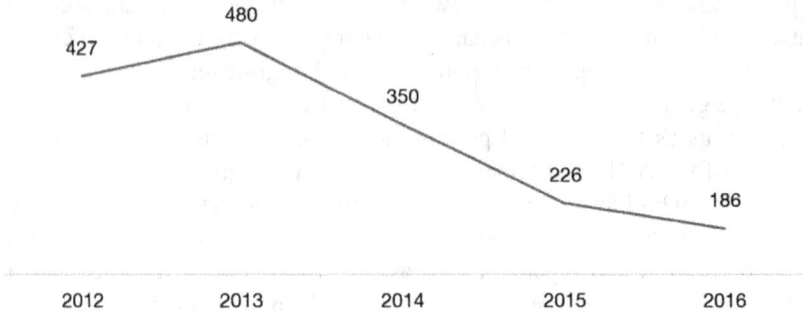

Figure 7.2 **The number of financial crimes investigation.** *Source: 2016 Turkish Report of ASOD*, 21.

Smuggling Cases

The government's purging of experienced police officers and its replacement of those individuals with inexperienced officers loyal to the government has allowed smuggling groups to flourish. First, the number of oil smuggling cases and suspects as well as the amount of oil seized decreased sharply in 2015 and 2016, despite the fact that Turkey had been exposed to more oil smuggling cases due to the ongoing civil war in Syria (see Figure 7.3).

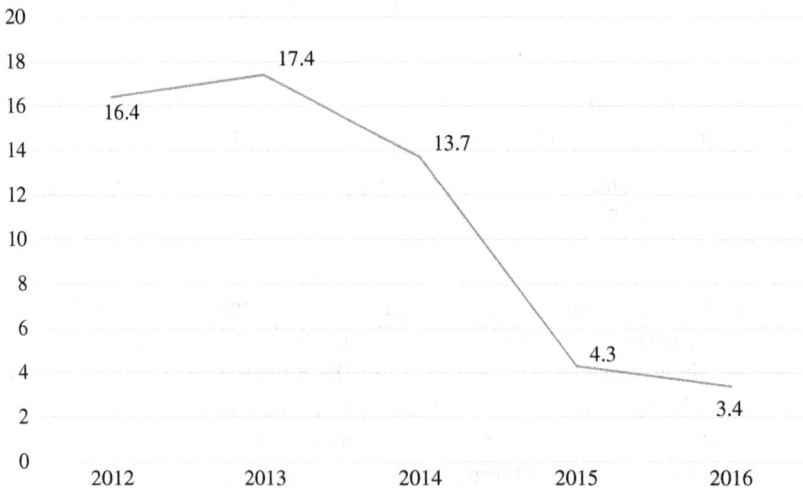

Figure 7.3 **The amount of oil (liters) confiscated between 2012 and 2016.** *Source: 2016 Turkish Report of ASOD*, 25.

Also demonstrating the inadequacy of the replacement police after the purges was the decrease in seizures of smuggled pharmaceuticals, antiquities, tobacco, and alcoholic beverages. The number of pharmaceuticals decreased 66.3 percent between 2013 and 2016.[15] Similarly, the number of suspects arrested in relation to antiquities trafficking decreased 43.5 percent in the same period.[16]

The purges also have paralyzed the capacity of Turkish police to suppress rampant and traditional smuggling activities in border provinces with neighboring Syria, Iraq, and Iran. For instance, the number of smuggling cases in four Turkish cities bordering Syria has confirmed the serious impact of the purges on crime control. As seen in Figure 7.4 below, the number of smuggling cases decreased 90.3 percent in Hatay, 72.6 percent in Gaziantep, 7 percent in Şanlıurfa, and 51.5 percent in Mardin between 2013 and 2016.[17]

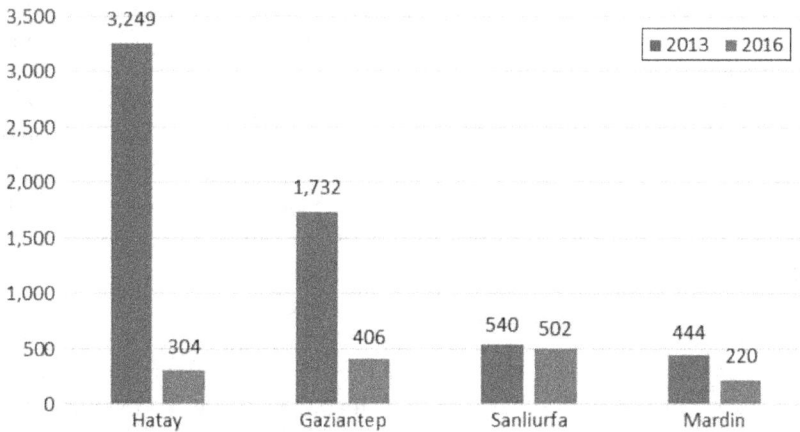

Figure 7.4 The comparison of smuggling cases in Turkish provinces bordering Syria. *Source: 2013 Turkish Report of ASOD, 80 and 2016 Turkish Report of ASOD, 42.*

In addition, it can be inferred that counter-smuggling activities in metropolitan centers such as Istanbul, Izmir, Ankara, Adana, and Antalya have been ineffective as witnessed by a 73.5 percent decrease in smuggling cases between 2013 and 2016.[18]

Drug Trafficking

The government crackdown on law enforcement and judiciary personnel has created vacuums in authority that drug traffickers easily exploit. The annual law enforcement report for 2014 illustrates the deleterious impact the government's campaign against its pre-purge police forces has had, which has hamstrung any campaigns to suppress drug trafficking and other crimes. In 2014, for example, seizures of cannabis declined by 49.5 percent compared to 2013, while captagon seizures declined by 94.5 percent, ecstasy by 53.6 percent, and acetic anhydride by 98.1 percent.[19] The seizure of heroin in high-volume cities such as in Van, Istanbul, and Hakkari was much lower between 2014 and 2016 compared with years before 2013. In Hakkari, one of the entry points for Iranian heroin, the police seized only 2.5 kg of heroin in the first three months of 2014 compared with around 500 kg during the same period in 2013.[20] The amount of heroin decreased 43.3 percent between 2013 and 2016.[21]

According to interviews by one of the authors,[22] the purges have destroyed the capacity of the police to fight drug trafficking. Some of the respondents' comments are paraphrased below:

- Turkey is on the verge of again being designated a heroin processing country because the police uncovered many heroin laboratories in the country in 2015, 2016, and 2017.[23]
- The police randomly made heroin seizures in large quantities in a few cases after the purges. Traffickers preferred transferring heroin in small amounts through Turkey before the purges because the police were skilled at conducting organized crime investigations and made frequent road checks. The police made road checks to search cars in each eastern province in 2013, enabling police to seize large quantities of heroin. Newly assigned police officials, however, repealed these former practices, allowing trafficking activities to continue unimpeded.[24]
- Methamphetamine laboratories mushroomed in Turkey. Iranian traffickers began to use Turkish routes more often than they did before the purges.[25]
- The crackdowns recklessly abolished an effective crime-fighting system established by the former police officers. In some provinces, newly assigned police chiefs were proud of purging not only entire drug units but also narcotics dogs.[26]
- Turkey lost its capacity to cooperate with other law enforcement agencies in the fight against drug trafficking. Controlled delivery investigations after the purges became rare. Newly assigned police officers lacked the skills needed to conduct international drug trafficking investigations, and European drug liaison officers complained about the current lack of cooperation.[27]
- Corruption has become a common issue again. The chiefs of the narcotics units in metropolitan cities have been bribed by traffickers.[28]
- The capacity of the police to focus on drug use decreased after the purges. Before the purges, officers were required to conduct at least one organized crime investigation of street dealers each year. The newly assigned police officers, however, care little about street dealers.[29]
- Police officers no longer focus their attention on drug trafficking because of the fear of being purged. Almost every month, the government exploits

the state of emergency and uses it as a tool to eliminate police officers who are not loyal to the government and to issue new lists of police officers who are subject to the purge. Police officers are fearful of being purged based on flimsy or fabricated evidence of disloyalty to the government.[30]

- The police have lost credibility in terms of drug investigations. The lack of a system to monitor police officers' actions creates opportunities for those officers who tend to traffic heroin.[31] After the purges, the number of police officers involved in drug trafficking increased. For example, two police officers and one prosecutor were arrested with 161 kg of cannabis and 13 kg of heroin in December 2014.[32] In 2015, one police officer was arrested after being seized driving a car loaded with 205 kg of cannabis.[33] In 2017, another police officer was arrested with 40 kg of heroin in Diyarbakir.[34]

Mafia-type Criminal Organizations

Turkey still hosts mafia-type criminal organizations based on kinship relations (see Chapter 1). They engage in traditional activities such as extortion, usury, robbery, and kidnapping by means of using force. Organized crime requires highly experienced investigators who know how to use wiretapping and surveillance techniques and capably deploy undercover agents. Decreases or increases in the number of investigations against mafia-type criminal organizations reflect the expertise of the investigators. Figure 7.5 implies that the ability of Turkish police investigators to combat organized crime has been paralyzed, with the number of investigations and suspects sharply decreasing after 2013.

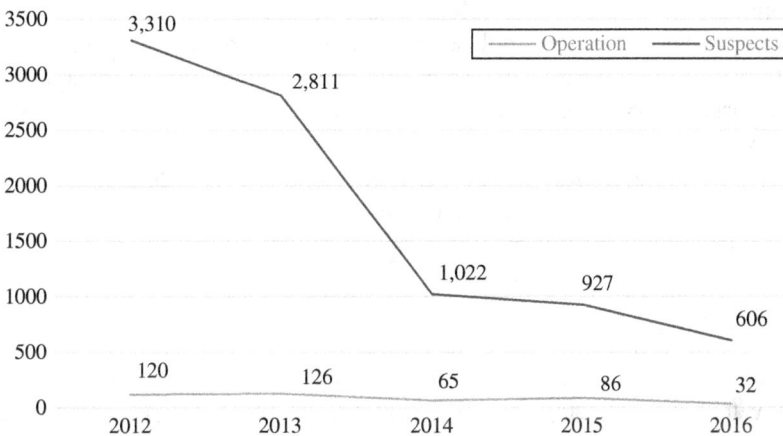

Figure 7.5 The number of cases and suspects in mafia-type criminal cases. *Source: Turkish Report of ASOD, 48.*

Confiscation of Crime Proceeds

It is vital for the police to confiscate criminal assets. This has proved the most effective strategy used against groups engaged in smuggling and trafficking. The purges of police investigators with expertise in confiscation strategies, however, have diminished the ability of the police to stop smuggling and trafficking operations. Whereas the number vehicles confiscated was 4,023 and properties was 618 in 2013, these dwindled to 871 vehicles and 0 property assets in 2016.[35]

International Crime Fighting Capacity

Over the years, Turkish police developed several policy models to improve its international crime-fighting capability. However, the police purges have dramatically impaired this capability. The purges had a similar effect on the experienced training officers at the Turkish International Academy against Drugs and Organized Crime (TADOC), which was established in 2000 with contributions from the United Nations and the United States in order to provide regional-level research and training programs for fighting transnational crime. The following statistics support these claims:

- The number of participants in training programs for fighting transnational crime decreased by 74 percent (1,471 participants in 2013[36] versus 386 participants in 2015), while the number of training programs held at the Turkish International Academy against Drugs and Organized Crime decreased by 59 percent (56 programs in 2013 versus 23 programs in 2015).[37]
- The number of times that Turkish police officers participated in international activities against smuggling and trafficking decreased by 41 percent, from 185 times in 2013[38] to 109 times in 2015.[39]
- The number of Turkish police officers who attended the meetings of international organizations responsible for fighting transnational crime decreased by 65 percent, with 192 attendees in 2013[40] and 68 attendees in 2015.[41]
- The number of controlled delivery operations against international drug trafficking groups decreased by 64 percent, with 25 operations in 2013[42] and 9 operations in 2014.[43]

Terrorist Financing

In recent years, organized crime fighting units have been reconfigured to deploy terrorist financing investigations against the perceived enemies of the state. There is enough evidence to suggest that these units are being exploited by the Erdoganist regime to repress opposition forces by means of demonizing them as terrorists. By doing this, the government has confiscated their assets by identifying these cases as terrorist financing investigations. The Financial Crimes Investigation Board recorded 14 terrorist financing cases in 2012, 6 cases in 2013, and in 2016 the number of cases grew to 6,265.[44] If these figures are correct, either there is a huge problem with the financing of terrorist groups, or these numbers suggest that the government has been busy targeting the assets of its perceived enemies, as illustrated above. Perhaps the best explanation is that the AKP government has used appropriation as one of the tactics of state terrorism to oppress its opponents.

Many statistics recorded after 2013 confirm that the December 17 and December 25 corruption investigations had a detrimental impact on the capacity of law enforcement to investigate and apprehend persons engaged in the country's illicit economy. The government's retaliation against the investigators involved (and even those not involved) in the two December investigations greatly diminished the capacity of the police.

NOTES

1. Louise Shelley, *Dirty Entanglements* (New York: Cambridge University Press, 2014), 5.

2. Jonathan White, *Terrorism and Homeland Security* (Independence, KY: Cengage Learning, 2017), 155.

3. "FDD's Alberto Nisman Award for Courage," *Foundation for Defense of Democracies*, accessed on October 26, 2018 from http://albertonisman.org/fdds-alber to-nisman-award-for-courage/. Although Turkish investigators, even their wives and children, were fired and put in the jails due to the Zarrab investigation, their efforts were recognized by their American collegues. During the award ceremony, FBI agent, Jennifer Mcreynolds, said, "We especially recognize the sacrifices of you, the innocent people in Turkey and Iran, who are persecuted for your struggles against oppression and corruption. What you and your families have endured, no one should have to, but even in the darkest hours you have courageously strived for truth and justice.Very much like Alberto Nisman."

4. "Kronoloji: Yolsuzluk ve rüşvet operasyonu." *Al Jazeera,* accessed on December 26, 2016, from http://www.aljazeera.com.tr/kronoloji/kronoloji-yolsuzluk-ve -rusvet-operasyonu.

5. "Efkan Ala Yolsuzlukları Örtmek İçin Polisleri Fizana Sürüyor." *YouTube,* accessed on December 26, 2016 from https://www.youtube.com/watch?v=yIRxIwV9 v00.

6. "Savcının 17 Aralık fikri 10 ayda değişti," *Gercek Gundem,* accessed on December 26, 2016 from http://www.gercekgundem.com/guncel/79662/savcinin-17-aralik-fikri-10-ayda-degisti.

7. "Savcı 17 Aralık'ı 'sıfırlamanın' ödülünü aldı: Sicili temizlendi," *Birgun,* accessed on December 26, 2016 from http://www.birgun.net/haber-detay/savci-17-aralik-i-sifirlamanin-odulunu-aldi-sicili-temizlendi-81818.html.

8. Reza Canikligil, "Reza Zarrab: Tahliye Icin Kismenn Rusvet Verdim," *Hurriyet,* accessed on April 6, 2018 from http://www.hurriyet.com.tr/dunya/reza-zarrab-tahliye-icin-kismen-rusvet-verdim-40667982.

9. Interviews with law enforcement officials and researchers, 2015-2016.

10. Toygun Atilla, "Bir Donemin Unlu Polis Seflerinin Esleri Gozaltina Alindi," *Hurriyet,* accessed on April 6, 2018, from http://www.hurriyet.com.tr/gundem/bir-donemin-unlu-polis-seflerinin-esleri-gozaltina-alindi-40640204.

11. "Corruption Perception Index 2017." *Transparency International,* accessed on April 5, 2018 from https://www.transparency.org/cpi2017/results.

12. *2013 Turkish Report of ASOD, 41.*

13. *2016 Turkish Report of ASOD, 5.*

14. *2016 Turkish Report of ASOD, 21.*

15. *2013 Turkish Report of ASOD, 61 and 2016 Turkish Report of ASOD 2016, 41.*

16. *2016 Turkish Report of ASOD, 39.*

17. *2013 Turkish Report of ASOD, 80 and 2016 Turkish Report of ASOD, 42.*

18. *2013 Turkish Report of ASOD, 80 and 2016 Turkish Report of ASOD, 42.*

19. Mahmut Cengiz, "Amped in Ankara: Drug Trade and Drug Policy in Turkey from the 1950s through Today," *Brookings Institution,* accessed on April 6, 2017, from https://www.brookings.edu/wp-content/uploads/2017/04/fp_201704_turkey_drug_policy.pdf, p. 12.

20. Mahmut Cengiz, "How the crackdown in Turkey created a permissive environment for drug trafficking." *Global Initiative,* accessed on April 6, 2016 from http://globalinitiative.net/how-the-crackdown-in-turkey-created-a-friendly-environment-for-drug-trafficking/

21. "2017 Turkish Drug Report," *Uyusuturucyla Mucadele Daire Baskanligi,* accessed on April 6, 2018, from (http://www.narkotik.pol.tr/TUBIM/Documents/TURKIYE%20UYUSTURUCU%20RAPORU%202017.pdf), and *2013 Turkish Report of ASOD,* 7.

22. This chapter used the same interviews described in Chapter 3.

23. DrLe2, DrLe3, DrLe5, Interview by Mahmut Cengiz, Personal Interview-Skype, July 29, 2017.

24. DrLe8, DrLe9, DrLe10, Interview by Mahmut Cengiz, Personal Interview-Skype, July 21, 2017.

25. DrLe1, DrLe4, DrLe6, Interview by Mahmut Cengiz, Personal Interview-Skype, July 25, 2017.

26. DrLe2, DrLe3, DrLe5, Interview by Mahmut Cengiz, Personal Interview-Skype, July 29, 2017.

27. DrLe6, DrLe12, DrLe13, Interview by Mahmut Cengiz, Personal Interview-Skype, July 27, 2017.

28. Interviews with law enforcement and customs officials, July-August, 2017.

29. DrLe1, DrLe4, DrLe6, Interview by Mahmut Cengiz, Personal Interview-Skype, July 25, 2017.

30. DrLe6, DrLe12, DrLe13, Interview by Mahmut Cengiz, Personal Interview-Skype, July 27, 2017.

31. DrLe2, DrLe3, DrLe5, Interview by Mahmut Cengiz, Personal Interview-Skype, July 29, 2017.

32. "Uyuşturucuyla yakalanan savcı ve polis tutuklandı," *Cumhuriyet*, accessed on December 30, 2017, from http://www.cumhuriyet.com.tr/haber/turkiye/167355/Uyusturucuyla_yakalanan_savci_ve_polis_tutuklandi.html

33. "Polis Memuru 205 Kilo Uyuşturucu ile Yakalandı," *Haberler,* accessed on December 12, 2017, from https://www.haberler.com/polis-memuru-205-kilo-uyusturucu-ile-yakalandi-6998024-haberi/

34. "Açığa alınan polis 40 kilogram eroinle yakalandı," YouTube, accessed on November 26, 2017, from https://www.youtube.com/watch?v=mxf7h22Mtgg

35. *2016 Turkish Report of ASOD, 57.*

36. *2013 Turkish Report of ASOD, 80.*

37. *2015 Turkish Report of ASOD, 75.*

38. *2013 Turkish Report of ASOD, 99.*

39. *2015 Turkish Report of ASOD, 82.*

40. *2013 Turkish Report of ASOD, 102.*

41. *2015 Turkish Report of ASOD, 85.*

42. *2013 Turkish Report of ASOD, 4.*

43. *2014 Turkish Report of ASOD, 27.*

44. *2012 MASAK Report, 28; 2013 MASAK Report, 32; and 2016 MASAK Report, 21.*

Chapter 8

Terrorists and the Illicit Economy

INTRODUCTION

Terrorist groups have engaged in a wide range of criminal activities to finance their operations. Early on, they focused primarily on extortion and robbery, eventually making the transformation into crime groups with operations in many areas of the illicit economy. The Revolutionary Armed Forces of Colombia (FARC), the Kurdistan Workers' Party (PKK), the Islamic State of Iraq and Syria (ISIS), Hezbollah, al Qaeda, and other terrorist groups generate vast amounts of money in the illicit economy.

Turkish terrorist groups such as the PKK are heavily involved in the illicit economy thanks to their strong linkages to diverse types of smuggling and trafficking networks that include cigarettes, drugs, humans, and arms. They are part of the global criminal network. In addition to being part of the illicit economy, terrorist groups in Turkey have undermined the country's economy. This chapter examines various types of terrorist groups in terms of how they are financed and their impact on the illicit economy in Turkey.

Terrorists in the Turkish Illicit Economy

It is widely accepted that terrorism not only imperils democratic institutions and undermines economies but also destabilizes regions.[1] In the economic realm, for example, terrorist groups provide funds for essentials such as food, lodging, transportation, and even materials used to make bombs. These groups also raise funds for terrorist operations, terrorism training, and propaganda. Funding sources include a wide array of illicit trafficking and smuggling activities.[2]

Links between terrorist and crime groups have evolved over several decades as both groups continued to develop in response to changes in geopolitics. Terrorist attacks in France and Belgium in 2016 revealed that terrorists with criminal backgrounds committed the attacks.[3] Terrorist organizations are essentially criminal organizations. While the actors in both are distinctive from one another, in the modern era they are both in the business of raising money, both illicitly and legitimately. Both raise money, transfer and store their assets. At the same time, they continually adopt new operational strategies and methods for avoiding detection.[4]

Since the 1960s Turkey has been challenged by a variety of terrorist organizations, including those categorized as revolutionary/left-wing, right-wing, religious/salafi-jihadist, and ethnic separatists. Starting in the 1990s, Turkey saw the rise of terrorist organizations sponsored by the Iranian Quds Force. Although Turkey has waged a strong fight against these organizations, the country has failed to eradicate terrorist groups within its borders. By some accounts the lack of success can be attributed to the failure of the Turkish government to suppress terrorist involvement in the illicit economy. That involvement dates back to the 1980s, when terrorist groups in Turkey turned to robbery, theft, and extortion to support their illegal activities. Funding sources, however, have evolved over time. Today, terrorist groups in Turkey finance their operations through various types of transnational smuggling and trafficking.

Revolutionary/Left-wing Terrorist Organizations

Terrorist groups based on the Marxist-Maoist ideology in Turkey emerged in the same period when the world witnessed the left-wing organizations in the 1960s and 1970s. This period of upheaval was part of a global movement against the Vietnam War, colonialism, and growing Western imperialism. Quixotically, some of these organizations attempted to seize power from legitimate states, hoping to spur political and social change.[5] Some of the left-wing terrorist groups that have operated in Turkey include the Maoist Communist Party (MKP), the Workers and Peasants Salvation Army (TIKKO), the Revolutionary People's Liberation Party Front (DHKP-C), and the Marxist-Leninist Communist Party (MLKP). Revolutionary groups such as FARC and the Shining Path successfully funded their activities through taxation, kidnapping, robbery, and drug trafficking. Likewise, their Turkish left-wing counterparts were funded similarly, before turning to more lucrative drug trafficking later on. Two cases recorded in 2007[6] and in 2011,[7] revealed that some militants of the DHKP-C were arrested because of their linkage to extortion.

Other financial sources for Turkish left-wing terrorist organizations involved theft (automobiles and goods), robbery (banks and jewelry), ransom demands, and the collection of so-called taxes. These groups rose to prominence in Turkey through their public criminal activities. For example, bank robberies financed the Turkey People's Liberation Party Front (TPLP/C) and the People's Liberation Army of Turkey (THKO), alerting the public that terrorist groups existed in Turkey.[8]

To expand their funding sources, left-wing terrorist organizations have engaged in arms and drug trafficking. In 1990, for example, the TIKKO militants smuggled heroin into Europe. One of the militants arrested in the operation verified the flow of a significant amount of the heroin income to the TIKKO. In addition, police seizures in Europe have linked arms and drug trafficking to financial support for the DHKP-C. European police, for example, seized 350 kg of heroin in a case linked to high-level militants of the DHKP-C.[9]

Religious Terrorist Groups

Kurdish Hezbollah and Al-Qaeda are among the most prominent religious terrorist organizations operating in Turkey. Kurdish Hezbollah emerged in the eastern portion of the country in the 1980s. It is distinct from the Lebanese Shi'ite group of the same name. The Kurdish incarnation's primary aim was to counter the PKK. Some speculated that this organization was clandestinely supported by the Turkish government. In the 1990s, Kurdish Hezbollah underwent a transformation and began to target businesses and other establishments that were deemed to be non-Islamic. Hezbollah kidnapped Muslim businesspersons who did not support its ideology. In the early 2000s, Hezbollah morphed into Turkish al Qaeda. Some of Hezbollah members who were trained in Pakistan returned to Turkey, having linkages with al Qaeda. One of them was Habib Aktas, who was following directives from Osama bin Laden. Aktas plotted the bombing of two synagogues and the British consulate in Istanbul in 2003 and 2004.[10]

Both of the former groups are similar to leftist terrorist groups in terms of financing and activities.[11] After the Syrian conflict began, ISIS and Al Nusra Front were added to this category because of their activities in Turkey (see Chapter 9). Revenue sources for ISIS include antiquities trafficking, oil smuggling, and trafficking of Yezidi women. Investigations into these activities in Turkey have significantly dropped off in recent years.[12] ISIS militants in Turkey have openly collected money for their terrorist activities.[13] Al Nusra Front is active in some regions of Turkey and along the Syrian border. The group's revenue source is a so-called GST (goods and services) customs tax on oil smugglers in the amount of 500 Syrian lira per container.[14]

The Kurdish Hezbollah has financed its activities mainly through extortion and smuggling. The organization exploited religious values to collect money in the form of zakat (under Islamic law, a tax levied as a percentage of personal income to help the poor) in large quantities in the southeastern region of Turkey in the 1990s. The organization also generated income by selling the skins of sacrificed animals during the Eid al-Fitr and Eid al-Adha religious holidays. Investigations conducted in Diyarbakir, Batman, Mardin, and Bingol provinces revealed much of its financing activities.[15] Moreover, donations collected voluntarily by the militants and their sympathizers have provided another financial source for the Kurdish Hezbollah. Each militant, depending on his economic situation, is required to pay monthly dues and a fee to join the organization. Sympathizers are required to make a donation of at least 10 percent of their monthly salary to the Kurdish Hezbollah.[16]

Additionally, Turkish Hezbollah has earned substantial profits from ciga-rette trafficking. Police seizures of illicit cigarettes have confirmed the active involvement of Hezbollah in cigarette trafficking. Members have been linked to the trafficking of cigarettes from Iraq and Syria and selling them in Turk-ish cities.[17] In a 2008 case, Kurdish Hezbollah militants engaged in cigarette trafficking in the Konya province of Turkey.[18]

Separatist Terrorist Organizations

The PKK, an ethnic terrorist organization in Turkey, has occupied a spe-cial place in terms of the devastating consequences of its activities. It has destroyed public facilities and killed more than 35,000 civilians and military personnel.[19] The organization has developed chameleon-like characteristics, using the languages of Marxism, nationalism, and religion since the 1990s.[20] The PKK is more prominent than any other Turkish group in terms of its activities linked to the illicit economy. It has transformed from a terrorist organization to hybrid organization that deals with crime and terrorism.[21]

The continued presence of the PKK in Turkey, despite the government's intense fight against it, results largely from its significant financial resources, including money collected from its militants and the organization's sympa-thizers, extortion, fraud, ongoing trafficking and smuggling along Turkey's eastern and southeastern borders, and involvement in transnational smuggling and trafficking.

In the early years of the PKK, the organization's main financial sources were donations and extortion.[22] In the 1990s, for example, the PKK collected 2.5 million pounds each year, mostly from Kurdish people living in the United Kingdom.[23] Investigations in Belgium and Germany revealed that extortion of enormous sums and the drug trade remain a fundamental financial source for the PKK.[24] Regular payments and donations remain important sources of income for the PKK. The scope of that income has expanded to include PKK sympathizers in Turkey and Europe who make periodic payments and donations to the PKK in the name of relief campaigns. It is estimated that huge amounts of money from these sources go to the PKK. In a fundraising campaign conducted in the 1990s, for example, the PKK announced that almost $2 million was collected from the organization's sympathizers.[25]

The PKK became actively involved in smuggling operations to bring goods and even people from Syria, Iran, and Iraq into Turkey. For example, the organization has taxed human smugglers, drug traffickers, and oil smugglers at border crossings, such as the eight so-called customs points set up by the PKK on the Iranian side of the Turkish border. When smugglers attempt to cross the border, the PKK exacts taxes from the smugglers before permission to cross is granted. The amount of tax required varies. For example, the PKK demands $3 per horse or mule from tobacco smugglers, $800 to $1,000 per person smuggled into Turkey, and $10,000 per person smuggled into Europe.[26]

The involvement of the PKK in illegal immigrant activities is well-documented.[27] A significant amount of the PKK's revenue comes from global human smuggling and trafficking activities. For example, the PKK is part of human-smuggling networks and receives tribute from migrants in areas controlled by the PKK.[28] The PKK also uses these transnational crime networks to smuggle immigrants into Western European countries through Romania.[29] In addition, the PKK plays an active role in smuggling people from Middle Eastern countries into Western Europe. That role has included preparing false documents and providing logistical support for Kurdish refugees who want to migrate to European countries.[30]

Global terrorist organizations, such as the PKK, tend to generate income through the forgery of official documents and several types of fraud (banking transactions, credit cards, identity cards, and passports).[31] The PKK specializes in identity-card and passport forgery and official documents needed for human smuggling.[32] In a 2006 case, the police arrested 38 human smugglers affiliated with the PKK and seized fake materials used to prepare counterfeit passports and travel documents. The smugglers received $10,000 from each immigrant.[33] According to Interpol estimates, the PKK makes around 2,000 and 3,000 euros for each individual.[34] Furthermore, the ongoing conflict in Syria has presented opportunities for the PKK to transfer refugees. The PKK is one of the main crime organizations responsible for organizing the smuggling of these refugees, earning a hefty sum of money in the process. As of 2015, the PKK had smuggled around 100,000 Syrians, earning an estimated $300 million for doing so.[35]

Cigarette smuggling is another revenue source for the PKK.[36] One case study showed that the PKK earned a substantial amount of revenue from two cigarette factories opened illegally in northern Iraq. The organization received taxes from these factories and became involved in the trafficking of the cigarettes. Moreover, the PKK became one of the links in the chains of cigarette-trafficking networks that originated in Puerto Rico.[37] In Turkey, the PKK is one of the beneficiaries of cigarette smuggling.[38] The organization benefits from the cross-border trade in counterfeit cigarettes as well as other commodities along the Turkish borders with Iraq, Iran, and Syria, facilitated by kinship ties among Kurds living in these areas.[39] The PKK taxes Kurdish smugglers $100 per mule, each capable of carrying up to 3,000 packages of cigarettes. On average in 2015, the PKK earned $500 million from taxes paid by cigarette smugglers.[40] The tax loss to the government totaled 520 million Turkish lira. With 80 percent of the cigarettes in Turkey coming from the country's eastern and southeastern borders where PKK militants are dominant, the magnitude of the PKK's revenue stream becomes clear.[41]

To make the illicit income appear to be legal, the PKK launders its revenue. A joint investigation by Scotland Yard and the Belgium police exposed the money-laundering capacity of the PKK. A 1996 investigation dubbed Sputnik, led authorities to Luxembourg and Germany, where the focus shifted to laundering allegations involving MED TV, an international Kurdish satellite television station financed by the PKK. At the end of the investigation, the police confiscated almost $11 million from MED TV bank accounts and determined that the money belonged to the PKK who laundered the money using 15 companies to deposit funds into the MED TV accounts. In another operation conducted in 2002, the police determined that a company connected to the PKK prepared false documents and laundered money for the terrorist organization. Early in the investigation, the police determined that revenues obtained from sympathizers or militants were being transferred to the PKK.[42]

PKK and Drug Trafficking

Given its geographical location, Turkey is a prime route for global drug trafficking. A significant part of that route is under the control of the PKK and other terrorist organizations.[43] According to the estimations, 80 percent of the drugs produced in the Golden Crescent—the region including Afghanistan, Pakistan, and Iran—are trafficked using the route crossing over Turkey, and the PKK plays a critical role in transferring these materials in Turkey.[44] In response to the PKK's involvement in global drug trafficking, the United States in 2008 added the PKK to the list of significant foreign narcotics traffickers subject to the provisions of the Foreign Narcotics Kingpin Designation Act (Kingpin Act).[45] The PKK's involvement in drug trafficking has a long and lucrative history, dating back to the 1980s. By the 1990s, the PKK was collecting around $300 million annually from drug trafficking.[46] Between 1984 and 2012, Turkish police seized the contraband from the PKK in the course of 377 drug-trafficking cases. A total of 1,232 traffickers were arrested in these cases as well. The seized drugs included 4.584 kg of heroin, 36.5 tons of cannabis, around 6 million cannabis plants, 4.305 kg of morphine base, 27.630 liters of acetic anhydrite, 22 kg of opium gum, 710 kg of cocaine, and around 350,000 tablets of synthetic drugs.[47] In 2016, the police estimated that the PKK earned 1.5 billion dollars yearly from drug trade.[48]

The PKK is involved in many sectors of the drug trade such as illicit drug trafficking, production, street dealings, and extortion of commissions.[49] Police seizures in Turkey have shown that the PKK is active in every stage of drug trafficking, that the organization receives taxes from drug traffickers, and that it controls the cannabis fields in the southeastern region of Turkey. Furthermore, the PKK is active in the distribution of drugs in European countries.[50] For example, French police estimated in the early 2000s that 65 to 70 percent of the heroin market is under the control of Turkish criminal groups; around half of this percentage is controlled by the PKK.[51]

Another important source of income for the PKK are taxes received from the traffickers. Taxation was common in the 1980s, and the PKK stipulated that traffickers share 10 percent of their income with the terrorist organization. In the 2000s, the amount of money that a trafficker was required to pay to the PKK for permission to cross the Turkish border was based on the number of kilograms of drugs being transported. Traffickers in drug cases connected to the PKK have said that the PKK controls borderlands on the Iranian side of the Turkish border, making it impossible to cross the border without paying a tax to the PKK. Traffickers who refused to pay the PKK-mandated tax were denied passage unless they were connected to the terrorist organization.[52]

Police operations between 2011 and 2014 in southeastern Turkey uncovered an additional revenue source for the PKK—income derived from the cultivation of cannabis plantations. According to police findings, the PKK controlled the cultivation of cannabis in rural areas of Bingol and Diyarbakir provinces and organized the making of marijuana from the dried flowers and leaves of the cannabis plants. The PKK then sold the drugs in metropolitan areas of Turkey. According to a law enforcement officer who had worked for many years in the Diyarbakir drug-trafficking unit:

The cultivation of the cannabis mushroomed around rural areas of Diyarbakir after the truce started in 1999. When the truce ended in 2004, it has become very common to cultivate in a wider area of southeastern of Turkey, controlled heavily by the PKK that stipulated farmers to pay taxes. The only way to cultivate cannabis is to make payment to the PKK. Currently, there is a cultivation of cannabis in at least 80 villages in Diyarbakir, which is the main income of farmers. When the police conducted a series of operations over these cannabis fields in 2011, the farmers rebelled to protest the police, indicating that cannabis cultivation was perceived like an occupation by the farmers [see Chapter 2]. The police seized around two tons of marijuana in 2001, followed by four tons in 2012. Seizing marijuana culminated in 2013, and the amount was 89 tons. Currently, there is an ongoing cultivation of cannabis in a wider area of southeastern Turkey, which five thousand acres of this land is controlled by the PKK, being a yearly $500 million revenue for the terrorist organization.[53]

According to a recent Turkish Drug Report, police recorded another case in 2016 that indicated the linkage between the PKK and cannabis cultivation. In this operation, police seized cannabis, ammonium nitrates, weapons, and stolen vehicles from the PKK.[54] Police cases substantiate the ongoing link of the PKK to drug trafficking. In a 2010 case, Diyarbakir police found 65 kg of marijuana and 64 kg of explosives in the oil tank of a truck, arresting three suspects linked to the PKK. Also, in Diyarbakir province in 2010, police seized 25 kg marijuana from a trafficker who was also a PKK militant. The police learned that the trafficker specialized in making bombs and detonating them in large cities for the PKK. A third case occurred in Kayseri province, which is located along one of the alternative routes used by drug traffickers in Turkey. Here the police seized 450 kg marijuana from a PKK-affiliated trafficker. A fourth case in 2012 verified the PKK's connection with cannabis fields in Turkey. The police arrested nine traffickers in possession of 500,000 cannabis plants, 4 tons of marijuana, and two weapons. Two of the nine traffickers were detected and indicated that they were taxed monthly by the PKK. A fifth case reaffirmed the link between the PKK and drug trafficking. Here the police seized 5 tons of marijuana that belonged to the PKK in Van province.[55]

Iranian-Sponsored Salam Tawhid Quds Force

For decades, Iran has been and continues to be the most prominent state sponsor of terrorism.[56] The Islamic Revolutionary Guard Corps (IRGC), which was established in 1979 to consolidate the Islamic Revolution and fight the country's enemies after the autocratic monarchy of Mohammed Reza Shah Pahlavi was overthrown, takes the leading role in Iranian terrorist activities.[57] It now provides training, arms, and financial support to terrorist organizations.[58] Iran has spent billions of dollars in its terrorist funding efforts around the world, including $200 million per year for Hezbollah, 26 million USD for Shiite militias in Iraq and Syria, 15 billion USD for Assad's forces in Syria, and 20 million USD for Houthi militias in Yemen.[59]

Terrorism has been a defining feature of the IRGC since its inception. The 125,000-member force has been used to repress dissent and perform assassinations of high-profile targets such as an American ambassador.[60] A special branch of the IRGC, the Quds Force (QF), is in charge of exporting the revolution abroad by training, financing, and sponsoring terrorist groups such as al-Qaeda, the Taliban, Hezbollah, Hamas, and several Shi'a militants in Iraq.[61] Salam Tawhid Quds Force (STQF) is the QF's Turkish branch.

Its terrorist activities in Turkey cover two periods: 1990 through 2000 and 2011 to the present. The first period was marked by violence, the assassination of secular academics and journalists (e.g., Ugur Mumcu, Bahriye Ucok, Muammer Aksoy, and Ahmet Taner Kislali), and increased Iranian influence over the Turkish government.[62] Court documents from 2000 illustrate that the goal of the STQF is to establish a new regime similar to the Shia-based one in Iran, by creating sectarian divisions within Turkey.[63] The STQF is controlled by Iran, and its members frequently visited Iran to receive political and military training. They also were provided with weapons and deployed for attacks against citizens of the United States, Israel, Iraq, and the United Kingdom.[64]

A new period of STQF activity in Turkey came to light in 2011 when an informant for the Turkish government complained about her husband being linked to Iranian intelligence officials. The informant said that her husband was spying on Iran and that he had organized activities aimed at spreading the influence of Shiism in Turkey. The husband had a prior conviction for anti-secular activities and was a member of an Iranian group responsible for carrying clandestine activities such as photographing a Turkish nuclear research center and producing satellite images of the U.S. Consulate in Istanbul. The husband also was linked to Iran's head of intelligence.[65] The informant's statement prompted the prosecutor in Istanbul to launch an investigation in 2011.[66] Investigators learned that the Iranian general, Mir Vekili, in charge of QF activities in Turkey was linked to the founder of the Turkish STQF.[67]

Further investigation revealed that the goal of the STQF was to spark an Iranian-like revolution in Turkey. The group operated in clandestine cells and used code names during phone conversations.[68] For example, one of the group's members who met with the general in charge of the STQF in Turkey changed buses and bus stops eight times to spy and provide the general with a clandestine file. Police video recorded the meeting.[69]

In another instance, Turkish STQF members attempted to observe and prepare reports on the U.S. Consulate and the Nuclear Research Center in Istanbul.[70] The government's reaction was to cover up the investigation of the Turkish STQF despite an abundance of solid evidence against the group. The investigation leaked unlawfully, and the government attempted to tamper with the facts and evidence obtained during the investigation. For example, pro-government news outlets reported that Gulenist police officers (i.e., followers of US-based cleric Fethullah Gulen) had wiretapped 7,000 people, including politicians, businessmen, and celebrities. The police, however, actually had only wiretapped 241 suspects. Erdogan and previous Minister of Justice Bekir Bozdag issued explanations that undermined the evidence and blamed the police officers involved in the investigation.[71] In a backhanded swipe at the police, Bozdag commented that three people came together and saluted each other saying, *"selamun aleykum* (peace be upon you)," after which the police filed papers to designate the trio as a crime organization.[72]

The IRGC controls between 25 and 40 percent of the Iranian economy today, a stark increase from the 5 percent it controlled in 1989.[73] Iran's Supreme Leader, Ali Khamenei, issued an executive order in 2005 to transfer 80 percent of Iranian economic enterprises to the control of the supreme leader and the IRGC.[74] Since then, any business dealings with Iran mean doing business with the IRGC and the country's supreme leader.[75] The IRGC is heavily involved in legal and illegal sectors of the economy, ranging from high-technology, social housing projects, and chain stores to telecommunications and oil and gas.[76] In the illegal arena, the IRGC is active in the Iranian underground economy. The organization engages in low-level smuggling of alcohol and other contraband as well as high-level smuggling of oil. The IRGC's smuggling activities generate an estimated $12 billion each year.[77]

The financing of STQF was provided by the IRGC. Turkish investigators discovered that members of the Turkish STQF used a hawala money-laundering system (i.e., an alternative remittance system, or informal banking arrangement that bypasses traditional financial institutions) to finance the group's activities. Investigators found that some exchange offices in Istanbul were linked to Iranian exchange offices in order to transfer the laundered money. If the Turkish government had not interfered with the investigation, the trail may well have led to the discovery of sources of money for the STQF in Turkey.

NOTES

1. Charles Tilly "Terror, Terrorism, Terrorists", *Sociological Theory*, Vol. 22, No. 1, Theories of Terrorism: A Symposium (Mar., 2004): 5-13.

2. Anne L. Clunan "The Fight against Terrorist Financing", *Political Science Quarterly*, Vol. 121, No. 4 (Winter, 2006/2007): 569-596.

3. Louise Shelley "Following the Money: Examining Current Terrorist Financing Trends and the Threat to the Homeland", *Homeland Security's Subcommittee on Counterterrorism and Intelligence*, May 12, 2016.

4. Marcy M. Forman, "Combating terrorist financing and other financial crimes through private sector partnerships", *Journal of Money Laundering Control*, Vol. 9, Issue 1, (2006): 112-118.

5. Jonathan White, *Terrorism and Homeland Security* (Independence, KY: Cengage Learning, 2017), 225.

6. "DHKP/C'li 10 kişi yakalandı", *Hurriyet,* accessed on March 7, 2017, from http://www.hurriyet.com.tr/dhkp-cli-10-kisi-yakalandi-6347357.

7. "DHKP-C Beyoğlu'nu haraca bağlamış", *Aksam,* accessed on March 7, 2017, from http://www.aksam.com.tr/guncel/dhkp-c-beyoglunu-haraca-baglamis--40226h/haber-40226.

8. Mahmut Cengiz, *Turkiye'de Organize Suc Gercegi ve Terorun Finansmani,* (Ankara, Seckin Yayincilik), 168.

9. Mahmut Cengiz, "Terörün Para Kaynağı Olarak Organize Suç", in *Terörizm Paradoksu ve Türkiye,* ed. S.Özeren and M. Sever, (Istanbul: Karinca Yayinevi, 2011): 235-260.

10. White, *Terrorism and Homeland Security,* 155-156.

11. Cengiz, *Turkiye'de Organize Suc Gercegi ve Terorun Finansmani,* 169.

12. "Türkiye kendi IŞİD'ini nasıl yarattı: Kent kent IŞİD hücreleri", *Birgun,* accessed on March 10, 2017, from http://www.birgun.net/haber-detay/turkiye-kendi-isid-ini-nasil-yaratti-kent-kent-isid-hucreleri-125232.html.

13. "IŞİD Türkiye'de posta numarası vererek açık açık para ve eleman topluyor", *ABC Gazetesi,* accessed on March 10, 2017, from http://www.abcgazetesi.com/isid-turkiyede-posta-numarasi-vererek-acik-acik-para-ve-eleman-topluyor-20289h.htm.

14. "Haraç El-Nusra'ya" *Cumhuriyet,* accessed on March 10, 2017, from http://www.cumhuriyet.com.tr/haber/diger/438796/Harac_El-Nusra_ya_.html.

15. Cengiz, *Turkiye'de Organize Suc Gercegi ve Terorun Finansmani,* 169.

16. Ibid., 169.

17. Sharon Melzer "Counterfeit and Contraband Cigarette Smuggling: Opportunities, Actors, and Guardianship". Unpublished Dissertation thesis submitted to American University, 2010.

18. "Hizbullah sigara kaçakçısı oldu", *Gazete Vatan,* accessed on March 1, 2017, from http://www.gazetevatan.com/hizbullah-sigara-kacakcisi-oldu-155270-gundem/.

19. Tuncay Durna, "Restoring Trust between the Public and the Police: Implementing Democratic Policing in Turkey's Terrorism Torn Areas." in *Combating Terrorism,* eds. Samih Teymur, H. Ozdemir, O. Basibuyuk, M. Ozer & M. Gunbeyi (Eds.), (Washington, DC: TISD Press, 2007): 11-23.

20. White, *Terrorism and Homeland Security,* 156.

21. Mitchel P. Roth, *Global Organized Crime* (New York: Routledge, 2017), 346.

22. Mitchel P. Roth and Murat Sever "The Kurdish Workers Party PKK as Criminal Syndicate: Funding Terrorism through Organized Crime: A Case Study". *Studies in Conflict and Terrorism,* 30, (2007): 901-920.

23. N.B. Criss "The Nature of PKK Terrorism in Turkey". *Studies in Conflict and Terrorism,* 18, (1995): 17–37.

24. Louise Shelley, *Dirty Entanglements* (London: Cambridge University Press, 2014), 137.

25. Cengiz, "Terörün Para Kaynağı Olarak Organize Suç."

26. UTSAM "Terörün Ekonomisi: Sınır İllerinde Kaçakçılık ve Terörün Finansmanı Raporu." (Polis Akademisi Yayınları, 2009).

27. Roth, *Global Organized Crime,* 347.

28. S. Janssens and J. Arsovska "People Carriers: Human Trafficking Networks Thrive in Turkey", *Jane's Intelligence Review,* 2008.

29. M. Gheordunescu, "Terrorism and Organized Crime: The Romanian Perspective". In M. Taylor and J. Morgan (Eds.). *The Future of Terrorism,* (London: Frank Cass Publishers, 2000).

30. S. E. Cornell, "The Interaction of Drug Smuggling, Human Trafficking, and Terrorism". In A. Jonsson (Ed.). *Human Trafficking and Human Security.* (New York: Routledge, 2009): 48-66.

31. F.S. Perri and R.G. Brody, "The Dark Triad: Organized Crime, Terror & Fraud." *Journal of Money Laundering Control,* 14, 1, (2011), pp. 44 – 59.

32. Cengiz, *Turkiye'de Organize Suc Gercegi ve Terorun Finansmani,* 171.

33. "İstanbul'da insan kaçakçılığı operasyonu", *CNN Turk,* http://www.cnnturk.com/video/turkiye/istanbulda-insan-kacakciligi-operasyonu, accessed on March 1, 2017.

34. Roth, *Global Organized Crime,* 347.

35. "PKK, göçmenlerin yılda 300 milyon $'ını çalıyor!", *Sabah Gazetesi,* http://www.sabah.com.tr/gundem/2015/09/05/pkk-gocmenlerin-yilda-300-milyon-inicaliyor, accessed on March 1, 2017.

36. Roth, *Global Organized Crime,* 347.

37. Sharon Melzer and Louise Shelley. "Nexus of Organized Crime and Terrorism: Two Case Studies in Cigarette Smuggling". *International Journal of Comparative and Applied Criminal Justice,* 32, 1, (2008 Spring), pp. 43-63.

38. "PKK'nın en büyük gelir kaynağı kaçak sigara", *Haber Turk,* (September 26, 2015), from http://www.haberturk.com/gundem/haber/1132720-pkknin-en-buyuk-gelir-kaynagi-kacak-sigara, accessed on March 1, 2017.

39. Shelley, *Dirty Entanglements,* 275.

40. "PKK'nın kaçak sigara gelirine ağır darbe!", *Yeni Cag,* (May 11, 2015) http://www.yenicaggazetesi.com.tr/pkknin-kacak-sigara-gelirine-agir-darbe-114113h.htm, accessed on March 1, 2017.

41. *2014 Turkish Report of Anti-Smuggling and Organized Crime* (Ankara: KOM Daire Baskanligi), 53.

42. Roth and Sever, "The Kurdish Workers Party," 901-920.

43. *2012 Turkish Report of Anti-Smuggling and Organized Crime* (Ankara: KOM Daire Baskanligi), 82.

44. Roth, *Global Organized Crime,* 346.

45. "Treasury Sanctions Supporters of the Kurdistan Workers Party (PKK) Tied to Drug Trafficking in Europe", US Department of the Treasury, accessed on March 7, 2017 from https://www.treasury.gov/press-center/press-releases/Pages/tg1406.aspx

46. Mark Galeotti, (1998 Spring). "Turkish Organized Crime: Where State, Crime, and Rebellion Conspire." *Transnational Organized Crime,* 4, 1, pp. 25-42.

47. *2013 Turkish Report of ASOD,* 4.

48. *2017 Turkish Drug Report,* 22.

49. Yvon Dandurand and Vivienne Chin, "Links between Terrorism and Other Forms of Crime." *International Centre for Criminal Law Reform and Criminal*

Justice Policy, December 2004, accessed on April 9, 2018 from https://icclr.law.ubc.ca/wp-content/uploads/2017/06/LinksBetweenTerrorismLatest_updated.pdf.

50. *2012 Turkish Report of ASOD,* 82.

51. Mahmut Cengiz, *Turkish Organized Crime from Local to Global,* (VDM Publishing, 2011), 79.

52. *2012 Turkish Report of ASOD,* 83.

53. Cengiz, *Turkiye'de Organize Suc Gercegi ve Terorun Finansmani,* 174.

54. *2017 Turkish Drug Report,* 22.

55. *2012 Turkish Report of ASOD,* 83 and 84.

56. "State Sponsors: Iran" *Council on Foreign Relations,* (October 13, 2011), http://www.cfr.org/iran/state-sponsors-iran/p9362, accessed on March 3, 2017.

57. Emmanuel Ottolenghi, *The Pasdaran Inside Iran's Islamic Revolutionary Guard Corpses* (Washington DC: FDD Press, 2011), iii.

58. Ibid., 12.

59. National Council of Resistance of Iran, *The Rise of the Revolutionary Guards' Financial Empire,* (Washington DC, National Council of Resistance of Iran, 2017), 148.

60. Mark Dubowitz, "Labeling Iran's Revolutionary Guard", *Foundation for Defense of Democracies,* (March 6, 2017), http://www.defenddemocracy.org/media-hit/dubowitz-mark-labeling-irans-revolutionary-guard/, accessed on March 6, 2017.

61. Ottolenghi, *The Pasdaran Inside Iran's Islamic Revolutionary Guard Corpses,* p. iii.

62. Emre Ercis, *Kara Kutu Selam Tevhid Kudus Ordusu* (Istanbul: Istiklal Matbaacilik, 2015), 37.

63. Ibid., 23.

64. Ibid., 25.

65. Ibid., 46-53.

66. Ibid., 14.

67. Ibid., 94.

68. Ibid., 15-16.

69. Ibid., 70-71.

70. Ibid., 66-67.

71. Ibid., 56.

72. Ibid., 22.

73. Ottolenghi, *The Pasdaran Inside Iran's Islamic Revolutionary Guard Corpses,* p. 43.

74. National Council of Resistance of Iran, *The Rise of the Revolutionary Guards' Financial Empire,* 7.

75. Ibid., 11.

76. Ali Alfoneh, *Iran Unveiled How the Revolutionary Guards is Turning Theocracy into Military Dictatorship* (Washington DC, The AEI Press, 2013), 165.

77. Ibid., 190.

Chapter 9

The Syrian Crisis and the Illicit Economy

Refugees and Terrorists (ISIS and Al Qaeda-Affiliates)

INTRODUCTION

The Arab Spring had several unintended consequences for a handful of Arab countries. Some countries have struggled to fight corruption and newly emergent terrorist groups, while others have turned into conflict regions. Perhaps none of these countries has been more affected than Syria. When demonstrations began in 2011, few expected such a long intractable conflict would follow.[1]

A security vacuum in Syria has led to the development and expansion of new Salafi-jihadist terrorist networks.[2] The Islamic State in Iraq and Syria (ISIS), a splinter organization of al Qaeda, first emerged in Iraq, subsequently proclaiming its independence in both Iraqi and Syrian territories.[3] ISIS's expansion efforts have waxed and waned over the past several years, but has continued to metastasize worldwide by giving rise to several franchises that have spread its ideology to other countries.[4] The purported demise of ISIS has resurrected al Qaeda affiliates in Syria.[5]

Turkey is among countries facing the increasing influence of ISIS ideology.[6] Moreover, the country has been exposed to the dire consequences of ISIS terror, as its members cross back and forth unimpeded across Turkish borders as they wage jihad in Syria. Meanwhile, the Turkish government has been charged with sending cash and weapons to ISIS,[7] as well as to other Salafist terrorist groups such as Jabhat al Nusra (JN) and Ahrar al-Sham affiliated with al Qaeda. The number of Turkish militants joining these terrorist groups has continued to increase.

The Turkish economy has been affected by the Syrian crisis in two ways. Besides hosting over three million Syrian refugees who contribute to a burgeoning underground economy, Turkey has been plagued by a growing number of trafficking, counterfeiting, and smuggling cases linked to Syrian criminal actors and ISIS. The quantitative data used in this chapter include smuggling, counterfeiting, and trafficking cases from five Turkish cities (Hatay, Gaziantep, Kilis, Şanlıurfa, Mardin) bordering Syria[8] before and after the Syrian crisis that started in 2011. The qualitative data were obtained in two rounds of research using ethnographic topical interviews.[9]

Syrian Refugees in the Illicit Economy

Similar to the impact of the Iraqi conflict on Turkey,[10] the Syrian crisis has also invigorated a growing illicit economy, helped along by the immigration of over three million Syrian refugees. The conflict has generated 7.6 million internally displaced Syrians.[11] As of October 2018, the number of Syrian refugees in different countries approached over 5.6 million people. Turkey is a leading destination country, hosting almost 3.6 million refugees, followed by Lebanon, Jordan, Iraq, and Egypt.[12] Ongoing conflicts in Syria have continued to displace Syrians or force them to immigrate to foreign countries.

Turkey has maintained its open-door-policy for Syrians, in stark contrast to the restrictions imposed by Lebanon and Jordan. According to the Turkish sources, the government has spent almost 6 billion USD settling these refugees, even though there is little clarity on how this money was spent.[13] Turkey has received modest support from other countries in coping with this burden, including 300 million USD from countries and 650 million USD from NGOs.[14] Only 10 percent of Syrian refugees in Turkey are accommodated in government-run camps, with the rest mostly dispersed in cities neighboring Syria (as well as other cities across the country).[15] Turkey has encountered increasing challenges stemming from Syrian refugees.

Currently, a considerable number of Syrians in Turkey have not been screened and registered. It is most likely that among them are Syrian criminals and terrorists.[16] Increasingly, Syrians in Turkey have become involved in crimes.[17] According to research conducted by Hacettepe University, 63 percent of the Turkish population are convinced that Syrians are ruining moral and social values by committing crimes such as robbery, prostitution, and smuggling.[18] Furthermore, the fact that Syrians live in rural ghettos frightens Turkish people in terms of their future propensities to commit crimes.[19] Turkish perceptions suggest that Syrian refugees represent more of a threat than ISIS in Turkey.[20]

Uncertainties on the duration of the Syrian refugee crisis in Turkey has only increased negative public reactions to the current situation. Most

Turkish people are against the influx of Syrians. According to the Hacettepe research findings, 61 percent of Turkish people are against continued government support for Syrians, particularly as Turkey is rife with poverty among its own citizens. Additionally, almost half of the Turkish population would be uncomfortable having Syrian refugees as neighbors.[21] Almost 80 percent of the surveys indicate that this refugee crisis and its concomitant crime wave remains an insurmountable issue.[22]

Syrians also are perceived as contributing to a strengthening underground economy. Turkey already has the worst unregistered economy among OECD countries with the ratio of 28.2 percent,[23] and Syrians are considered to be exacerbating this economy. Almost 82 percent of Turks are against any government policy that grants Turkish citizenship to Syrians because of the perception that they are burdens on the Turkish economy.[24] Many refugees work illegally and for lower wages without making any contribution to the tax base or social security. This situation makes Syrians vulnerable to exploitation.[25] Unemployment and inflation rates have risen wherever there is a large number of Syrians, while the price of apartments continues to skyrocket in these regions.[26]

ISIS: Recruitment in Turkey and Its Involvement in the Illicit Economy

Salafi jihadist groups such as "al Qaeda in Iraq" (AQI) started to fill vacuums created following American troop withdrawals from Iraq in 2005. Considering it as an opportunity, the leader of AQI developed strategies to fill security vacuums in Iraq and expanded its territories towards Syria.[27] At its zenith, ISIS had become such a well-financed and organized terrorist group that observers expected it to supplant al Qaeda.[28] ISIS terror has contributed to a burgeoning Turkish illicit economy that includes the smuggling and trafficking of drugs, oil, antiquities, cigarettes, and pharmaceuticals. It is crucial to analyze ISIS in Turkey with its different dimensions in order to figure out what presents opportunities for ISIS to influence the illicit economy.

Radicalization continues to increase in Turkey. While there were historically fewer Turkish people joining salafi-jihadist terrorist organizations such as al Qaeda, more people recently have become involved in other terrorist groups. The number of Turkish people in ISIS demonstrates the radicalization trends in Turkey as its civil society undergoes a radical evolution, as does its political institutions under the Justice and Development Party (Adalet ve Kalkinma Partisi-AKP) ruling the country since 2002.

Some of the generally accepted explanations for radicalization have included relative deprivation, the lack of a robust middle class, alienating social networks, and victimization caused by authoritarian regimes.

The Turkish case goes against these accepted justifications. It is becoming increasingly clear that Turkish radicalization has been influenced by the actions of the AKP that has sponsored Islamic organizations in return for their unconditional support, more specifically, obeying President Erdogan who has increasingly consolidated his power. In this period, institutional (registered organizations) and informal (street gatherings, café groups, mosque groups) types of Islamic activism have flourished.[29] These groups have taken the role of defending the regime of Erdogan in exchange for freely carrying out their radical activities.[30]

The favorite path for Turkish radicals is to join ISIS and JN in Syria. Radical extremists are a diverse population, making it impossible to profile recruits.[31] Militants come from all levels of social and economic standing, including lawyers, government and private service employees, merchants, small-shop owners, and university students. The average age of militants participating from Turkey is 27 years, with Kurds overrepresented in the sample.[32]

Similar to other countries, Turkish women tend to join ISIS as opposed to other comparable jihadist groups.[33] The motivations of women in joining ISIS are similar to men. Women who have joined violent movements and militias in different countries are often responding to the conditions inherent in living in conservative social spaces, facing constant threats to their ethnic, religious, or political identities. More specifically, sectarian struggles in Iraq and *fatwas* inviting young women to join are effective in recruiting women to join ISIS.[34] In Turkey, the main motivation pushing women to ISIS is related to the increasing radicalism. Women who are oppressed by conservative environments are more likely to join ISIS.[35] Some cases in the media confirm the relationship between radicalism and joining ISIS. For example, the husband of a young woman who joined ISIS with her two-year-old son explained that his wife came under the influence of Islamic organizations and joined ISIS.[36]

Turkish militants in salafi-jihadist groups in Syria fall into three categories: The first is the group of militants who were involved in recent conflicts in Afghanistan, Bosnia, and elsewhere.[37] Research also confirms the existence of Turkish veterans who previously fought in jihadi regions. In one of these studies, one-third of the veterans examined became involved in jihadi groups in Bosnia, Chechnya, Afghanistan, and Iraq.[38] The second category consists of younger people who have touched base with extremists. As a result of being influenced by ISIS, these young people perceive it as a successful organization and aim to contribute to its mission in the region. The third category is made up of people who are recruited by ISIS and linked to or affiliated with organizations operating in Turkey. ISIS is well-organized in Turkey, using recruiters, social media activities, propaganda mechanisms, magazines, journals,[39] websites, and videos prepared to propagate ISIS ideology. Alternatively, most people belonging to the third category have been recruited in cafes located in suburban areas. This category hosted ISIS attackers who became involved in Diyarbakir, Suruc, and Ankara attacks in 2014 and 2015. In these three attacks, the perpetrators originally from Gaziantep and Adiyaman, were recruited by salafi extremists in cafes.

Several factors lead to involvement in salafi-jihadist groups in Turkey. A desire for martyrdom motivates some people in their involvement. However, many others are attracted to "living under the rule of a caliphate"[40] stemming from the historical inspiration inherited from the Ottoman Empire.[41] Still others, as Turkish Islamists,[42] are inspired to "fight against the Democratic Union Party (PYD)" which is perceived as fighting against the Kurdistan Workers Party (PKK).[43] It is worth mentioning that some people, including officials, join ISIS to earn money. The terrorist organization pays based on the skills of the militants. Some Turkish militants were paid 5,000 USD to 8,000 USD to provide training programs.[44] Some of these were allegedly involved in the siege of Kobane and fought for ISIS.[45]

Radical salafi groups have settled in metropolitan cities and have used connections in universities to gain influence. They have contacted students who are susceptible to radicalization and involvement in terrorist groups.[46] For instance, in Adiyaman city, which hosts a considerable number of ISIS militants and perpetrators who plotted ISIS attacks in Turkey, salafi groups are active and easily infiltrate society. In one case, militants from this city were influenced by salafi groups operating locally.[47]

There is no consensus as to the total number of ISIS fighters. In recent years it has become increasingly dangerous (if not suicidal) for journalists and intelligence operatives to study ISIS. Likewise, the number of Turkish militants in ISIS remains unknown. According to open sources, Turkish militants are one of the most highly represented groups. Estimates of the number of Turks fighting for ISIS and JN range between 2000 and 2200, and the number of Turkish militants killed are around 400 since the beginning of Syrian conflict.[48]

ISIS effectively employs social media in its Turkish recruitment campaign to attract and recruit followers. Its goal is to gain sympathy and strengthen its perception as a successful organization. According to analysis,[49] ISIS was fixated on using social media to gain sympathy and support in 2014 and 2015. This is perhaps best exemplified by the sheer number of ISIS-connected Twitter accounts opened in these years. The mean number of followers of the 290 accounts sampled is 990, which indicates that a considerable number of people are at least partially under the influence of ISIS. The most frequently mentioned terms in these accounts were the "PKK/PYD," "Islamic State," "Takfir/Apostasy/Infidel," "USA," "AK Party," "Martyr/Martyrdom," "Kill," and "ISIS," confirming acceptances of ISIS ideology. Popular hashtags used by these accounts included "#IslamicState," "#FreedomtoIslamicWebsites," and "#FollowingCaliphate," indicating a radicalizing mission of these accounts in Turkey.[50] Turkey was the seventh country in terms of locations claimed in profiles listed in 2014.[51] The Turkish government interestingly does not have a strategy to combat ISIS propaganda tools, nor any answers to controlling its use of social media.[52]

Why Turks Join ISIS

Scholars and policymakers point to a host of factors that lead to involvement in salafi-jihadist organizations. Generally accepted factors are weak states, education, and social and economic disadvantage as well as specific situations such as military conflict and genocidal campaigns. Different motives prompt Turks to join ISIS. One of them is the Turkish border with Syria that presents a natural environment for Turks living in borderlands. Turkey has been frequently used as an entry point to Syria for ISIS militants. The networks established among foreign militants, local smugglers, and citizens create a favorable environment for them to encounter each other. The other motive is related to the backgrounds of some Turkish militants who previously battled in jihadi regions. Turkish involvement in these regions has a legacy going back to the Turks who fought in the 1980s Afghan-Soviet conflict. Some of them joined al Qaeda after the war and began a cycle of moving from conflict to conflict in other jihadi regions such as Bosnia, Chechnya, and Iraq. In much the same way, Turks subsequently join salafi-jihadist groups in Syria. ISIS seems to be the most attractive group to Turkish veterans due to its achievements and relative popularity.[53] High unemployment among young people also has helped ISIS recruitment efforts. Recruiters lure uneducated and unemployed people in cafes, mosques, and bookstores, particularly in the southeastern regions of the country and motivate them to become involved in ISIS. Additionally, social structure in Turkey contributes to recruitment successes of ISIS. Familial and kinship relations resulting from marriages or from tribal and sectarian relationships, help ISIS recruiters lure more people into its ranks.[54]

The perception of ISIS as a group fighting against the PYD also motivates some Turks. More concretely, the so-called Kobane uprising in 2014 triggered more people to join not only PYD in Syria but also ISIS. Kobane is a northern Kurdish Syrian city. When it was besieged by ISIS militants, it increased tension among Kurds.[55] Protesting Ankara's inaction against this siege, Kurds took to the streets and held demonstrations against the government, resulting in the death of 50 people. A considerable number of schools, banks, and health centers were damaged by the demonstrators.[56] The Kobane incidents split the Kurdish people between PKK and Hezbollah-in-Turkey[57] supporters. Extremists from both groups tended to become involved in ISIS and PYD. Also, these events reinforced the perception that PYD is linked to the PKK. ISIS recruiters exploited this perception and invited more Turks into ISIS. In this context, it should be noted that ISIS deliberately perpetrated attacks in the Turkish cities of Diyarbakir and Suruc in order to increase ethnic tensions. ISIS viewed these attacks as a way to punish Kurds in Turkey for attacks made by the PYD in Syria.[58]

Lastly, the attitude of the government toward ISIS militants in Turkey encourages more ISIS support. Nonfunctioning police units have led to increasing support for ISIS in parts of Turkey. For instance, in most cases ISIS militants are released from custody after a few days of detention. A considerable number of people believe that strong ISIS support within the government bureaucracy has allowed the terrorist organization to operate more freely.[59]

Structure of ISIS in Turkey

ISIS in Turkey was established on the ashes of al Qaeda operating in Turkey. In addition to the opportunities presented through the reluctance of the Turkish government and ineffective law enforcement, ISIS has also benefited from previous al Qaeda militants who have played a key role in developing ISIS cells. Many high-level ISIS leaders apprehended in Turkey have previous criminal convictions arising from their relationship with al Qaeda and had trained in Afghanistan or Pakistan.[60]

ISIS structure is based on three groups in Turkey: "core cadres," "active cadres," and "sympathizers." The first group includes core cadres who are directly connected to the ISIS headquarters in Raqqa. They organize different sub-groups.[61] One of them is *Dokumacilar* operated in Tel Abyad in Syria. This group started to establish networks in the outskirts of Adiyaman city in order to recruit militants for ISIS in 2013.[62] The most fatal ISIS attacks in Turkey were conducted by the members of this cadre.[63] The core cadre is regarded as the most effective of the three structures identified above and are often responsible for organizing and facilitating ISIS activities.

The second cadre is made up militants whose responsibility is to gather intelligence and conduct terrorist attacks using suicide bombers and other strategies meant to produce mass casualties. The third cadre consists of ISIS sympathizers, divided into active and passive supporters. Whereas active supporters are assigned to provide logistical support such as financing, transportation, and making propaganda for the organization, passive supporters are bystanders who are sympathetic to the goals and ideology of ISIS.[64]

ISIS is well-entrenched in Turkey, having established sub-regions and assigned *Emirs* representing ISIS ideology. The fact that ISIS has assigned Emirs in territories that proclaim its own area means that ISIS has a developed structure in Turkey.[65] For example, ISIS has a so-called Emir in Gaziantep city of Turkey who is also responsible for controlling Turkish and Syrian borders. According to interviews, when this Emir shut down the border, his command was more effective than the command of a Turkish military commander. Upon command of the Emir, smugglers and traffickers refrain from crossing the border because ISIS militants on the Syrian side shoot trespassers. Furthermore, ISIS has assigned other Emirs in different Turkish metropolitan cities. ISIS's expanding power in Turkey is understandable due to the reluctance of the government to confront ISIS as well as the state policies that have bolstered ISIS recruitment.[66] Although there have been half-hearted attempts at securing borders around ISIS territory, including the Turkish-Syrian border, by-and-large the Turkish government remains reluctant to become too involved in suppressing the illicit activities of ISIS in the border regions.[67]

The Perpetrators and Timeline of ISIS Attacks in Turkey

The perpetrators involved in ISIS attacks in Turkey came out of Syria and Iraq. They can be categorized into three groups: recruits who return home bringing their holy war, homegrown actors inspired and influenced by ISIS, and militants who are directed by ISIS. Western countries have witnessed perpetrators that belong to the first and second categories.[68] Turkey is mostly exposed to the third one, the attacks of perpetrators directed by ISIS.[69]

There has been controversy over the timeline of ISIS attacks. It has been asserted that ISIS has made attacks in Turkey when it is both beneficial for its organization and the AKP government. The pattern of previous ISIS attacks indicates a relationship based on reciprocal interests between the AKP government and ISIS. More concretely, when there is an international meeting in Turkey or criticism about weak performances of the government, ISIS has detonated bombs or deployed suicide attacks in Turkey, or the AKP government has detained some ISIS militants. For example, subsequent to the Brussels airport attack in March 2016 that left 35 dead, ISIS detonated a bomb in Istanbul that killed 11 tourists. This attack took place before Erdogan attended the Nuclear Summit held in Washington, DC in March 2016. Likewise, Turkish police detained some militants in Antalya before the G20 summit in February 2016, and the police detained ISIS militants just before President Erdogan attended the UN Assembly held in New York in September 2016.

Critics assert that these police operations strategically aim to alleviate criticisms on weak Turkish performances in its fight against ISIS.[70] Almost 45 percent of the Turkish public believes that the government response to ISIS has been inadequate. Conversely, 9.3 percent of the Turkish people do not regard ISIS as a terrorist organization.[71]

The first fatal ISIS attack in Turkey was in Reyhanli, a district of Hatay province in 2013. The militants detonated two car bombs and killed 52 people. Even though the investigation failed to identify the perpetrators, ISIS was among terrorist organizations suspected of being behind the attack.[72] In 2014, two ISIS attacks took place in Turkey. In the first attack, two Albanian ISIS militants attacked a security checkpoint killing three people in the central Anatolian city of Nigde in March 2014.[73] Three months later ISIS operatives invaded the Turkish Consulate in Mosul and took 49 consulate employees hostage.[74]

Suspicions of collaboration between the AKP government and ISIS led some observers to conclude that it was no coincidence that ISIS attacks took place around the time of elections in 2015. In the June 7th elections, the AKP lost its majority at the parliament because of increasing popularity of the Pro-Kurdish Peoples' Democratic Party (HDP). By some accounts, the AKP exploited its relationship with ISIS to escalate tensions. For instance, ISIS detonated several bombs at election offices of the HDP in Adana and Mersin cities. Several people were wounded before the June 7th elections. Another ISIS attack occurred right before the June 7th elections. The ISIS militant, Orhan Gonder, who belonged to the *Dokumacilar* cell, exploded two bombs at an HDP rally on June 5, 2015. In this attack, four Kurdish people lost their lives. Subsequent to the AKP's failure at the June 7th elections, Turkey witnessed the bloodiest ISIS attacks, that is, until the November 1st elections were repeated due to the fact no political party succeeded in setting up a new government.[75]

In Suruc in July 2015, a suicide bomber, Abdurrahman Alagoz, killed 34 others. The perpetrator was also a member of the *Dokumacilar* cell. Another ISIS attack that points to possible links between the government and ISIS took place on October 10, 2015, right before the November 1st elections, killing 102 Kurdish people who attended a peace rally in Ankara. The two suicide bombers implicated in this attack were also members of the *Dokumacilar* cell. As a result, the AKP used the fear of terror in its campaign messages, warning that Turkey could only be a secure country if there was a strong single party government. Under these circumstances, the AKP won the majority in parliament in the second round of elections on November 1st. While not substantiated with solid evidence, the fact that ISIS attacks revolved around elections and targeted the HDP are considered indicators of possible linkages between the government and ISIS.[76] Besides the aforementioned ISIS attacks, possibly related to the elections, the terrorist organization made other attacks in 2015, including an attack on a police station perpetrated by a foreign suicide bomber in January 2015 and the killing of a Turkish soldier in Kilis city bordering Syria in July 2015.[77]

In 2016, ISIS concentrated its attacks on foreign targets. For instance, ISIS killed 10 people in a suicide bombing perpetrated by a Saudi-born Syrian in the Sultan Ahmet (Blue Mosque) district of Istanbul. In March 2016, ISIS continued to attack foreign targets. The bombing in Istanbul killed 5 people. In another attack in June 2016, three suicide bombers blew themselves up, killing 41 people.[78]

The honeymoon based on reciprocal interests between Turkey and ISIS ended when the Turkish military plunged into Syria to clear ISIS militants from its border stronghold and halt the advancement of Kurdish forces in northern Syria in late 2016. In this period, ISIS made one of its deadliest attacks in the first hours of 2017. A mass shooting was carried out in an attack on the Reina night club in Istanbul, killing 39 and injuring nearly 70 others. Soon after the attack, ISIS claimed responsibility.

In its new relationship, Turkey is paying the cost of its alleged collaboration with salafi-jihadist groups operating in Syria. Turkey's close friendship with Russia and Iran has resulted in the loss of ISIS territory, particularly in Aleppo. This situation has sparked tensions between Turkey and jihadist groups. In December 2016, JN militants attacked Turkish forces in Syria and killed 16 soldiers, and the Russian ambassador to Ankara was killed by a JN-affiliated police officer in Turkey.

Examination of cases mentioned above indicates that Turkish and foreign national suicide bombers were deployed in terrorist attacks. Those that took place in 2015 seemed more localized and targeted HDP supporters. Attacks in 2016 seemed more focused on international targets. These attacks demonstrated the high operational capacity that ISIS was able to project in Turkey. Research suggests that 49.2 percent of the survey respondents believed ISIS is going to increase its attacks in Turkey,[79] underlining at least a belief in the capacity of ISIS in Turkey.

Why ISIS Finds Favorable Ground in Illicit Economy

ISIS militants and ISIS-affiliated criminals have found an environment favorable to their counterfeiting, smuggling, and trafficking activities in Turkey. More specifically, the attitude of the government in some cases mentioned below have created opportunities for these criminals, particularly those operating in southern cities bordering Syria.

The Impacts of the Qassap Case

ISIS and JN are believed to be engaged in the acquisition of weapons of mass destruction (WMD). ISIS, by most accounts, possesses materials for WMD.[80] It is believed that ISIS used mustard gas in one of its attacks near Aleppo.[81] These terrorist organizations also made attempts to possess WMD materials for other attacks, including one in Turkey.[82] The prosecutor in Adana city launched an investigation on criminals who attempted to procure some materials used in manufacturing chemical weapons in 2013. Investigation revealed that Syrian and Turkish criminals found some materials and attempted to transfer them to al Ahrar al-Sham and JN terrorist organizations. The anti-terror police detained six criminals including the Syrian leader Hytham Qassap. However, all other suspects were released after one week and the prosecutor of the investigation was reassigned. After laboratory results of the materials in 2015 demonstrated they were genuine and could be used to make a chemical weapon, the judge sentenced Qassap to 12 years of imprisonment.[83] This case was a turning point in Turkey's counter terrorist activities directed at organizations operating in cities bordering Syria. Government efforts to obstruct justice sent a clear message to law enforcement—that is, "not investigate any criminals linked to Syria."[84]

The Scandal of the MIT Rigs

Acting on tips about the looming transfer of some weapons to terrorist organizations in Syria on January 19, 2014, a prosecutor ordered check points to search lorries in Adana city on the way to Syria. Lorries were stopped by over 100 military personnel and searched. No sooner had the search begun than the mayor of Adana city, Hüseyin Avni Coş, arrived at the scene and intervened, violating a court decision. The mayor stated that the materials in the lorries belonged to the MIT (Milli Istihbarat Teskilati - National Intelligence Agency of Turkey). In response the chief of law enforcement asked for proof of the legal linkage of these materials with MIT. Nonetheless, as a result of the mayor's intervention, the lorries proceeded to the border.

The government maintained that the cargo in the lorries was a national secret, followed by contradictory statements made from the cabinet. One of the explanations was that the cargo was food and medical aid being transferred to Bayirbucak Turkmens. Another suggested that only rifles for sporting purposes were included in the cargo. The other minister, Tugrul Turkes in the AKP cabinet said, "I swear these weapons were not transferred to Turkmens in Syria."[85] On the other hand, the opposition parties asserted that the vehicles were transferring weapons to JN and ISIS. Turkmens clarified that they did not get any humanitarian aid from Turkey,[86] confirmed by leaking footage in May 29, 2015 right before the June 7th elections. Can Dundar from the *Cumhuriyet Daily* newspaper released the footage which showed weapons placed beneath the humanitarian aid.[87]

In addition to contradictory explanations coming from different ministers, the government issued a ban on both written and visual reporting. Also, the government punished all of the personnel involved in the search. Even though the tipoff was verified when the weapons were found in the lorries, all the personnel, including prosecutors and judges were suspended, forced out of their jobs, and even put in jail.

The prosecutors spoke about how they enforced the rule of law in searching the lorries in court. One of them, Ozcan Sisman, who prosecuted lorries in Hatay on January 1, 2014 said that he received a tipoff regarding lorries carrying weapons through Kilis city to ISIS controlled territory in Syria. Sisman issued a search warrant. However, before he could intervene he was contacted by a MIT official who insisted that these lorries were carrying humanitarian aid to Syrians. Thereupon, he responded to the official saying "...if there were humanitarian aid, I would let the lorries proceed." In the meantime, he was called by the prosecutor and military commander who were at the scene. Both reported interference and that they were not allowed to conduct a search. Then Sisman decided to travel to the scene. Although the official of MIT said to him that these lorries belonged to MIT, the drivers of the lorries refused to show their ID cards. Also, the military at the scene told Sisman that these drivers looked more like al Qaeda militants than truck drivers. Sisman's only goal was to find out whether criminals were transporting weapons or whether official complicity was involved. If these drivers were official officers, they had to present their documents and IDs.[88]

Prosecutor Sisman's previous experiences motivated him to go further in searching the lorries, despite the barriers thrown up by high level governmental officials. In another investigation he made several months ago, he found out how weapons under the supervision of governmental officials were transferred from Konya to Reyhanli district of Hatay city en route to Syrian territory controlled by al Ahrar al-Sham.[89] The prosecutor Sisman, in his defense, stated that a number of wiretappings confirmed that transporting weapons to Syria turned out to be a permanent job for some criminals. He also found a linkage between MIT officers and a 2011 kidnapping case, based on wiretappings. In this case, Colonel Huseyin Harmush, the founder of the Free Syrian Army and Mustafa Qassom were kidnapped from the Hatay refugee camp with assistance from MIT officers and then turned over to the Syrian Intelligence Service. Furthermore, in an attack made at the Hatay Cilvegozu border gate in February 2013, an informant linked to the MIT handed a SIMS card to four Syrians who perpetrated this attack, which killed 14 people. Additionally, Sisman prosecuted the explosion in Reyhanli that killed 52 people and determined the traces of MIT's involvement in this case.[90]

Prosecutor Sisman responded to the accusations of being a spy and disclosing state secrets, declaring that "...finding out weapons in a lorry destined to ISIS territory is not a state secret. It is the effort to uncover some officials who exploited their positions. It is clear in Turkish laws who [is] authorized to carry weapons. They are only law enforcement, not MIT officers." He also said that in another case recorded January 19th in Adana, the search found weapons in trucks being transferred to Syria. He concluded there was collusion between some officials at the government and terrorist groups.[91]

The other prosecutor, Aziz Takci, testified in court that he saw all the ammunition and weapons in the aforementioned truck searched on January 19, 2016. After getting a search warrant for the truck, a car arrived at the scene with individuals who identified themselves as MIT officers. It was determined that this car had been connected to a previous case and was linked to a suspect convicted for his al Qaeda connections.[92]

To sum up, the two prosecutors, allegedly connected to the MIT, who investigated both weapons trafficking cases, confirmed at court hearings that the trucks were indeed loaded with weapons intended for Syrian territories mostly under the control of ISIS or al Qaeda affiliates. Can Dundar, editor-in-chief of *Cumhuriyet Daily* stated that this footage demonstrated the methods used by intelligence units to illegally smuggle weapons to be used in the Syrian conflict. Subsequently, President Erdogan did not refute the news reports, instead he threatened the journalist.[93] Dundar was arrested and imprisoned for three months on charges of spying and disclosing government secrets. Following his release he fled to Germany.

Ineffective Investigations against ISIS

The reluctance of the government to confront terrorism has ultimately hampered any ISIS investigations and has diminished the capacity of law enforcement to counter terrorist activities. For instance, one opposition party member, Eren Erdem, addressed these shortcomings in June 2016. According to his speech to parliament,[94] wiretappings and surveillances indicated that ISIS was a well-structured terrorist organization with terrorist cells active in Turkey. The country launched 14 different ISIS investigations. One recently disclosed indictment focused on an ISIS attack near the main train station in Ankara.[95] It reported that one of the suspected perpetrators, IB,[96] organized the illegal crossing of 1,800 ISIS militants on the Turkish-Syrian border.[97] The indictments suggested that the police not only knew of IB's involvement through wiretappings but made no attempt to prevent it. What's more, though

IB provided a specific address directing his accomplices in the illegal border crossings, not one persons was arrested.[98]

According to Erdem, although police indictments included many addresses, no officials acted on the information. Despite the overwhelming evidence against IB in three different investigations, he was released in Turkey. He was also considered an al Qaeda recruiter. In another investigation, a suspect recruited Turkish militants and sent them to Raqqa, Syria. Police discovered explosives and other weapons at their Turkish safe house. Police not only linked IB to the aforementioned Gaziantep case, he was also named as an accomplice in the Suruc attack. IB avoided prison for these activities, as did most of the ISIS militants connected to terrorist attacks in Turkey.[99]

ISIS militants have been treated in Turkish hospitals (Gaziantep), and then permitted to travel back to Syria.[100] One 2014 investigation revealed that wounded ISIS militants were transported to some hospitals in Gaziantep from Kilis, which borders ISIS-controlled territory in Syria. By most accounts, their treatment expenses were covered by the so-called "Emir of Gaziantep." In one of the wiretappings, the Emir is recorded bargaining with the hospital in order to reduce his bill from 68,000 to 40,000 USD.[101] One of the hospitals that served rebel fighters was located in Reyhanli, Hatay city. Rebel fighters, some of whom were the members of Ahrar al-Sham, were treated there. In this instance, the Turkish humanitarian aid organization, Insani Yardim vakfi (IHH),[102] funded the medical treatment.[103] In addition to hospitals, other buildings were transformed into hospitals to treat ISIS militants. One police officer recounted the treatment of ISIS actors in a building that he protected for two years. Coincidentally, the chief of the Gaziantep city police resided at this building as well.[104]

The government's interventionist policies toward ISIS investigations as well as its support to ISIS had caused untold harm to the Turkish capacity to fight terrorist activities. As a result, the government has spoiled the impartiality of the judiciary. In cities bordering Syria, no prosecutors and judges dare to issue any search warrant or start investigations. This attitude created authority vacuums filled by criminals and terrorists operating in border cities. According to one interview, the respondent claimed to have travelled across the Turkish and Syrian borders on several occasions, but never saw a single road check point.[105] These developments have also had a parallel negative effect on the ability of law enforcement to investigate other types of trafficking and smuggling cases.

The Linkages of Criminal Actors and ISIS in the Illicit Economy

For most of its history ISIS has been a self-sufficient terrorist organization thanks to its various financial resources. At its apogee it was probably the richest terrorist group ever. In addition to revenue obtained in occupied territories in Iraq and Syria, there was a steady flow of income from the sale of crude oil, extortion, kidnapping for ransom, bank robbing, donations, smuggling, and trafficking activities.[106] The terrorist organization also sold electric power and economic assets, and controlled banks in its territories.[107]

According to some calculations, daily revenues of ISIS varied from 1–4 million USD.[108] Therefore, ISIS, in its prime, was considered to be the richest terrorist organization in the world.[109] By contrast, al Qaeda-linked JN has very limited financial resources, mostly from donations and kidnappings for ransom.[110] ISIS does not make any distinction in choosing its financial resources.[111] The organization increasingly has become involved in the sales of counterfeit cigarettes, cell phones, pharmaceuticals,[112] foreign passports, and antiquities in Turkey,[113] benefiting from the favorable environment provided by the government.[114] Also, ineffective regulations and weak law enforcement have left vast territories open to weapons and narcotic trafficking.[115]

Gulf States are continuing to support ISIS and JN. Some Middle Eastern countries have provided weapons and ammunition, whereas others are complicit by allowing their lands to be used in the transfer of arms and new militants to jihadi regions. Interestingly, supporting countries do not make any distinction whether these arms or militants are linked to radical or moderate groups. Turkey occupies a special place among sponsoring countries because it is linked to JN and Ahrar al-Sham. It is a source country for ISIS to recruit, a transit country to assist ISIS militants who enter Syria, and a so-called ally that provides weapons.[116]

Petroleum has been one of the most lucrative financial resources for ISIS.[117] A tremendous amount of the revenue came from the confiscations of lucrative oil fields in Iraq and Syria.[118] ISIS is estimated to have confiscated 3 million barrels of petroleum from storage tanks in Iraq and Syria. Initially, this was expected to provide a long-term revenue source for ISIS.[119] In the early years it was selling 47 thousand barrels daily thanks to the cooperation of smuggling groups.[120] Another source placed the daily amount at almost 100,000 barrels in a day,[121] bringing in a reported 500 million USD in oil revenue in December 2015 alone.[122] Operationally, ISIS typically sells this petroleum to intermediaries in Syria. They then use smugglers,[123] who easily bypass checkpoints after 5,000 USD bribes are paid to transport crude oil outside of territory controlled by ISIS. For instance, Kurdish oil smugglers can earn up to 300,000 USD each month.[124] ISIS has made a habit of selling barrels of petroleum at prices below market value. In spite of this lower price, at one time ISIS was bringing in between 850,000 USD and 1.5 million USD per month.[125]

The increase in oil seizures in Turkish cities neighboring Syria has confirmed the intensive transfer of Syrian petroleum into Turkey. A comparison of oil seizures between the two years leading up to the Syrian civil war (2009-2011) and the two years after it began in 2011, indicates a 900 percent increase after the conflict broke out.[126] Traditional smuggling networks active in the region have facilitated the sale of ISIS controlled petroleum, taking advantage of porous borders.

Turkey's borders with Syria have been historically unsecured, contributing to recent border security issues after the outbreak of hostilities in Syria.[127] Revelations from interviews and focus group studies demonstrate the relationship between the Turkish government and ISIS, particularly in their cooperation selling ISIS petroleum. Middlemen and smugglers are key operators in this sector, eliminating any obstacles to ISIS petroleum trucks destined for Turkey. They easily pass border gates without being checked. This petroleum is processed in rural areas and sold to some petroleum stations.[128]

Comparisons of petroleum seizures between 2013 and 2015 in Şanlıurfa, Gaziantep, and Mardin, Turkish cities bordering Syria, suggest a dramatic decrease in the amount of oil seized of late, plummeting from 1.7 tons in 2013 to 1.4 tons in 2014, and to 0.6 tons in 2015.[129] This decrease does not necessarily mean that petroleum sales between Turkey and ISIS plummeted in 2014 and 2015. According to interviews, one of the best explanations for the decline in seizures stems from intimidation from the central government, which created vacuums in authority filled by petroleum middlemen and smugglers. In contrast to lower seizure amounts, the amount of illicit petroleum trade on the Turkish-Syrian border increased in 2015.[130] Nonetheless, one ISIS member admitted that ISIS earned a tremendous amount of money from petroleum sales thanks to the involvement of regional middlemen.[131]

The Syrian conflict has created an environment for the looting of the country's tremendous historical heritage, leading to the unparalleled plundering of Syrian antiquities. ISIS has been among the most active groups taking advantage of the utter lack of security at archeological sites, museums, and other prominent hunting grounds. Police seized an ISIS computer in one raid. A scan of the computer's files revealed that antiquities smuggling was a significant revenue source for ISIS, indicating that in one year, the organization made 36 million USD in revenue from the sales of antiquities in just one region.[132] The combined value of this activity when taking account other regions indicates a revenue stream between 150 and 200 million USD per year.[133] Documents found in one raid of an ISIS cell revealed that ISIS is well organized in the trafficking of antiquities through its established administrative and logistical resources. According to the documents, ISIS has set up sub-units responsible for marketing, excavation, and identification of new sites, research and investigation of known sites, and administration.[134]

A comparison of antiquities seizures in two Turkish cities neighboring Syria, Gaziantep and Hatay, points to the increase in trafficking. Whereas the combined number of antiquities seized was 878 in 2010, the year before the Syrian war started, that number rose sharply to 4,524 pieces in 2012.[135] News reports indicate that there were seizures of antiquities being trafficked by Syrians in Gaziantep in 2015, as evidenced by the arrest of a Syrian smuggler in possession of antiquities and a statue.[136]

ISIS has emboldened thieves and smugglers in the plundering of archeological sites, earning commissions in the process. Moreover, ISIS is using bulldozers to enable its own archeological excavations, selling antiquities to local middlemen, who market the loot in neighboring countries.[137] At this point, Turkey generally serves as a gateway for connecting the plundered antiquities to international markets.[138] A report by the ASOD Department confirms the impact of the Syrian conflict. Its findings offer more evidence of the looting of Syria's cultural and historical heritage, how traffickers market the treasures in Turkey, and then transfer them to Western countries via a Turkish pipeline.[139]

According to 2015 research,[140] ISIS militants exploited previously established criminal networks between Turkey and Syria in 2013 and 2014 to move looted antiquities. These criminals were predominantly smugglers well versed in different types of smuggling. Local smugglers transfer antiquities to brokers linked to antiquities trafficking groups. More recently, ISIS has eliminated the use of local smugglers; instead, the organization has used ISIS actors in Turkey in order to increase the amount of revenue by cutting out middlemen.[141] From Turkey these antiquities have been transported to Western countries, including the UK.[142] Media reports confirm the research findings. In one story a correspondent contacted an ISIS smuggler in a southern Turkish town near the Syrian border who attempted to sell a relief statue trafficked from Palmyra.[143] According to field research conducted by one of the authors, Syrian antiquities have been transferred to Gaziantep city and sold in auctions. Then these materials have been moved to Istanbul, Antalya, or Izmir to prepare falsified documents in order to market those internationally using different routes.[144]

ISIS, like other terrorist groups, generates revenue from donations. According to a report from a UN member state, ISIS has been funded by businessmen in Gulf States who actively direct fundraising campaigns for ISIS and al Qaeda.[145] This money has been used to some degree as seed capital for recruitment and the acquisition of military equipment.[146] Donations have been collected through internet campaigns and social media and then transferred to ISIS in cash.[147] Turkey increasingly hosts individuals who support political Islam and jihadist ideology. Some not only sympathize with salafi-jihadist terrorist organizations such as Boko Haram,[148] al Qaeda, and ISIS, but donate money in the name of zakat. ISIS militants also use cafés and mosques in order to organize people to fundraise money for ISIS in Turkey.[149]

Ongoing conflict in Syria and Iraq has made women and children more vulnerable to trafficking. The number of children who are recruited by terrorist groups has increased as well. The Assad government, PYD, JN, ISIS, and FSA have employed underage children as fighters. Syrian women in particular constitute a risk group for human trafficking. Customers from Gulf States and states neighboring Syria are buying young girls, mostly at refugee camps, through intermediaries. This situation has created a dependable means of financing for terrorist organizations,[150] including ISIS.[151] ISIS is forcing non-Muslims to convert to Islam. Men who reject conversion have been killed by ISIS. But what is probably most disturbing has been its practice of selling women and children. The plight of the Yazidis exemplifies this phenomenon. Hundreds of Yazidi men who rejected conversion have been killed, and their wives, daughters, and even mothers have been sold to ISIS fighters.[152] ISIS commonly forces Syrian girls to marry its fighters and has purportedly forced some into sex-related activities to earn more cash. The terrorist organization routinely forces Syrian and Iraqi girls to undergo virginity tests before trading them.[153] One of the markets for ISIS is Turkey. According to interviews, ISIS has established some centers in Hatay city[154] to sell Yazidi women who are illegally transferred to Turkey.[155]

ISIS participates in the drug trade in two ways, either by participating directly in the trafficking of illicit drugs or by taxing smugglers and traffickers. According to interviews made with FSA members, ISIS has generated revenue from cannabis, heroin, and captagon trafficking.[156] It has also allowed drug traffickers to open drug labs in their territories in return for commissions. By most accounts these traffickers all had had backgrounds as jihadists.[157]

Drug seizures in Turkey have confirmed an increase in the smuggling of synthetic drugs in or through Syria.[158] Turkish drug seizures in cities neighboring Syria have increased substantially. Whereas only four Syrians were arrested with 26 kg of cannabis in 2009-2010, prior to the outbreak of hostilities, the amount of drug activity increased after the war began. In 2011-2013, for example, 36 Syrians were arrested with 1.7 tons.[159] Syrian involvement in drug trafficking continued to rise across the country in 2014 with 86 percent of foreign cannabis traffickers and 80 percent of foreign captagon traffickers arrested in Turkey being of Syrian descent.[160]

Drug seizures made in Turkey in December 2013 speak to the effectiveness of drug trafficking networks in the Middle East. In Gaziantep, in neighboring Syria, the police seized 48 kg of heroin destined to be smuggled to Lebanon through Iran, Turkey, and Syria. The group had also planned to smuggle cocaine from Lebanon to Iran.[161] This case demonstrates the persistence of transnational drug traffickers as they work closely with each other.

Captagon seizures in Turkey also provide data with respect to the drug trade potential in Syria. Captagon pills transferred from Syria were captured mainly in Turkish provinces neighboring Syria. In 2014, 96 percent of Turkish captagon seizures were made in Gaziantep, Hatay, and Kilis. Captagon, a form of amphetamine, is reportedly manufactured in Syrian drug labs.[162] In 2013, 4.2 million captagon pills were seized in Hatay, before they could be shipped to their ultimate destination in the Gulf States.[163] Syrian criminals increasingly dominate captagon trafficking, exemplified by the fact that in 2014, 80 percent of captagon traffickers were Syrians.[164]

ISIS militants have been known to be consumers of several types of drugs, especially methamphetamine. According to a Syrian refugee interviewed for this study, it is very common to consume methamphetamine and cannabis among ISIS militants.[165] Kurdish Peshmerga who made a raid on an ISIS leader's house found heroin stored in a bag for the purpose of distributing it to militants. It is known that ISIS is allowing its followers to use drugs hoping to make them more fearless in battle.[166] According to some media accounts, opium has been discovered stashed in Qur'ans in the shelters of ISIS militants after they left Kobane.[167]

ISIS plays an active role in many smuggling activities on the Turkish-Syrian border.[168] It has linkages in the area to human smugglers, cell phone smuggling, and cigarette trafficking.[169] Cigarette smuggling cases perpetrated by Syrians spiked in Turkey. According to recent seizure reports, routes to transfer smuggled cigarettes to Turkey moved from Iran to Syria. Cigarette seizures in Turkish cities neighboring Syria indicates that the number of cigarette packages seized in Turkish cities increased 900 percent in two years after the beginning of the Syrian war in comparison to two years before the war.[170]

Similar to other illicit trade activity during the years of the Syrian conflict, the number of cell phones smuggled from Syria to Turkey by Syrians has increased as well.[171] Turkish smuggling data indicate that the number of cell phones smuggled increased almost tenfold in 2012 and 2013 in comparison to 2009 and 2010, and a significant amount of these cases occurred in Turkish cities neighboring the Syrian border, and committed by Syrians.[172] There were also increases in the number of Chinese-made counterfeit pharmaceuticals in Turkey after the Syrian war started, from 1.5 million tablets in 2009 and 2010, to 11.2 million in 2012 and 2013, and the number of Syrian smugglers operating in this area increased as well.[173] Syrians are involved in the Turkish illicit economy, making counterfeit passports, money, and documents. In 2013, 249 Syrians were arrested in Turkey because of their linkages with counterfeit money, passports, and visas. These arrests require a specific analysis in the context of ISIS.[174] The number of Syrians arrested in 2015 was 491.[175] It should be noted that ISIS militants sell their passports for huge amounts of money in Turkey before entering Syria.[176]

The fact that Syrians in refugee camps in Turkey and Lebanon have sold their transplantable organs, such as kidneys and corneas, has helped pave the way for organ trafficking. The price of a kidney is around 1,000 USD in Iraq and 10,000 USD in Turkey. Close to 18,000 Syrians have sold their organs.[177] According to interviews, some Syrian and Turkish brokers mediate between organ traffickers and Syrian victims at refugee camps. After negotiations about the price, these traffickers acquire the organs from Syrians with the assistance of doctors on their payroll. Some Syrians pay this money to human smugglers to travel to the European countries.[178]

NOTES

1. Charles Glass, *Syria Burning: A Short History of a Catastrophe* (London: Verso, 2016).

2. Abdullahi Alazreg, *ISIS Management of Savagery* (Pittsburgh, PA: Dorrance Publishing, 2016).

3. Mark Hitchcock, *ISIS, IRAN, ISRAEL: And the End of Days* (Eugene, OR: Harvest House Publishers, 2016).

4. Sanserif, *ISIS The Face of Terrorism.*

5. Bruce Hoffman, "Al-Qaeda's Resurrection," *Council on Foreign Relations,* accessed on April 14, 2018 from https://www.cfr.org/expert-brief/al-qaedas-resurre ction?utm_medium=social_share&utm_source=emailfwd.

6. Focus Group Study with Free Syrian Army (FSA) Members by Mahmut Cengiz, April 12, 2015, Sanliurfa.

7. Jobby Warrick, *Black Flags: The Rise of ISIS* (New York: Penguin House LLC, 2015).

8. The first category includes cases in 2009 and 2010, and the second one in 2012 and 2013. These data are extracted from the yearly reports of Turkish Anti-Smuggling and Organized Crime Department (ASOD). Both categories are compared to see crime trends before and after the Syrian crisis started.

9. The theoretical framework in obtaining these data is based on qualitative techniques which primarily focus on open-ended and ethnographic topical interviews. The first research was a focus group study done with the members of the Free Syrian Army (FSA). Six people from this organization attended focus groups conducted in Sanliurfa city of Turkey on April 12, 2015. The second data set is composed of 7 interviews conducted with law enforcement in Turkey on May 18, 2015. Respondents are experts on terrorist financing issues and well-informed about illicit trade activities of ISIS. They were selected with snowballing technique because it was the best technique to reach experts about the topic. They voluntarily participated in the research, and each interview lasted three hours. Every individual was reassured that their interview details were confidential. They were coded from Le1 to Le7.

10. Unending conflicts in countries have national, regional, and global impact. Turkey was exposed to the unintended consequences of the conflict in Iraq after the 2003 U.S. invasion. A substantial number of Iraqis immigrated to Turkey, as regional smugglers and traffickers expanded their turf and terrorist organizations became embroiled in illicit trade. Turkish government statistics confirmed the rise in

the number of smuggling and trafficking cases post-2003. For instance, the number of arms trafficking cases transferring weapons from Iraq to Turkey increased 120% between 2003 and 2004. The number of weapons smuggled into Turkey rose from 237 in 2002 to 1,066 in 2004. Whereas the amount of heroin was 2.1 tons in 2002, it increased to 6.5 tons in 2004. A significant amount of this heroin entered Turkey across the Iraqi border. Similarly, the number of cigarette trafficking cases in Turkey increased from 1,120 in 2003 to 2,084 in 2004, again, mostly trafficked from Iraq. An interesting aberration took place, in which the amount of legal cigarettes consumed in the Turkish cities of Sirnak and Hakkari, bordering Iraq, dropped by 80% in 2004 in comparison to the sales in 2002, indicating that this was probably due to cigarette smokers purchasing more cigarettes from the illegal market linked to Iraq.

11. Kemal Kirisci and E. Ferris, "What Turkey's open-door policy means for Syrian refugees" (July 8, 2015), accessed on October 11, 2017 from https://www.brookings.edu/blog/order-from-chaos/2015/07/08/what-turkeys-open-door-policy-means-for-syrian-refugees/.

12. "Syria Regional Refugee Response", accessed on October 25, 2018, from http://data.unhcr.org/syrianrefugees/regional.php.

13. Kirisci and Ferris, "What Turkey's open-door policy means for Syrian refugees."

14. Oguzhan O. Demir, "Göç Politikaları, Toplumsal Kaygılar ve Suriyeli Mülteciler", accessed on October 3, 2017 from http://globalpse.org/goc-politikalari-toplumsal-kaygilar-ve-suriyeli-multeciler/.

15. Kirisci and Ferris, "What Turkey's open-door policy means for Syrian refugees".

16. Demir "Göç Politikaları, Toplumsal Kaygılar ve Suriyeli Mülteciler".

17. Kirisci and Ferris, "What Turkey's open-door policy means for Syrian refugees".

18. Murat Erdoğan "Türkiye'deki Suriyeliler: Toplumsal Kabul Ve Uyum Araştırma Raporu", (Hacettepe Üniversitesi Göç Araştırmaları Merkezi, 2014).

19. Demir, "Göç Politikaları, Toplumsal Kaygılar ve Suriyeli Mülteciler".

20. "Türkiye Toplumsal Eğilimler Anketi 2015", (Global Politika ve Strateji, 2015).

21. Erdoğan, "Türkiye'deki Suriyeliler: Toplumsal Kabul Ve Uyum Araştırma Raporu".

22. Demir, "Göç Politikaları, Toplumsal Kaygılar ve Suriyeli Mülteciler"

23. "Turkey worst in OECD for unregistered economy: Study," *Hurriyet Gazetesi*, accessed on October 10, 2017 from http://www.hurriyetdailynews.com/turkey-worst-in-oecd-for-unregistered-economy-study.aspx?pageID=238&nID=94026&NewsCatID=347.

24. Demir, "Göç Politikaları, Toplumsal Kaygılar ve Suriyeli Mülteciler".

25. Kirisci and Ferris, "What Turkey's open-door policy means for Syrian refugees".

26. Demir, "Göç Politikaları, Toplumsal Kaygılar ve Suriyeli Mülteciler".

27. William McCants, "State of Confusion", in *The ISIS Crisis*, ed. G. Rose, (Foreign Affairs, 2015): 14-18.

28. Barak Mendelsohn, "Collateral Damage in Iraq?", in *The ISIS Crisis*, ed. G. Rose, (Foreign Affairs,2015): 10-13.

29. Gunes M.Tezcur and Sabri Ciftci "Why Turkish Citizens are Joining ISIS?", in *The ISIS Crisis*, ed. G. Rose, (Foreign Affairs,2015): 45-50.

30. Le2, Le4, and Le7, Interview by Mahmut Cengiz, Personal Interviews, May 18, 2018, Gaziantep.

31. Tezcur and Ciftci (2015) examined 112 individuals at jihadist organizations based on data gathered from open spurces such as newspapers, magazines, and blogs.

32. Tezcur and Ciftci "Why Turkish Citizens are Joining ISIS?"

33. Interviews with law enforcement and researchers 2014-2016.

34. Nimmi Gowrinathan "The Women of ISIS: Understanding and Combating Female Extremism", in *The ISIS Crisis*, ed. G. Rose, (Foreign Affairs,2015), pp. 19-23.

35. Interviews with law enforcement and researchers 2014-2016.

36. "2 Yaşındaki Oğluyla IŞİD'e Katılan Kadın, Kocasına Mesaj Yolladı", (October 23, 2015), accessed on August 5, 2016 from http://www.haberler.com/2-yasindaki-ogluyla-isid-e-katildigi-iddia-edilen-7806628-haberi/.

37. Suleyman Ozeren, Hakan. Hekim, M.S. Elmas, and H.Canbegi "ISIS in Cyberspace: Findings from Social Media Research", *Global Policy and Strategy,* (February 2016), accessed on August 11, 2016 from http://globalpse.org/en/isis-in-cyberspace-findings-from-social-media-research.

38. Tezcur and Ciftci "Why Turkish Citizens are Joining ISIS?"

39. ISIS has periodically published a magazine in Turkey whose name is Konstantiniyye. http://www.amerikaninsesi.com/a/isidden-turkce-dergi-konsatantinniye/2807520.html This journal aims to radicalize people in Turkey and finally lure them to ISIS. It published its fifth edition in 2016.

40. Ozeren and Hekim, "ISIS in Cyberspace: Findings from Social Media Research".

41. When the Ottoman Empire was defeated in World War I, a newly established secular Turkish republic repealed the caliphate system. Conservative Muslims protested this transition, embarking on several unsuccessful attempts to reestablish the caliphate. Well aware of its historical resonance, ISIS proclaimed itself caliphate in the world. (McCants, *The ISIS Apocalypse)* Abubakr al-Baghdadi declared himself as a Caliph in 2014 as a result of its organization's success in securing wealth and strengthening its military. J. Sekulow, *Rise of ISIS A New Threat We Cannot Ignore*, (New York: Howard Books, 2014).

42. N. Danforth "The Myth of the Caliphate", in *The ISIS Crisis*, ed. G. Rose, (Foreign Affairs, 2015), pp. 3-10.

43. Ozeren and Hekim, "ISIS in Cyberspace: Findings from Social Media Research"

44. Le1, Le3, Le5, and Le7, Interview by Mahmut Cengiz, Personal Interviews, May 18, 2018, Gaziantep.

45. "IŞİD saflarında savaşan Türkiyeli resmi görevliler var" (September 30, 2014), accessed on October 05, 2016 from http://odatv.com/n.php?n=isid-saflarinda-savasan-turkiyeli-resmi-gorevliler-var--3009141200.

46. Le1, Le3, Le5, and Le7, Interview by Mahmut Cengiz, Personal Interviews, May 18, 2018, Gaziantep.

47. "IŞİD saflarına katılan Adıyamanlılar", *Haberturk,* (July 14, 2016), accessed on September 13, 2016 from http://www.haberturk.com/gundem/haber/1102784-isid -saflarina-katilan-adiyamanlilar.

48. Ozeren and Hekim, "ISIS in Cyberspace: Findings from Social Media Research".

49. The Global Policy and Strategy Institute conducted research on seed accounts that are deemed to be linked to ISIS. This research examined 290 accounts, most of which used religious symbols and quotations from Quran as well as historical figures or ISIS leaders. (Ozeren and Hekim, "ISIS in Cyberspace: Findings from Social Media Research").

50. Ozeren and Hekim, "ISIS in Cyberspace: Findings from Social Media Research".

51. J. Morgan and J.M. Berger, "The ISIS Twitter census: Defining and describing the population of ISIS supporters on Twitter", *Report*, (The Brookings Institution, 2015).

52. Le2, Le4, and Le7, Interview by Mahmut Cengiz, Personal Interviews, May 18, 2018, Gaziantep.

53. This popularity leads to the influx of Al Nusra militants to the ISIS. When both terrorist organizations parted ways in 2013, 60 percent of JN militants moved to ISIS. (McCants, *The ISIS Apocalypse*).

54. Le2, Le4, and Le7, Interview by Mahmut Cengiz, Personal Interviews, May 18, 2018, Gaziantep. This social structure has been used by other criminal and terrorist organizations. For example, Turkish criminal groups were formed by familial relations and illustrated as family type criminal organizations (Cengiz, *Turkiye"de Organize Suc Gercegi*).

55. Ozeren and Hekim, "ISIS in Cyberspace: Findings from Social Media Research".

56. Tezcur and Ciftci, "Why Turkish Citizens are Joining ISIS?"

57. It is a radical terrorist organization composed of Sunni Turks and Kurds and operating in the southeastern region of Turkey (see Chapter 6).

58. Ozeren and Hekim, "ISIS in Cyberspace: Findings from Social Media Research".

59. Le1, Le3, Le5, and Le7, Interview by Mahmut Cengiz, Personal Interviews, May 18, 2018, Gaziantep.

60. Le1, Le3, Le5, and Le7, Interview by Mahmut Cengiz, Personal Interviews, May 18, 2018, Gaziantep.

61. Ozeren and Hekim, "ISIS in Cyberspace: Findings from Social Media Research".

62. "Kim bu dokumacılar" *Hurriyet Gazetesi*, (October 12, 2015), accessed on October 21, 2016 from http://www.hurriyet.com.tr/kim-bu-dokumacilar-30290471

63. Le2, Le4, and Le7, Interview by Mahmut Cengiz, Personal Interviews, May 18, 2018, Gaziantep.

64. Ozeren and Hekim, "ISIS in Cyberspace: Findings from Social Media Research".

65. Focus Group Study with FSA Members by Mahmut Cengiz, April 12, 2015, Sanliurfa.

66. Le2, Le4, and Le7, Interview by Mahmut Cengiz, Personal Interviews, May 18, 2018, Gaziantep.

67. A. J. Tabler, "Securing al-Sham" in *The ISIS Crisis*, ed. G. Rose, *Foreign Affairs*, 38-45.

68. Stern and Berger, *ISIS The State of Terror*

69. Le1, Le3, Le5, and Le7, Interview by Mahmut Cengiz, Personal Interviews, May 18, 2018, Gaziantep.

70. Le2, Le4, and Le7, Interview by Mahmut Cengiz, Personal Interviews, May 18, 2018, Gaziantep.

71. Ozeren and Hekim, "ISIS in Cyberspace: Findings from Social Media Research".

72. "Reyhanlı saldırısı için vahim iddialar", *Cumhuriyet Gazetesi*, accessed on October 21, 2016 from http://www.cumhuriyet.com.tr/haber/turkiye/274009/Reyha nli_saldirisi_icin_vahim_iddialar.html

73. "Niğde saldırganları tutuklandı", *Hurriyet Gazetesi*, accessed on October 21, 2016 from http://www.hurriyet.com.tr/nigde-saldirganlari-tutuklandi-26078888.

74. "IŞİD, Musul'da Türkiye konsolosluğunu bastı, 49 kişi rehin", *Evrensel*, accessed on October 21, 2017 from https://www.evrensel.net/haber/86093/isid-mus ulda-turkiye-konsoslugunu-basti-49-kisi-rehin.

75. According to the Turkish constitution, the threshold to set up a government requires one member more than one half of members at the parliament, which it is 276.

76. Ozeren and Hekim, "ISIS in Cyberspace: Findings from Social Media Research".

77. Ozeren and Hekim, "ISIS in Cyberspace: Findings from Social Media Research".

78. "41 killed in suicide attack at Istanbul airport", *USA Today*, (June 29, 2016), accessed on July 21, 2017 from http://www.usatoday.com/story/news/2016/06/28/ reports-least-10-dead-blast-istanbul-airport/86481174/

79. Ozeren and Hekim, "ISIS in Cyberspace: Findings from Social Media Research".

80. Sekulow, *Rise of ISIS*.

81. "UN Watchdog Confirms Mustard Gas Attack in Syria" *Guardian*, accessed on June 13, 2016 from http://www.theguardian.com/world/2015/nov/06/un-watchdog -confirms-mustard-gas-attack-in-syria.

82. M. Cengiz, *Orta Dogu'da Kuresel Tehditler Suriye Krizi ve ISID Teroru*, (Ankara: Adalet Yayinevi, 2016).

83. "Sarin gazı' davasında Qassap'a 12 yıl hapis, 5 Türk'e beraat", *Habertürk*, accessed on September 2, 2017 from http://www.haberturk.com/gundem/haber/11 73861-Sarin-gazi-davasinda-5-turk-beraat-etti.

84. Le1, Le3, Le5, and Le7, Interview by Mahmut Cengiz, Personal Interviews, May 18, 2018, Gaziantep.

85. "Yeminini yutan Türkeş kabinede, sevkiyat haberini yapan gazeteciler hapiste", *YouTube*, accessed on October 1, 2016 from https://www.youtube.com/watch?v=XtVnuNbW4ho

86. "Turkey declares vanishing truck to Syria 'state secret'," *Al Monitor,* accessed on October 21, 2016 from http://www.al-monitor.com/pulse/originals/201 4/01/vanished-turkish-truck-state-secret.html#ixzz4NmGMiN1Q.

87. "MİT TIR'LARIYLA ILGILI videolar ortaya cikti", *YouTube*, accessed on August 23, 2016 from https://www.youtube.com/watch?v=3YRduO2yWgU

88. "Savcı Özcan Şişman'dan tarihi 01 savunma", *YouTube*, accessed on September 15, 2016 from https://www.youtube.com/watch?v=iL-L-1DfZ3I

89. "Savcı Özcan Şişman'dan tarihi 01 savunma"

90. "Savcı Özcan Şişman'dan tarihi 01 savunma"

91. "Savcı Özcan Şişman'dan tarihi 01 savunma"

92. "Savcı Aziz Takçı'nın 02 savunması", *YouTube*, accessed on September 17, 2016 from https://www.youtube.com/watch?v=0aFYy_NJsl8.

93. "I revealed the truth about President Erdogan and Syria. For that, he had me jailed", *The Guardian,* (December 28, 2015) accessed on September 28, 2016 from https://www.theguardian.com/commentisfree/2015/dec/28/truth-president-erdog an-jailed-turkey-regime-state-security-crime.

94. "EREN ERDEM AKP-IŞİD ilişkisini BELGELERİYLE ispat etti !!!", *YouTube,* accessed on September 29, 2016 from https://www.youtube.com/watch? v=EcBUrIGbGmI.

95. This ISIS attack in October 10, 2015 killed 102 Kurdish people near the main station in Ankara.

96. IB is the abbreviation of the name of the suspect.

97. These militants sometimes carried weapons when crossing the border. Even though the police identified these militants before crossing the border, nobody intervened ("Lav silahlarıyla sınırı geçmişler!") *Cumhuriyet,* accessed on October 13, 2016, from http://www.cumhuriyet.com.tr/haber/siyaset/532704/Lav_silahlariyla_sin iri_gecmisler_.html.

98. "EREN ERDEM AKP-IŞİD ilişkisini BELGELERİYLE ispat etti !!!"

99. "EREN ERDEM AKP-IŞİD ilişkisini BELGELERİYLE ispat etti !!!". Another investigation revealed the linkage of transferring weapons from Turkey to ISIS. Allegedly, intelligence officers organized the transfer of arms which were seized in September 2015. Some amount of ammunitions that are used to make bombs was found in a truck hidden beneath the sacks of onions ("İşte IŞİD'e soğan altında giden silahlar", *Cumhuriyet Gazetesi.* accessed on October 13, 2017 from http://www.cumhuriyet.com .tr/haber/turkiye/523452/iste_ISiD_e_sogan_altinda_giden_silahlar.html)

100. "EREN ERDEM AKP-IŞİD ilişkisini BELGELERİYLE ispat etti!!!".

101. "IŞİD'in yaralıları Antep'te özel hastanede tedavi görüyor, şebekede insani yardım dernekleri de var", *Birgun Gazetesi,* accessed on October 4, 2016 from http://www.birgun.net/haber-detay/isid-in-yaralilari-antep-te-ozel-hastanede-tedavi-goruyor-sebekede-insani-yardim-dernekleri-de-var-113107.html.

102. There are other allegations about the relationship between IHH and ISIS. In one of the investigations against ISIS, the leader of the organization linked to ISIS said that we could employ IHH to transfer ISIS militants and transport materials to

Syria ("İHH yardım eder TIR'ları geçiririz", *Cumhuriyet Gazetesi,* accessed on June, 15, 2016 from http://www.cumhuriyet.com.tr/haber/dunya/550737/_iHH_yardim_eder_TIR_lari_geciririz_.html).

103. "Underground clinics in Turkey treating Syria's wounded to fight on", *Middle East Eye,* accessed on October 3, 2016 from http://www.middleeasteye.net/news/illegal-medical-clinics-turkey-healing-syrian-militants-fight-another-day-1980097 915.

104. "Polisten IŞİD itirafı: 2 yıl böyleydi, orada nöbet tuttum", Cumhuriyet Gazetesi, accessed on October 5, 2016 from www.cumhuriyet.com.tr/haber/turkiye/5266 27/Polisten_ISiD_itirafi__2_yil_boyleydi__orada_nobet_tuttum.html.

105. Le1, Le3, Le5, and Le7, Interview by Mahmut Cengiz, Personal Interviews, May 18, 2018, Gaziantep.

106. "The Islamic State in Iraq and the Levant and the Al-Nusrah Front for the People of the Levant: report and recommendations submitted pursuant to resolution 2170 (2014)", *United Nations Security Council Syrian Report,* http://www.securityc ouncilreport.org/atf/cf/%7B65BFCF9B-6D27-4E9C-8CD3-.

107. Sanserif, *ISIS The Face of Terrorism.*

108. A. Macias and J. Bender, "Here's How The World's Richest Terrorist Group Makes Millions Every Day", *Business Insider,* 2014.

109. "ISIS an unprecedented threat, wealthiest terrorist group in the world", *New York Daily News*, (February 6, 2016), accessed on October 12, 2016 from http://www.nydailynews.com/news/world/isis-world-wealthiest-terrorist-organization-u-n-article-1.2522284.

110. United Nations Security Council Syrian Report, 2014.

111. Macias and Bender, "Here's How the World's Richest Terrorist Group Makes Millions Every Day".

112. ISIS generates 10%-35% taxes from pharmaceuticals from people who live in its territory ("Inside the $2 Billion ISIS War Machine", *CNN,* accessed on October 7, 2016 from http://money.cnn.com/2015/12/06/news/isis-funding/).

113. Louise Shelley, "Blood Money How ISIS Makes Bank", in *The ISIS Crisis*, ed. G. Rose, (Foreign Affairs,2015): 28-31.

114. Le1, Le3, Le5, and Le7, Interview by Mahmut Cengiz, Personal Interviews, May 18, 2018, Gaziantep.

115. Shelley, "Blood Money How ISIS Makes Bank".

116. A. Burweila, "How to lose a war: when your allies are your enemies", *Research Institute for European and American Studies*, 2014.

117. Macias and Bender, "Here's How The World's Richest Terrorist Group Makes Millions Every Day".

118. Shelley, "Blood Money How ISIS Makes Bank".

119. International Energy Agency, "Oil market report", accessed on July 25, 2016 from https://www.iea.org/oilmarketreport/omrpublic/.

120. "United Nations Security Council Syrian Report".

121. B. Foucan and A. Albayrak, "Islamic State Funds Push Into Syria and Iraq With Labyrinthine Oil-Smuggling Operation", *The Wall Street Journal,* accessed on

September 2, 2016 from http://www.wsj.com/articles/islamic-state-funds-push-in to-syria-and-iraq-with-labyrinthine-oil-smuggling-operation-1410826325.

122. "Inside the $2 Billion ISIS War Machine".

123. Macias and Bender, "Here's How The World's Richest Terrorist Group Makes Millions Every Day".

124. Shelley, "Blood Money How ISIS Makes Bank".

125. "United Nations Security Council Syrian Report".

126. *2009, 2010, 2012, and 2013 Turkish Report of ASOD.*

127. United Nations Security Council Syrian Report, 2014.

128. Le1, Le3, Le5, and Le7, Interview by Mahmut Cengiz, Personal Interviews, May 18, 2018, Gaziantep.

129. *2013, 2014, and 2015 Turkish Reports of ASOD.*

130. Le1, Le3, Le5, and Le7, Interview by Mahmut Cengiz, Personal Interviews, May 18, 2018, Gaziantep.

131. "İŞİD'in Adıyamanlı üyesi konuştu: Petrol Türkiye'ye satılıyor", *Sputnik News,* (December 12, 2015). accessed on October 5, 2016 from https://tr.sputnikne ws.com/ortadogu/201512221019810620-isid-adiyamanli-uye-konustu-petrol-turki ye-satiliyor.

132. "ISIS Cashing in on Looted Antiquities to Fuel Iraq Insurgency".

133. "How ISIS Makes Millions From Stolen Antiquities", accessed on October 18, 2016 from http://www.newsweek.com/isis-syria-antiquities-millions-profit-mo ney-russia-islamic-state-palmyra-444805.

134. A. Keller, "Documenting ISIL's antiquities trafficking: The looting and destruction of Iraqi and Syrian cultural heritage", *US State Department.* accessed on June 2916 from http://www.state.gov/e/eb/rls/rm/2015/247610.htm

135. *2010 and 2012 Turkish Reports of ASOD.*

136. "Gaziantep'te tarihi eser kaçakçılığı" Sabah Gazetesi, accessed on October 24, 2016 from http://www.sabah.com.tr/yasam/2015/05/06/gaziantepte-tarihi-eser-kacakciligi

137. "United Nations Security Council Syrian Report".

138. L. Amineddoleh, "How western art collectors are helping to fund Isis", *The Guardian,* accessed on July 5, 2016 from https://www.theguardian.com/artanddesign /2016/feb/26/western-art-funding-terrorism-isis-middle-east.

139. *2015 Turkish Report of ASOD.*

140. Focus Group Study with FSA Members by Mahmut Cengiz, April 12, 2015, Sanliurfa.

141. Le2, Le4, and Le7, Interview by Mahmut Cengiz, Personal Interviews, May 18, 2018, Gaziantep.

142. "Looted in Syria – and sold in London: The British antiques shops dealing in artefacts smuggled by Isis". *The Guardian,* accessed on August 25, 2016 from https ://www.theguardian.com/world/2015/jul/03/antiquities-looted-by-isis-end-up-in-london-shops.

143. "Smuggler of stolen artifacts from Palmyra speaks out about ISIS' illicit operation" *NBC News,* accessed on July 28, 2016 from http://www.nbcnews.com/

storyline/isis-terror/smuggler-stolen-artifacts-palmyra-speaks-out-about-isis-illicit-operation-n551806.

144. Le1, Le3, Le5, and Le7, Interview by Mahmut Cengiz, Personal Interviews, May 18, 2018, Gaziantep. According to media reports, Turkey is a center to transit the antiquities marketed by ISIS. After being transferred to Turkey, ISIS antiquities have been sold in international markets. "Rusya: IŞİD, Suriye'den çaldığı tarihi eserleri Gaziantep'te satıyor" accessed on October 17, 2016 from https://tr.sputnikne ws.com/ortadogu/201604071021992258-suriye-rusya-isid-turkiye-sanat-eseri-satisi/. Moreover, ISIS militants are linked to Turkish antiquities traders to transit antiquities. "IŞİD, Türkiye üzerinden tarihi eser kaçırıyordu", accessed on October 18, 2016 from https://tr.sputniknews.com/ortadogu/201603311021860246-suriye-sedade-turkiye-isid/.

145. "United Nations Security Council Syrian Report".

146. Shelley "Blood Money How ISIS Makes Bank".

147. United Nations Security Council Syrian Report, 2014.

148. It should be noted that the Turkish government allegedly has linkage with conflicts in Nigeria. In a wiretapping released in 2014, the official from Turkish Airlines says "we are carrying tons of equipment and we do not know who these materials will kill either Muslims or Christians". Thereon the chief advisor to President Erdogan says "I need to ask to chief of intelligence and get back to you". "Türk Hava Yollari Nijerya ya silah tasiyor" accessed on October 13, 2017 from https://www.you tube.com/watch?v=1nT4-IwEKts. According to some comments, the address for these weapons was Boko Haram. "118 kişiyi öldüren bombaları Türk Hava Yolları mı taşıdı" accessed on October 13, 2017 from http://odatv.com/118-kisiyi-olduren-bomb alari-turk-hava-yollari-mi-tasidi--2105141200.html.

149. Le2, Le4, and Le7, Interview by Mahmut Cengiz, Personal Interviews, May 18, 2018, Gaziantep.

150. Human Trafficking Syria Report, 2014. http://www.state.gov/documents/organization/226848.pdf

151. Macias and Bender, "Here's How The World's Richest Terrorist Group Makes Millions Every Day".

152. United Nations Human Rights Report, 2014. http://www.ohchr.org/Docu ments/Countries/IQ/UNAMI_OHCHR_POC_Report_FINAL_6July_10September 2014.pdf.

153. "2016 Trafficking in Persons Report", *Syrian Report*, accessed on October 22, 2016 from http://www.state.gov/j/tip/rls/tiprpt/countries/2016/258872.htm.

154. The number of Syrian traffickers and victims has risen exponentially in Turkey. Syrian women, including underage girls, have been sold to wealthy individuals in Gaziantep and Kilis. Prices vary between 2,000 USD and 15,000 USD. The brokers connect the customers and Syrian victims. Poor Syrians who live out of refugee camps are especially vulnerable to human trafficking. A considerable number of Syrians have been detained in Turkey on charges of prostitution. Police detained 11 Syrian women on prostitution charges in one case in Hatay. Hotels and private houses have been used by traffickers to facilitate a large number of Syrian women in Gaziantep city.

155. Le2, Le4, and Le7, Interview by Mahmut Cengiz, Personal Interviews, May 18, 2018, Gaziantep.

156. Captagon is a form of amphetamine popular with ISIS fighters.

157. Focus Group Study with FSA Members by Mahmut Cengiz, April 12, 2015, Sanliurfa.

158. *2013 Turkish Report of ASOD.*

159. *2009, 2010, 2011, and 2013 Turkish Reports of ASOD.*

160. *2014 Turkish Report of ASOD.*

161. *2013 Turkish Report of ASOD.*

162. *2014 Turkish Report of ASOD.*

163. *2013 Turkish Report of ASOD.*

164. *2014 Turkish Report of ASOD.*

165. Le1, Le3, Le5, and Le7, Interview by Mahmut Cengiz, Personal Interviews, May 18, 2018, Gaziantep.

166. "Isis fighters 'high on cocaine: Drugs found at home of isis fighters", accessed on June 13, 2016 from http://ukmagazine.org/u-s/isis-fighters-high-on-cocaine-drugs-found-at-home-of-islamic-state-leader

167. "IŞİD kaçarken cinsel haplarını unuttu", *Internethaber,* accessed on June 23, 2016 from http://www.internethaber.com/isid-kacarken-cinsel-haplarini-unuttu-761596h.htm, 2 Şubat 2015.

168. Le2, Le4, and Le7, Interview by Mahmut Cengiz, Personal Interviews, May 18, 2018, Gaziantep.

169. "Islamic State Is a Diversified Criminal Operation". *Der Spiegel*, accessed on July 23, 2016 from http://www.spiegel.de/international/business/terror-expert-shelley-speaks-of-islamic-state-business-model-a-1011492.html.

170. *2009, 2010, 2012, and 2013 Turkish Reports of ASOD.*

171. *2013 Turkish Report of ASOD.*

172. *2009, 2010, 2012, and 2013 Turkish Reports of ASOD.*

173. *2009, 2010, 2012, and 2013 Turkish Reports of ASOD.*

174. *2013 Turkish Report of ASOD.*

175. *2015 Turkish Report of ASOD.*

176. Shelley, "Blood Money How ISIS Makes Bank".

177. "Syrian Refugees Are Selling Their Organs to Survive", *Newsweek*, accessed on October 20, 2016 from http://www.newsweek.com/syrian-refugees-selling-organs-survive-459745

178. Le2, Le4, and Le7, Interview by Mahmut Cengiz, Personal Interviews, May 18, 2018, Gaziantep.

Chapter 10

Money Laundering

INTRODUCTION

Criminals and terrorists, forever watchful for new ways to finance their activities, have turned to money laundering in Turkey's illicit economy to protect their finances from government watchdogs. Endemic corruption and the lack of effective anti-money laundering strategies in Turkey play into the hands of criminals and terrorists, making their ability to operate in Turkey's illicit economy that much easier. The free flow of unregistered money into Turkey reflects the country's vulnerability to money laundering.

Money launderers—a mix of criminals, terrorists, and corrupt officials—resort to different methods to "clean" their money, ranging from cash or bank transfers to underground systems for transferring funds. These methods apparently have been successful. While it may seem that the Turkish banking system is compliant with international standards, the results of police investigations in Turkey demonstrate that the country's politicians exploit the banking system. The lack of a due diligence system combined with political corruption provides a favorable environment for money launderers. This chapter examines the sources of dirty money, what the government is doing to combat money laundering, and how money launderers operate in the country, using interviews[1] conducted with money laundering experts.

The Flow of Illicit Money in Turkey

Global money laundering has increased astronomically as world economies became increasingly more interconnected in recent years. It increased from 273 billion USD in 1995 to 603 billion USD in 2006 for twenty OECD countries.[2] The amount of global money laundering amounted to 5-6 percent of

GDP in 2006.[3] An overwhelming number of Turkish money laundering cases in the 1960s were related to drug trafficking. Most of them involved Turks who had immigrated to European countries. The problem was pervasive and long-standing. Drug trafficking reigned as the single largest source of illegal proceeds until the situation shifted in the 1990s, when tax-evasion cases rose to the top of the list. This shift was precipitated by a substantial amount of money laundering activity through the fictitious exportation of goods. In the 1990s, it was estimated that 50 percent of the Turkish economy was unregistered.[4]

Turkey is an important regional financial center for countries in Central Asia, the Caucasus, the Middle East, and Eastern Europe.[5] Corrupt officials, criminals, and terrorists who use banks, nonbank financial institutions, and the informal economy to hide their illegal activities have exploited Turkey's stature in the financial sector.[6] According to government officials, unregistered businesses are responsible for one-quarter to one-third of the country's economic activity. Criminals use various money laundering methods, including large-scale cross-border currency smuggling, bank transfers into and out of the country, trade fraud, and the purchase of high-value items such as real estate, gold, and luxury automobiles.[7] Recent cases demonstrate that criminal organizations are prone to using smurfing and structuring money laundering techniques. Meanwhile, they integrate dirty money into the transportation sector and restaurant industry.[8]

In 2013, 1.1 trillion USD in illicit money came from developing and emerging economies, mainly stemming from tax evasion, corruption, and other crimes.[9] The value of illicit money worldwide is estimated at 1.4 trillion to 2.5 trillion USD.[10] In a December 2015 report on illicit financial flows from developing countries between 2004 and 2013 published by Global Financial Integrity, Turkey was ranked 12th in terms of the largest average illicit outflow of money among the 149 countries studied, an amount indicative of high-volume money laundering in Turkey.[11]

During the tenure of the ruling Justice and Development Party (AKP), the amount of money flowing out of the country between 2004 and 2013 increased steadily.[12] Turkey was 26th on the list of 145 countries between 2003 and 2012. Turkey became more vulnerable to money laundering and the inflow of illicit money in 2013.[13] The amount of illicit money flowing out of Turkey during the study period was $227 million in 2006. Illicit outflow for all other years of the study period was zero.[14] The total amount of illicit money flowing into the country because of fraudulent invoices between 2004 and 2013 reached $345.5 billion, while the amount of illicit money going out of the country for the same reason was $154.3 billion.[15] The organization's report for 2005 to 2014 showed that the flow of illicit money out of Turkey was as high as 3 percent (low of 1 percent) of the country's total trade, while the inflow of illicit money was as high as 13 percent (low of 6 percent) of the country's total trade.[16] Data from a Turkish news report disclosed that the amount of illicit money flowing into the country was 10.2 billion USD in 2015 and 11.7 billion USD in 2016—an increase of almost 400 percent.[17]

Although a huge amount of illicit money flows into the country, the Central Bank of the Republic of Turkey does not elucidate the source of this money on its financial statements, presenting it instead under the "Net Errors and Omissions" column. An increase in the Net Errors and Omissions column indicates that money is flowing into a country, while a decrease in this column indicates that money is flowing out of a country. During the AKP's time in office, the flow of illicit money into the country has increased considerably. The AKP government has legitimized the inflow of illicit money by issuing tax amnesties. While the inflow of illicit money was 3.5 billion USD between 2002 and 2012, it grew to 29.4 USD between 2003 and 2013. The AKP has reduced government account deficits by using illicit money inflows. For example, 26 of every 100 USD that an account was deficient in 2014 was paid for by illicit money entering the country.[18]

Different explanations have been offered for the source of illicit money flows into Turkey. One explanation posits that the inflows are remittances from Turkish people abroad who transfer money when the economy needs a boost. This explanation, however, is not convincing because little evidence exists to validate such big money transfers from Turkish immigrants abroad. A second explanation is that Iraqis, Syrians, and people from other war-torn Arabic countries transfer money to a secure country—in this case, Turkey. Again, the explanation is not credible. Such money would need to be deposited into a bank account, but it is not. The money remains outside the legal financial system and is treated as errors and omissions. A third explanation holds that Muslim countries in the Gulf States transfer money to support the Turkish economy.[19]

For many years, the source of illicit money flowing into Turkey had been Iran. Now the Gulf States play that role. A significant amount of the illicit money into Turkey belongs to Qatar,[20] which sends the money to Turkey on its way to Syria in support of opposition groups fighting in the Syrian civil war.[21] According to one official who worked on the Syrian border in 2013, his team arrested a courier with a huge amount of money in a suitcase. The courier's interrogation revealed that he brought the money from Qatar in order to transfer it to the jihadist groups fighting in Syria.[22] Additional evidence of the Qatar connection occurred in 2016. A Qatari Airbus A319 aircraft landed late at night, cabin curtains closed, in Gaziantep, Turkey, on the border of ISIS territory—even though the airline had no scheduled flights between any Qatari city and Gaziantep.[23] Qatar's close relationship with terrorist organizations in Syria and the mysterious appearance of the aircraft in Gaziantep suggest that money or weapons were being transferred to Syria via Turkey.[24] The close friendships among Turkish and Qatari leaders who are considered major funders of terrorism[25] have made this speculation seem more plausible.

The Sources of Illicit Money

The sources for money laundered in Turkey include narcotics trafficking, smuggling, invoice fraud, tax evasion, and, to a lesser extent, counterfeit goods, forgery, highway robbery, and kidnapping.[26] Other sources include terrorist financing, corruption, and suspicious money transfers between Turkey and Gulf States.[27] Turkish-based traffickers use couriers to transfer money and gold and the underground banking system and bank transfers to pay drug suppliers in Pakistan and Afghanistan. The traffickers frequently transfer funds to accounts in Pakistan, the United Arab Emirates, and other Middle Eastern countries.[28]

In addition, criminal groups have exploited Turkish government policies that permit the conveyance of unlimited amounts of money into the country. According to a regulation adopted in 2015, the government repealed money transfer limits into the country.[29] Criminal groups operating abroad took advantage of the opportunity to do so. For example, Turkish organized crime groups that dominate heroin trafficking in European countries have transferred drug money into Turkey. That money typically makes its way into the tourism and real estate sectors. By most accounts, Antalya is a safe haven for Turkish drug traffickers interested in buying hotels and Russian criminal groups transferring cash for the same purpose.[30]

Police seizures of large sums of money in the luggage of Turkish passengers at European airports confirm the flow of money from Europe to Turkey. For example, German customs officials in June of 2016 seized 450,000 euros from a Turkish passenger who attempted to fly to Turkey. In his statement, the passenger acknowledged that his intention was to transfer the money to Turkey to buy real estate.[31] The following year, Russian customs officials arrested a passenger and seized the 200,000 USD he was attempting to transfer to Turkey. This passenger also admitted that he planned to buy real estate in Turkey.[32]

The numerous casinos in Northern Cyprus attract Turkish criminals needing a place to transfer money for laundering. According to law enforcement officials in Cyprus, the main requirement for opening a hotel is sufficient occupancy and therefore sufficient income to provide hotel services. Visitors who use the casinos, however, occupy hotels in the country only on weekends. Revenue from hotel services is quite limited compared to revenue generated by the casinos.[33] In August 2014, for example, the law enforcement officials at the airport in Northern Cyprus seized almost 1 million USD in cash from money launderers who had attempted to transfer money from the casinos.[34]

Smuggling is another crime that is linked to money laundering. In 2013, Turkish police recorded around 25,000 smuggling cases and arrested more than 40,000 smugglers illegally transporting oil, cigarettes, people, contraband, pharmaceuticals, and antiquities.[35] In 2016, Turkish customs officials recorded 4,424 smuggling cases involving 2.6 billion Turkish liras.[36] Smugglers have transferred the money in cash, via couriers from source countries and transit countries. It should be noted that Turkey has a strong preference for cash transactions. Smugglers also use the Hawala system, banks, and exchange offices to launder money.[37]

Tax evasion is another activity that often involves money laundering. Turkish people do not consider tax evasion as a serious crime according to the results of research published in 2008[38] and 2015.[39] Government data show that the police arrested an average of around 500 criminals each year between 2010 and 2015.[40] Most of the cases referred to the Financial Crimes Investigation Board (MASAK) between 2010 and 2014 involved tax evasion, including 117 cases in 2014.[41] According to the minister of finance, the yearly tax loss in Turkey is around 90 billion Turkish liras (approximately 30 billion USD).[42] The cost of tax loss from smuggled and counterfeit goods is 7.2 billion USD.[43]

Front companies set up by Iranians also are a source for money laundering. Sanctions imposed on Iran by the United Nations and the United States locked Iranian currency in overseas escrow accounts. Front companies in Turkey enable Iranians to access the frozen funds. These companies issued fraudulent invoices in 2013 for food and medicines that were exempt from the rules of the sanctions and exploited state-owned banks in return for giving bribes (see the Zarrab case in Chapter 6).[44]

Although the Turkish banking system operates according to global standards, it lacks the oversight needed to detect suspicious money transfer systems. The money transfer system in Western countries is based on flagging, whereby law enforcement investigators attempt to detect money transfers that exceed a specified limit set by law. For example, the U.S. system considers money transfers of more than $10,000 to be suspicious.[45] Banks in Turkey, however, are required to notify the central bank only when money transfers exceed $50,000 and are not part of an export or import transaction.[46]

Turkish banks also lack an effective due diligence system for detecting suspicious money transfers. Businesspersons affiliated with the ruling political party are not subject to due diligence scrutiny. The authority of the ruling party to appoint executive boards of state banks makes the appointees more vulnerable to exploitation.[47] As the December 17 and December

25 corruption scandals (see Chapter 6) indicated, Turkish state banks were exploited to allow corrupt politicians to make illegal money transactions. While state-owned Halkbank was used to launder Iranian money with fraudulent transactions, another state-owned financial institution, Ziraat Bank, was used to provide improper credits for businesspersons linked to President Erdogan.[48] Also, Turkish state banks have been used in corrupt transactions. Dictators in Africa and Asia use their relationships with Erdogan to illegally transfer their money to Turkish state banks.[49]

Terrorist groups such as the PKK, al-Qaeda affiliates, ISIS, and some leftist organizations generate revenue from various areas of the illicit economy (see Chapters 8 and 9).[50] Some of these groups transfer cash across Turkey's southern border into Syria. Ongoing conflicts at the Turkish borders with Iraq and Syria have presented opportunities for terrorist groups to generate income from oil and antiquities smuggling and human trafficking operations stretching from the region to Europe.[51] Both ISIS and PKK militants use money funneled through accounts in Turkey. After opening bank accounts in Turkey by either themselves or their networks, the two terrorist groups use their bank debit cards in Turkey and northern Iraq to withdraw funds. Terrorists also have used Turkish state banks with branches in northern Iraq.[52] Some currency exchange offices in the Turkish cities of Gaziantep, Kilis, and Hatay operate as hawaladars for ISIS. For example, the exchange office in Gaziantep, which is linked to an exchange office in Tunisia, transfers money in return for receiving commissions from ISIS.[53] A police investigation conducted in 2018 verified how terrorists used the hawala system in Turkey. Investigation revealed that ISIS militants opened a hawala office in Istanbul, where police arrested two militants and seized gold and money in various currencies.[54]

Despite the high volume of smuggling, drug trafficking, corruption, tax evasion, and terrorist financing in Turkey, the government's efforts to fight these crimes have been ineffective. One remedy would be to increase the number of money-related crimes reported to MASAK, the government agency in charge of examining suspicious money transfers and detecting the linkages in money laundering operations. Only a handful of cases are reported to MASAK. In 2016, for example, only 11 drug trafficking cases, 21 smuggling cases, 32 corruption cases, and 34 tax evasion cases out of tens of thousands of cases were referred to MASAK.[55]

Anti-Money Laundering Efforts and Criminal Proceeds

Turkey has experienced advances and setbacks in its fight against criminals and terrorists. The country's failure to incorporate anticorruption and anti-money laundering strategies in the fight against crime and terrorism has played into the hands of corrupt government officials. Although criminals and terrorists generated revenue elsewhere and laundered it in Turkey, no anti-money laundering investigations had been conducted by the time Turkey's Anti-Money Laundering Law was passed in 1996.[56] Passage of the law was the result of Turkey's efforts to join the international community. Five years earlier, Turkey had become a member of the Financial Action Task Force, an inter-governmental body established in 1989 to set standards for effective efforts against money-related crimes.

A 1999 ASOD report noted that Turkey's anti-smuggling and organized crime police units referred 72 cases to MASAK between 1997 and 1999, but MASAK found suspicious money transfers in only five of those cases. In 1999, out of 72 predicate offenses (crimes underlying money laundering or terrorist financing activity) four were for drug trafficking,[57] even though the total number of drug trafficking cases in the entire country was 3,345 that year.[58] The numbers suggest that the police found suspicious money in only 0.1 percent of all drug cases. MASAK's inefficiency continued over the following years. According to the U.S. Department of State International Narcotics Control Strategy Report published in 2003, MASAK examined more than 500 cases in 2003. It prosecuted 59 of those cases and won a conviction in only two of them. The failure of convictions stemmed from deficiencies and loopholes in anti-money laundering law and the lack of technical personnel.[59]

No data on money laundering were available until 2006 when the Turkish government enacted the Prevention of Laundering of Criminal Proceeds law. That same year, law enforcement and units in the Ministry of Finance were reorganized based on the new legislation, spurred on by a European Union Twinning project that aimed to integrate the Turkish anti-money laundering system into the international community.[60] One requirement of the project was to enhance the investigative capacity of Turkish law enforcement. In response to that requirement, in 2010 law enforcement officials established a section that would specialize in probing criminal proceeds.[61]

Anti-money laundering strategies in Turkey are twofold: direct confiscation of criminal proceeds and investigation of suspicious money laundering cases. Turkish police have used anti-smuggling and anti-trafficking laws to justify the confiscation of criminal goods. For example, Turkey's anti-smuggling law permits officers to confiscate a vehicle if the vehicle has been used in two smuggling operations. In 2011, the police confiscated 716 vehicles and 82 real estate properties in the investigations of financial, narcotics, mafia-type, and smuggling crimes.[62] The police increased their confiscation capacity in 2012 and 2013, with the total number of vehicles and real estate properties confiscated rising to 2,884 in 2012[63] and 4,641 in 2013.[64] Unfortunately, these totals dropped sharply when the government responded to the two corruption investigations in December 2013 by firing entire crime-fighting units (see Chapter 7). Confiscations decreased to 2,451 in 2014[65] and to 1,771 in 2015.[66] The amount of money confiscated in 2014 and 2015 dropped to 9.3 million Turkish liras (approximately $3.1 million) from 85 million Turkish liras (approximately $28 million) in 2012 and 2013.[67]

Turkey's success in tracing the source of criminal revenue is as dismal as it is for confiscating criminal assets. This can be explained in part by the fact that Turkish anti-money laundering laws require conviction on the predicate offense before a money laundering investigation can be started. Given that it takes several years to obtain a conviction in a criminal case, money laundering investigations are ignored. It should be noted that unlike their Western counterparts, Turkish laws require the police to prove that the assets were obtained from a crime rather than the criminal to prove that the assets were not obtained from a crime. The country's weak and incompetent judicial infrastructure therefore makes it difficult to trace illicit profits.[68]

In a 2012 case, the police found solid evidence that an oil station sold smuggled oil between 2008 and 2012 and earned 12 million Turkish liras, or approximately 5 million USD. The oil smugglers bribed members of the Turkish Supreme Court, convincing the court to drop the case despite overwhelming evidence proving that oil smuggling had occurred, and that illegal money had been generated from the crime. In another case, the police found the linkages of a currency exchange office that had been used in a hawala system. The smugglers transferred money obtained from cigarette trafficking through the exchange office. When the police dug deeper, they found that human traffickers used the same exchange office to transfer money from Turkey to Azerbaijan; however, the investigation failed to proceed once more because of the country's weak judicial infrastructure.[69]

Turkish Capacity to Fight Money Laundering

Serious issues hamper the anti-money laundering system in Turkey from reaching its full potential. The country lacks effective investigative units, interagency cooperation, oversight, and law enforcement capability.[70] Moreover, the country does not have a cash reporting system, even though the laws require reporting of suspicious transactions.[71] According to an interim compliance report from the Council of Europe's anti-corruption Group of States against Corruption (GRECO) in June 2017, Turkey failed to comply with any of the group's 17 recommendations pertaining to "incrimination" and "transparency of political funding."[72]

Furthermore, the U.S. State Department's 2016 International Narcotics Control Strategy Report (INCSR) has asserted that Turkey's nonprofit sector is not audited adequately in terms of its linkages to terrorist financing and money laundering primarily because there are not enough auditors to review the country's more than 70,000 nonprofit institutions.[73] Other weaknesses identified in the report include ineffective due diligence of politically exposed persons, lack of international standards on cross-border wire transfers and cash transfers, lack of scrutiny of nonfinancial businesses and professions, inability of MASAK to conduct sufficient data collection and analysis, and ineffective interagency cooperation for implementing existing laws and regulations.[74]

The aforementioned INCSR report also faults Turkish institutions responsible for suppressing money laundering for not publishing adequate statistical data since 2009, making it difficult, if not impossible, to get a clear picture of the number of investigations, prosecutions, and convictions those institutions handled. These shortcomings are made clear, as exemplified by the lack of data for 2014 and 2015, although 387 suspects were purportedly charged with money laundering and 61 individuals charged with terrorism, all referred to MASAK. The report further criticized Turkey for its lack of civil asset forfeiture procedures and for having only rudimentary criminal procedures and practices.[75]

MASAK chides Turkey for its failure to regulate cash transaction reports. Without cash transaction reports, it is not possible to conduct trend analyses that could show the crime categories and terrorist regions where the majority of cash transactions occur. Turkey's poor implementation of international sanctions makes the country appear unreliable in the eyes of international institutions. At one point, MASAK noted, Turkey had been at risk of being blacklisted.[76] In 2013, the Financial Action Task Force listed Turkey among the countries not committed to a plan of action developed with the FATF, to address deficiencies in efforts to fight money laundering and other money-related crimes.[77] Turkey remained on the list in 2014.[78]

It is urgent for Turkey to create an independent anti-money laundering institution that complies with international standards. Recent events demonstrate that MASAK is an institution vulnerable to government exploitation, as exemplified by the announcement of corruption investigations in December 2013. Since then, the government has redesigned MASAK, replacing its highly experienced personnel with individuals who are unconditionally obedient to the AKP government. The vernacular used in recent MASAK reports indicates that MASAK is dependent on the government, politicized, and is firmly under the control of the AKP. Officers in this unit now focus on the government's political agenda rather than on efforts to trace illegal money obtained from various criminal, terrorism, and corruption sources.

NOTES

1. Mahmut Cengiz conducted these interviews with four former officials who worked for Turkey's Financial Investigation Board (MASAK) in July 2015. Similar to other chapters, this chapter also codified the identity details of respondents. The codes given them are ML1, ML2, ML3, and ML4.

2. Fredrich Schneider "The Hidden Financial Flows of Organized Crime: A Literature Review and Some Preliminary Empirical Results" in Illicit Trade and Global Economy, eds C. Storti and P. Grauwe, (London: The MIT Press, 2012) pp. 31-48.

3. Mohammad Reza Farzanegan "Dark Side of Trade in Iran: Evidence from a Structural Equation Model" in Illicit Trade and Global Economy, eds C. Storti and P. Grauwe, (London: The MIT Press, 2012): 31-48. 73-118.

4. Bahadir Küçükuysal, "Karaparanin Aklanmasi Sorunu: Bir Türkiye Perspektifi/Money Laundering Problem: A Turkey Perspective," *Selçuk Üniversitesi Sosyal Bilimler Enstitüsü dergisi*, Vol. 28 (July 1, 2012): 125-134.

5. "2016 International Narcotics Control Strategy Report (INCSR)," *U.S. Department of State*, accessed on July 21, 2013, from https://www.state.gov/j/inl/rls/nrcrpt/2016/vol2/253435.htm.

6. ML1 and ML3, Interview by Mahmut Cengiz, Personal Interview-Skype, July 29, 2016.

7. "2016 International Narcotics Control Strategy Report (INCSR)," U.S. Department of State, accessed on July 21, 2013, from https://www.state.gov/j/inl/rls/nrcrpt/2016/vol2/253435.htm.

8. ML2 and ML4, Interview by Mahmut Cengiz, Personal Interview-Skype, July 28, 2016.

9. Dev Kar and Joseph Spanjers, "Illicit Financial Flows to and from Developing Countries: 2004-2013," *Global Financial Integrity*, (December 8, 2015), accessed on July 19, 2017, from http://www.gfintegrity.org/report/illicit-financial-flows-from-developing-countries-2004-2013/.

10. Dev Kar and Joseph Spanjers, "Illicit Financial Flows to and from Developing Countries: 2005-2014," *Global Financial Integrity*, (April 2017), accessed on July 19, 2017, from http://www.gfintegrity.org/wp-content/uploads/2017/05/GFI-IFF-Report-2017_final.pdf, iii.

11. Kar and Spanjers, "Illicit Financial Flows to and from Developing Countries: 2004-2013," 28.

12. Dev Kar and Joseph Spanjers, "Illicit Financial Flows to and from Developing Countries: 2004-2013," *Global Financial Integrity*, (December 8, 2015), accessed on July 19, 2017, from http://www.gfintegrity.org/wp-content/uploads/2015/12/IFF-Update_2015-Final-1.pdf, p. 28.

13. "Kara para en çok 17-25 Aralık döneminde aklandı," *Cumhuriyet*, (February 3, 2016), accessed on July 19, 2017, from http://www.cumhuriyet.com.tr/haber/ekonomi/475077/Kara_para_en_cok_17-25_Aralik_doneminde_aklandi.html.

14. Dev Kar and Joseph Spanjers, "Illicit Financial Flows to and from Developing Countries: 2004-2013," *Global Financial Integrity*, (December 8, 2015), accessed on July 19, 2017, from http://www.gfintegrity.org/report/illicit-financial-flows-from-developing-countries-2004-2013/, 41.

15. Dev Kar and Joseph Spanjers, "Illicit Financial Flows to and from Developing Countries: 2004-2013," (December 8, 2015), accessed on July 19, 2017, from http://www.gfintegrity.org/report/illicit-financial-flows-from-developing-countries-2004-2013/, 45.

16. Dev Kar and Joseph Spanjers, "Illicit Financial Flows to and from Developing Countries: 2005-2014," *Global Financial Integrity*, (April 2017), accessed on July 19, 2017, from http://www.gfintegrity.org/wp-content/uploads/2017/05/GFI-IFF-Report-2017_final.pdf, 31.

17. "Ekonomiye 41 milyar dolarlık 'gizemli' doping," *Cumhuriyet*, (February 22, 2017), accessed on July 19, 2017, from http://www.cumhuriyet.com.tr/haber/ekono mi/681798/Ekonomiye_41_milyar_dolarlik__gizemli__doping.html.

18. Mehmet Çetingüleç, "Türkiye kayıt dışı parada rekora koşuyor," *Al Monitor*, (September 10, 2014), accessed on July 19, 2017, from http://www.al-monitor.com/pulse/tr/originals/2014/09/turkey-central-bank-mystery-funds.html.

19. Sumer Meric, "Nereden geliyor bu dolarlar?," *Kronos*, (February 17, 2017), accessed on July 24, 2017, from http://www.kronos.news/tr/nereden-geliyor-bu-dolar lar/.

20. Mehmet Çetingüleç "Türkiye kayıt dışı parada rekora koşuyor," *Al Monitor*, (September 10, 2014), accessed on July 19, 2017, from http://www.al-monitor.com/pulse/tr/originals/2014/09/turkey-central-bank-mystery-funds.html.

21. "İranlı Komutan: Türkiye, Katar'dan 5 Milyar Dolar Aldı," *Nerianazad*, (March 5, 2014), accessed on July 24, 2017, from http://www.nerinaazad.net/news/regions/turkey/iranli-komutan-turkiye-katardan-5-milyar-dolar-aldi.

22. Le1, Interview by Mahmut Cengiz, Personal Interview, May 29, 2015.

23. "Gaziantep'te Katar uçağı gizemi," *Yenicag Gazetesi*, (May 31, 2016), accessed on July 26, 2017, from http://www.yenicaggazetesi.com.tr/gaziantepte-katar -ucagi-gizemi-138578h.htm.

24. ML1 and ML3, Interview by Mahmut Cengiz, Personal Interview-Skype, July 29, 2016.

25. Zakir Gul, "Erdogan and Tamim: A Case for International Criminal Court?," *Vocale Europe*, (February 6, 2017), accessed on July 26, 2017, from http://www.voca leurope.eu/erdogan-and-tamim-a-case-for-international-criminal-court/.

26. "2016 International Narcotics Control Strategy Report (INCSR)," U.S. Department of State, accessed on July 21, 2013, from https://www.state.gov/j/inl/rls/nrcrpt/2016/vol2/253435.htm.

27. ML2 and ML4, Interview by Mahmut Cengiz, Personal Interview-Skype, July 2, 2016.

28. "2016 International Narcotics Control Strategy Report (INCSR)," U.S. Department of State, accessed on July 21, 2013, from https://www.state.gov/j/inl/rls/nrcrpt/2 016/vol2/253435.htm.

29. "Getirmek serbest götürmek beyanla," *Gazetevatan*, (December 31, 2015), accessed on July 25, 2017, from http://www.gazetevatan.com/getirmek-serbest-goturmek-beyanla-900009-ekonomi/.

30. ML1 and ML3, Interview by Mahmut Cengiz, Personal Interview-Skype, July 29, 2016.

31. "Türkiye'ye 450 bin Euro ile girmek istedi," *Airline Haber*, (June 11, 2016), accessed on July 24, 2017, from https://www.airlinehaber.com/turkiyeye-450-bin-euro-ile-girmek-istedi/.

32. "Para Dolu Çantayı İstanbul'a Getirmeye Çalıştı Havalimanında Yakalandı," *Airline Haber*, (March 19, 2017), accessed on July 24, 2017, from https://www.airlineh aber.com/para-dolu-cantayi-istanbula-getirmeye-calisti-havalimaninda-yakalandi/.

33. ML1 and ML3, Interview by Mahmut Cengiz, Personal Interview-Skype, July 29, 2016.

34. Filiz Seyis, "10 Ayda 3 milyon TL'ye el konuldu!," *Kibris Postasi*, (November 12, 2014), accessed on July 24, 2017, from http://www.kibrispostasi.com/index.php/cat/35/news/147069.

35. *2013 Turkish Report of Anti-Smuggling and Organized Crime*, 56.

36. "Bülent Tüfenkci: Gümrüklerde 2,6 milyar liralık kaçakçılık önlendi," *NTV*, (January 15, 2017), accessed on June 5, 2017, from http://www.ntv.com.tr/ekonomi/bulent-tufenkci-gumruklerde-2-6-milyar-liralik-kacakcilik-onlendi,UshGX6jRb kmqeuqopcRXdg?_ref=infinite.

37. ML2 and ML4, Interview by Mahmut Cengiz, Personal Interview-Skype, July 28, 2016.

38. F. Saracoglu, "Cevre, adalet algisi, sucun algilanis bicimi ile vergi kaçakci-ligina iliskin tutumlar arasindaki iliskiler," *Eskisehir Osmangazi Universitesi IIBF Dergisi*, Vol. 3, No. 1, (2008), pp. 59-74.

39. Serkan Benk, "Perception of Tax Evasion as a Crime in Turkey," *Journal of Money Laundering Control*, Vol. 18, No. 1 (January 2015): 99-111.

40. *2015 Turkish Report of Anti-Smuggling and Organized Crime*, 15.

41. "2014 MASAK Faaliyet Raporu," *MASAK*, accessed on July 27, 2017, from http://www.masak.gov.tr/userfiles/file/MASAK%202014%20FAAL%C4%B0Y ET%20RAPORU.pdf, p. 29.

42. "Maliye Bakanı Mehmet Şimşek, "Türkiye'nin kayıt dışı vergi kaybının 90 milyar lira olduğunu söyledi," *Finans Gundem*, (June 5, 2013), accessed on July 24, 2017, from http://www.finansgundem.com/haber/kayit-disi-vergi-kaybi-90-milyar-lira /384016.

43. "Kacak ve sahte urunde vergi kaybi 7.2 milyar dolar," *Ajans Press*, (March 27, 2017), accessed on July 24, 2017, from, http://www.turkonfed.org/tr/fotograflar/155/turkiyede-marka-olmak-calistayi-medya-yansimalari-23-mart-2017-istanbul/.

44. John A. Cassara, *Trade-Based Money Laundering*, (2015, Hoboken, NJ: John Wiley & Sons) 26.

45. ML2 and ML4, Interview by Mahmut Cengiz, Personal Interview-Skype, July 28, 2016.

46. Yilmaz Sezer, "Yurtdışına para transferinde bunlara dikkat!," *Dunya*, accessed on July 25, 2017, from https://www.dunya.com/gundem/yurtdisina-para-transferin de-bunlara-dikkat-haberi-327366.

47. ML1 and ML3, Interview by Mahmut Cengiz, Personal Interview-Skype, July 29, 2016.

48. ML2 and ML4, Interview by Mahmut Cengiz, Personal Interview-Skype, July 28, 2016.

49. ML1 and ML3, Interview by Mahmut Cengiz, Personal Interview-Skype, July 29, 2016.

50. ML2 and ML4, Interview by Mahmut Cengiz, Personal Interview-Skype, July 28, 2016.

51. "2016 International Narcotics Control Strategy Report (INCSR)," U.S. Department of State, accessed on July 21, 2013, from https://www.state.gov/j/inl/rls/nrcrpt/2016/vol2/253435.htm.

52. ML1 and ML3, Interview by Mahmut Cengiz, Personal Interview-Skype, July 29, 2016.

53. ML2 and ML4, Interview by Mahmut Cengiz, Personal Interview-Skype, July 28, 2016.

54. "IŞİD'in İstanbul'daki kasasına baskın," *Gazeteduvar*, (April 4, 2018), accessed on October 25, 2018, from https://www.gazeteduvar.com.tr/gundem/20 18/04/04/isidin-istanbuldaki-kasasina-baskin/.

55. *2016 MASAK Faaliyet Raporu, 21.*

56. *1997 Turkish Report of ASOD*, 66.

57. *1999 Turkish Report of ASOD*, 97.

58. *1999 Turkish Report of ASOD*, 23.

59. Bahadir Küçükuysal, Küçükuysal, "Karaparanin Aklanmasi Sorunu: Bir Türkiye Perspektifi/Money Laundering Problem: A Turkey Perspective," *Selçuk Üniversitesi Sosyal Bilimler Enstitüsü dergisi*, Vol. 28 (July 1, 2012), 129.

60. *2007 Turkish Report of ASOD*, 98.

61. *2010 Turkish Report of ASOD*, 107.

62. *2011 Turkish Report of ASOD*, 13.

63. *2012 Turkish Report of ASOD*, 24.

64. *2013 Turkish Report of ASOD*, 94.

65. *2014 Turkish Report of ASOD*, 88.

66. *2015 Turkish Report of ASOD*, 60.

67. *2015 Turkish Report of ASOD*, 60.

68. Mahmut Cengiz, *Turkiye'de Organize Suc Gercegi ve Terorun Finansmani*, (Ankara: Seckin Yayincilik, 2015).

69. Mahmut Cengiz's field experience, 2011-2014. Igdir.

70. "2016 International Narcotics Control Strategy Report (INCSR)," U.S. Department of State, accessed on July 21, 2013, from https://www.state.gov/j/inl/rls/nrcrpt/2016/vol2/253435.htm.

71. ML1 and ML3, Interview by Mahmut Cengiz, Personal Interview-Skype, July 29, 2016.

72. "GRECO: Turkey's Compliance with Recommendations to Fight Corruption Is Globally Unsatisfactory," *Turkish Minute*, (June 12, 2017), accessed on July 23, 2017, from https://www.turkishminute.com/2017/06/12/greco-turkeys-compliance -with-recommendations-to-fight-corruption-is-globally-unsatisfactory/.

73. "2016 International Narcotics Control Strategy Report (INCSR)."

74. "2016 International Narcotics Control Strategy Report (INCSR)."

75. "2016 International Narcotics Control Strategy Report (INCSR)."

76. ML2 and ML4, Interview by Mahmut Cengiz, Personal Interview-Skype, July 28, 2016.

77. "FATF Public Statement - 21 June 2013," *FATF*, accessed on July 27, 2017, from http://www.fatf-gafi.org/publications/high-riskandnon-cooperativejurisdictions/ documents/public-statement-june-2013.html.

78. "FATF Public Statement - 14 February 2014," *FATF*, accessed on July 27, 2017, from http://www.fatf-gafi.org/publications/high-riskandnon-cooperativejuris dictions/documents/public-statement-feb-2014.html.

Conclusion

Turkey's illicit economy continues to increase and expand. Triggered by various factors, such as its strategic geographic position of the country, high taxes on commodities subject to smuggling, well-developed transnational criminal networks in the region, the lack of law enforcement cooperation between Turkey and its neighboring countries, and endemic corruption as well as ongoing conflicts in Iraq and Syria, Turkey has become a hotbed for illicit trade. Various criminal groups, Syrian refugees, facilitators, and terrorist organizations have actively participated in the illicit economy.

CRIMINALS

Smuggling and trafficking remain the purview of traditional criminal groups. The drug trade remains the oldest and far-reaching sector of Turkey's illicit economy. It is a multidimensional issue where drug use, production, and trafficking concurrently take place. No one knows the exact number of drug addicts in the country. Former governments as well as the current Justice and Development Party (AKP) have been reluctant to examine the addictive nature of the drug problem, with little attention paid to treatment or rehabilitation. According to some modest estimates, Turkey hosts several hundred thousand heroin addicts. There is a growing interest in the use of methamphetamine and bonsai. Despite the frightening trends in drug use, the government's approach remains laissez-faire at best, with too few addiction treatment centers to treat the growing legions of drug addicts.

Fortunately for the rising number of drug sides there are more than enough traffickers to supply them. With drug traffickers the most common variety of prisoners, there are always criminals waiting to take their places on the supply

229

side of the drug trafficking equation. Each year, law enforcement detains over 100,000 drug traffickers including foreign nationals. Turkish drug trafficking groups are among the most active runners on the Balkans route. The diversity of the Balkans drug trade is exemplified by the variety of drugs pouring into the country, including heroin, cocaine, synthetics, and cannabis. Turkey also must face the unanticipated consequences of its position, creating a huge domestic demand for the end products. In the 1970s and 80s heroin was processed in Turkish facilities as more domestic groups entered the production side of the drug trade. This was brought home to the public and the international community after police operations seized heroin and methamphetamine labs in various parts of the country. The government's traditional approach, ignoring the demand side of the equation, as well as its reluctance to increase international police cooperation or improve the capacity of police to make organized crime investigations means that Turkey will continue to grapple with the grave consequences of the drug trade in the years to come.

One of the constant themes in this book has been the fact that pervasive smuggling activity in Turkey has not just threatened the country's security but its economy as well. The illegal market for cigarettes, oil, and pharmaceuticals is incalculable, but by most accounts is surely in the billions of dollars. Demand for cheaper goods and the relative acceptance of smuggling as a legitimate activity have presented continuing opportunities for criminals. This is exemplified in the oil sector, where Turks pay considerably more for the oil it consumes than its neighbors Iran, Iraq, and Syria. This juxtaposition of pricing offers opportunities to smuggle oil from these countries into Turkey.

Similar to the tax evasion motivations of oil smugglers, cigarette smuggling results from a similar desire to avoid paying high government taxes. Cigarettes originating in China, Indonesia, and Bulgaria have been smuggled into Turkey by criminals using various land and sea routes. Furthermore, criminals benefit from the favorable environment in Turkey for the smuggling of counterfeit pharmaceuticals, though the process for doing so is complicated. Some counterfeit pharmaceuticals have been smuggled into Turkey from countries on its eastern and southern borders or transferred from Turkey to other Middle Eastern countries. Syrians are recent entrants, operating pharmaceutical smuggling networks between Turkey and Syria. Indications are that smuggling will increasingly threaten Turkey's legal economy and offer a revenue stream for the country's illicit economy.

Turkey occupies a critical position in terms of the trafficking of antiquities. Its rich historical legacy remains vulnerable to trafficking as a result of increasing interest in antiquities and the presence of highly developed transnational criminal groups who operate in this area. Recently, Turkish law enforcement has detected international trafficking groups operating in Turkey, with capabilities to sell and transport antiquities anywhere in the world.

Utilizing diverse sea and land routes, much of the looted antiquities are destined for the U.S. and Western European buyers and collectors. It is clear that antiquities trafficking will continue in Turkey as a result of its rich potential, the adaptability of traffickers, the inadequate attention of policy makers, and the existence of weak policies.

SYRIAN REFUGEES

Since this monograph was first conceived there have been a number of geopolitical developments that have long-term implications for Turkey's illicit economy. One major result of the Arab Spring was the "geopolitical tumult" and its unanticipated consequences for the illicit economy. According to Colin P. Clarke, "new smuggling and trafficking routes and networks throughout the Mideast and North Africa have emerged, with criminal and terrorist groups taking advantage of continued instability in key geographic hubs throughout the Mediterranean region."[1]

Turkey has been increasingly affected by the consequences of the ongoing Syrian conflict. The country hosts over three million Syrian refugees whose involvement in the underground economy is expanding. Many Syrians have been smuggled to Greece on routes through Turkey. The use of the Turkish route by illegal immigrants from eastern and western African countries reflects the transnational reach of human smuggling groups in Turkey. Syrians have been subjected to exploitation in the sex sector, with thousands of Syrians residing in or outside of refugee camps targeted for sale in the sex sector by traffickers. Syrians also comprise a significant portion of the victims of labor trafficking. What's more, a substantial number of underage Syrians do not attend school and have been exploited in the labor sector.

Syrian criminals have become increasingly involved in a number of smuggling and trafficking activities. They are the leading actors among foreign national criminals operating in drug trafficking, people smuggling, antiquities smuggling, counterfeiting, and kidnapping. This state of affairs is likely to continue as increasing numbers of Syrian refugees and criminals who are part of the underground economy and illicit economy take refuge across national borders.

TERRORISTS

Terrorist organizations, mainly the PKK and ISIS, have impacted the Turkish illicit economy. The PKK transformed itself over time into a criminal organization heavily funded by various kinds of trafficking and smuggling.

The terrorist organization's involvement in drug trafficking and cigarette smuggling remains visible throughout the country. The PKK also engages in the smuggling of Syrian immigrants to Western European countries, making the terrorist organization an important link in the chain of global smuggling networks. Terrorist groups have affected Turkey's illicit economy in many ways, ranging from increasing the size and scope of the illicit economy to normalizing smuggling and hindering the development of eastern and south-eastern cities.

It seems that after three years of conflict, ISIS, which once controlled almost one third of Iraq's and Syria's territory, has now been removed from its havens, including Iraq's second largest city, Mosul, and its stronghold in Syria, Raqqa. Surely, many of the militants have escaped underground to the vast border areas between Syria and Iraq. As ISIS is continually pressed in Iraq and Syria, many of its previous revenue streams chronicled earlier in the book have dried up. The diminished lucre coming from oil and gas extortion, trafficking of antiquities, taxation of residents, and so forth has forced the pragmatic terrorists to seek new income streams, particularly drug trafficking. Lest one look for any peace dividends too soon in Iraq, most military commanders have warned that the ISIS threat is far from over. As one Iraqi observer put it, "The battles against Daesh are over, but the war is not."[2]

The focus of much of the criticism of the Turkish government has been on how the AKP policies have opened opportunities for ISIS to thrive in Turkey. Radicalization has become increasingly tolerated under the eyes of the AKP regime; some critics suggest that its policies may have driven Turkish subjects into the hands of ISIS recruiters. Moreover, the reluctant attitude of the government and inadequate police investigations against salafi-jihadist terrorist groups have created a favorable environment for ISIS fundraising activities Nowhere was this clearer than in the trafficking of illicit petroleum and the antiquities trade at the zenith of ISIS power. It is in these activities that the most observable links between the Turkish criminals and ISIS are most obvious. But further investigation is needed to determine direct connections between ISIS and Turkish actors in a host of other funding streams.

The illicit economy will continue unimpeded until several major factors are addressed, beginning with the current counter-productive policies of the Erdogan government. More effective policies are desperately needed to handle ISIS and the Syrian refugee crisis. Lack of state strategies for suppressing ISIS activity in Turkey and its border regions increases the likelihood of Turkey one day being labelled as a state supporter of terrorism. Until steps in this direction are taken, these policies will continue to provide a favorable environment for salafi-jihadist terrorist organizations to recruit more Turkish people.

FACILITATORS

Corrupt politicians and bureaucrats as well as money launderers in Turkey facilitate criminals and terrorists to operate throughout most of the country. Political corruption has presented these criminals with further opportunities, as the dual corruption investigations in December 2013 have shown. Police investigators uncovered a systemic corruption system created by President Erdogan in 1994. When the system burgeoned into an international operation with activities such as transfers of Iranian and Saudi Arabian dirty money, the police conducted two investigations. The December 17 investigation found that Islamic revolutionary guards had developed a project to break the embargo imposed on Iran because of its adamant desire to possess nuclear weapons. The December 25 investigation disclosed a money pool system whose beneficiaries were AKP-linked businessmen who procured government contracts in return for giving bribes.

No criminal case exemplifies the widespread corruption and money laundering in Turkey more than the case of Reza Zarrab. In December 2017, the 34-year old Iranian-Turkish gold dealer, arrested during a trip to Florida, went on trial in the United States, accused of a litany of crimes linked to the current Turkish regime. At the center of the trial was his involvement in a conspiracy to violate U.S. Iranian sanctions in a billion-dollar laundering scheme to convert revenues from sales of Iranian gas to Turkey into gold, then shipping the gold to Dubai and selling it for billions of dollars.[3] Zarrab confessed that between 2010 and 2016 he had conspired with others to obstruct the U.S. Treasury Department enforcement of Iran sanctions. As a result of his testimony, it has only further ratcheted up tensions between the two countries.

According to Zarrab, the economy minister implicated President Erdogan in the scheme as well. This marked the first time that Erdogan was implicated in sanctions busting. However, this probably would have been revealed in 2013, when Turkish police uncovered his complicity, but were prevented from investigating by the president. According to one reporter who assiduously followed the trial, Zarrab only gave "brief testimony" on Erdogan.

The December 2013 investigations made Turkey more vulnerable in terms of the illicit economy when President Erdogan retaliated against thousands of individuals within its own institutions—even those who had not participated in the two police operations. The investigators involved in the operations were suspended, while others were forced out of their jobs, and many were tortured and incarcerated, creating weaknesses and a vacuum that criminals and terrorist groups were quick to exploit. Turkey now is a country much less safe than it was just a few years ago.

Turkey has a massive money-laundering problem created and sustained by a weak judicial infrastructure and a lack of highly skilled police officers to investigate financial crimes. Meanwhile, Turkey is exposed to the nefarious activities of money launderers, whose ranks include criminals, terrorists, tax evaders, and corrupt officials. A vulnerable banking system under the control of corrupt politicians, exchange offices that are subject to little or no oversight, and ineffective border controls enable money launderers to easily transfer illegal money into the country and send it outside the country to destinations both near and far.

Despite money launderers' historical preference for transferring illegal money in the form of cash, the criminals have started to use Turkish state banks to launder money. Evidence exists that politicians have processed fraudulent transactions and provided improper loans to corrupt businesspersons by exploiting state banks. In addition to illegal money obtained from crimes and for use as terrorist financing, Turkey has received cash from foreign countries. One commonly held belief in the international community is that the Gulf States have poured illegal money into Turkey in return for exploiting Turkey's support of opposition groups fighting in war-torn Syria, thereby creating favorable ground to spread their Salafism-based ideology.

Turkey has long been considered the only secular and democratic Islamic country. But this position is being threatened by an increasingly authoritarian state led by President Erdogan. In the early years of his leadership he was regarded as a liberal pro-European democrat, but in recent years has increasingly embraced "a nationalist, neo-Ottoman posture," presenting himself as "a leader who can recreate some of Turkey's lost empire."[4] Erdogan has continued to augment his powers as the country's relations with Europe and the United States are much diminished. Critics argue that Turkey's democratic gains are in serious jeopardy under the current regime.

NOTES

1. Colin P. Clarke, "ISIS Is so Desperate Its Turning to the Drug Trade," *Fortune*, July 24, 2017.

2. Daesh is the Arabic acronym for the Islamic State. Margaret Coker and Falih Hassan, "Iraq Premier Declares End of ISIS War," *New York Times*, December 12, 2017, 14.

3. "Plot of Gold," *The Economist*, December 9, 2017, 53.

4. Niki Kitsantonis and Carlotta Gall, "On Visit to Greece, Erdogan Irks His Hosts With Calls to Change a Treaty," *New York Times*, December 8, 2017, A6.

Index

About the Authors

Mahmut Cengiz spent many years in the headquarters of the Turkish Anti-Smuggling and Organized Crime Department (ASOD). In this capacity he was tasked with developing strategies and policies to better suppress organized crime and terrorist financing. His varied research has included investigations and interviews related to the trafficking of drugs, WMD materials, cigarettes, pharmaceuticals, antiquities, and arms as well as smuggling and trafficking of human beings. The Turkish National Police has adopted several crime control models directed against smugglers and traffickers based on his research. His last research was related to ISIS financing in 2014 and 2015. Holding two master's and two doctorate degrees from Turkey and the United States, he has been working at the Terrorism, Transnational Crime, and Corruption Center (TraCCC) of George Mason University and has also been involved in projects for the Brookings Institution, European Union, and U.S. State Department. He is teaching terrorism and homeland security courses at George Mason University.

Mitchel P. Roth is the former president of the International Association for the Study of Organized Crime (IASOC) and is the author of more than 15 books, including most recently, *Global Organized Crime: A 21st Century Approach.* His research on the PKK is widely cited and before the recent events in Turkey was a regular speaker and participant at Turkish conferences related to terrorism and organized crime. He is Professor of Criminal Justice and Criminology at Sam Houston State University, where he has taught graduate and undergraduate courses on organized crime and terrorism for more than 20 years.

www.ingramcontent.com/pod-product-compliance
Lightning Source LLC
Chambersburg PA
CBHW050639280326
41932CB00015B/2712